How You Can Make $25,000 a Year

Writing

(No matter where you live)

Nancy Edmonds Hanson

Writer's
Digest
Books

Cincinnati, Ohio

93 92   5 4

Library of Congress Cataloging in Publication Data
Hanson, Nancy Edmonds
   How you can make $25,000 a year writing (no matter where you live)
Includes index.
1. Authorship. I. Title
PN147.H313   808'.025   79-22725
ISBN 0-89879-405-6 paperback
ISBN 0-89879-557-5

Design by Barron Krody.

To Russ, who keeps me on my toes, and Patti, who keeps me laughing.

About the Author

Nancy Edmonds Hanson was a newspaper woman before beginning her successful freelance career 12 years ago. She has authored hundreds of magazine articles and six books, worked as a PR practitioner, taught workshops in six states, and served as an editor for a variety of periodicals.

Contents

3

Look Like a Winner

Creative overhead—your office and how you present yourself. Your "look" and your portfolio. Furnishings, supplies, and stationery. Hardware: computers and other chips off the writer's block. Services—telephone and mail/express. The boonie writer's guide to T&E. Deductive reasoning—why you need a good accountant now.

4

The Bottom Line Says More Than "The End"

Money's not a four-letter word. The genuine and timely appeal of free-lancers. You're selling a tangible service. Consciousness raising—preparing your clients to hire you. Positioning, marketing and the sales pitch. Boutique versus department store. The art of selling: coping with yes and no. Financial goals in broad sweeps and excruciating detail. Pricing your services. Sales you can't afford to make. Concept of "best use" of your time. What you're worth—hourly wages, benefits, and overhead. An eye to growth and profits.

5

Magazine Writing: Think Like a Farmer

The truth about magazine writing and how it fits your plans. A go-ahead isn't always good enough. Yourself, as seen by the editor. Bad bets and even ones. All-but-irresistible you. The six best-bet magazine categories for writers from afar.

6

The Markets Next Door

Regional magazines . . . tracking them down and making them happy. Newspaper pluses and pitfalls. Sows' ears and silk purses (making marginal markets better). Stringing along with unexpected clients.

Introduction:
In Pursuit of the Great Adventure

Just two words, and I fell in love.

Freelance writer.

The notion fairly smacked of high adventure. I could see gorgeous possibilities in that single phrase—a life that combined writing, real writing, with the sort of jaunty bravado that might do a buccaneer proud.

I was whittling away my teens in a tiny prairie farm town, caught up between a drought of role models and an excess of ambition and in hot pursuit of something to do with my life. It would have to be appropriately dramatic, of course, falling well short of typing other people's letters or teaching English to future generations.

Freelance writing! Here was a route around chalkboards and dictation! Here was a chance to fight dragons, scale mountains, and pursue the golden fleece . . . all, presumably, while collecting a living wage.

A pretty picture. I could almost smell the scent of fresh-bound books and roses tossed by critics. It was true love, for sure.

Love may be blind, but that doesn't mean it's lost its mind entirely. Even then and there—Streeter, North Dakota, in the middle 1960's—I knew there was a flaw in my perfect premise. As any jolly buccaneer requires his high seas and bounding main, my fantastical freelancer was clearly cast adrift far from the would-be author's natural element—the hum and rumble of the publishing industry, parked solidly in New York City.

Or Chicago, or Toronto, or even Fargo (the metropolis of choice for daydreaming girls in darkest North Dakota). Exactly where the scene was staged made little difference. No matter. It was somewhere else.

One point, at least, was clear: Somewhere amidst those glassy office towers and fern-bedecked bistros, erudite editors were surely meeting debonair freelance writers to negotiate the finer points of Great Ideas, and then sipping martinis over a literary lunch. (It was an article of faith that such lofty literati would forgo Hamm's beer.)

It could never happen here. Not in North Dakota—not in a one-grocery-store town utterly bereft of major publishing houses, where not a soul subscribed to the *Atlantic Monthly* and even "lunch" was a foreign concept. (We called it "dinner" and ate it at noon around the kitchen table.)

Yet the notion persisted, as it has across the years for countless writers who honed their dreams in corners of America every bit as obscure as my own.

What I didn't know then, and what I do know now, is this: Geography takes away certain dreams, but it endows you with new possibilities.

You *can* assault the grim grey fortresses of big-city publishing from afar. You *can* write books that earn respect—both fiction and nonfiction. You *can* score sales to magazines, not only *Turkey Call* and *Grit* but a good share of the entire gamut of periodicals, even unto the glossy high-profile newsstand names.

You *can* pursue the craft and the perplexing business of touching strangers' lives with well-shaped words. You can learn, and experiment, and create, and sell your writing to your heart's content.

You can, in short, carve out a successful career for yourself as a freelance writer . . . no matter where you live.

You're not the first to try. You're not alone. And you're on the verge of a great adventure.

For the past twenty years I have lived by my own words. I have worked as a newspaper reporter, an advertising executive, and a management-level cog in state government's slow-grinding gears. As a full-time freelancer, I have written hundreds of magazine articles and six books; produced a weekly TV show; edited wildly different periodicals for wildly different reasons; taught workshops in six states; cooked up public relations campaigns both vivid and subtle; offered advice to sundry public and private clients as a consultant; and bumped against the edges of a couple of political quests.

I have hatched more ideas than I can count. I've road-tested a good share of them. My résumé is as long as your Ford's front fender, and I'm not done yet.

What you should note from all of this is that I've accumulated every scrap of my experience right here in North Dakota.

Yes, North Dakota—land of wide-open spaces, potholes, Herefords, a couple million mallard ducks, and enough wheat to turn the Red River gold. Not incidentally, North Dakota ranks at the very bottom in the number of homegrown publishing markets and Number One among postmarks unlikely to impress an urbane editor in Manhattan.

I didn't choose my address to prove a point. I've been quietly making a living doing work I love, and this is where I'm planted. But here in good old North Dakota I've established beyond the shadow of a doubt that your address means beans when it comes to freelance writing.

What counts is, first, your delight in language; second, your eagerness to sample new and different applications of your craft; and finally, the enthusiasm and energy that arm you to take the freelance offensive.

What struggling writers have always known in their drafty New York lofts and garrets is that they've arrived in the absolute hub of the publishing world.

What I know in North Dakota is that the hub is vital but it takes a lot more to turn the wheel.

You can make a good living as a freelance writer in the boonies, in the towns and suburbs, in the great American cities that do not happen to be New York. Like all of life's best dreams, it's up to you to forge ahead and make it happen.

If I can live the comfortable, satisfying, exciting freelance life here on the prairie (and I'm coming up on fifteen years now), it's a foregone conclusion that you can do it, too—wherever you live right now or want to live in the future.

You *can* overcome your terror of abject poverty as a freelancer of unconventional address and high-numbered zip code, no matter how much your decision to quit your job horrifies your mother.

You *can* support a family as a full-time freelancer, even if you've never witnessed the feat firsthand before.

You *can* live as you choose to live, and earn the income you desire, without selling yourself to a corporate or governmental bidder. You can equal or surpass the income you receive in a more normal mode of work. And double the emotional rewards. And provide for all the benefits, and more.

Not only that. There are occasions when you *can* sleep until ten in the morning if you feel like it.

The prerequisites include no great mysteries. You accept the risk of being on your own and display the confidence you'll need to prepare to explore the possibilities. You develop your skills as a writer. And you resolve to stay flexible so that you can enjoy and evolve with the challenging, shifting markets that are your best bets.

There are just two key principles you'll have to adhere to like the True Faith, two keys that make the freelance life possible anywhere in the country.

One is that you must be as creative in the kinds of jobs you'll ferret out and tackle as you are in the "serious" creative writing you've produced in the past. I don't mean developing a sideline driving a street sweeper or rustling cattle. I do mean to include the enormous range of assignments that require solid research and writing, that challenge your skills perhaps as dramatically as a major magazine article or book but are unconventional enough to remain fallow until you set out to invent or uncover them.

The second principle is that freelance writing is a business. Not a calling. Not a lifetime date with the Muse. Not some kind of sacred quest that's somehow cleaner and more noble than the jobs you've held in the past (depending on just what those jobs amounted to).

Nor is it a permanent respite from the pressures of employment which you now lament as roadblocks to the flow of your creative juice.

If you choose full-time freelancing, you're embarking on a *business*. Your own bottom line can be survival, if you habitually choose only easy targets, or considerably better if you intend to soar.

You are selling your time, your unique background and insights, and—yes—your precious daily ration of inspiration in return for a living and a lifestyle that offers returns like no other. You're leasing those same natural assets no matter what kinds of assignments you tackle: articles for major magazines, books, commercial writing jobs, video and AV programs, conducting workshops, or whatever permutations appeal to you.

If you're ready to get out and hustle, if you're serious about freelancing right in your own community—well, then, I have some tested ideas for you to apply in your own setting and among your own cast of characters.

Every word in this book is based on my experience and that of our counterparts who've taken up the writing challenge and made it work in their own settings. In some cases we had prior work experience to use as a foundation. We came to others with only the will to master the essentials of a new writing application.

Some methods I've invented (or thought I had, until I began hearing from other successful freelancers in isolated locales who swore they invented them themselves). Others were inspired by the long list of guides to ever-more-specific aspects of this writing business, as well as books on small business and the whole curious mishmash of thought-provoking information afloat in one medium or another. But sooner or later I've tried every one of them, and I offer my hands-on experience candidly.

To hell with Manhattan! Here in North Dakota, and from the rangelands to the moss-draped boulevards of equally non-metropolitan America, writers are engaged in demonstrating that the myths about how to make it as a freelancer knocking on the doors of Publishers Row are seriously out-of-date and irrelevant.

Like all of life's most intoxicating dreams, you have to forge ahead on your own to make this one happen.

Ten years ago when I wrote the first edition of this book, the notion of freelance writing as a full-time career choice still seemed like a radical idea . . . at least when practiced in nontraditional locales like Idaho or Oklahoma or Georgia.

Then, I felt a little like a missionary. Now, the principles that motivate the choice to freelance have evolved into the next thing to a state religion.

Freelance writers were entrepreneurs when entrepreneurship was still a misty concept in the public mind. We operated home-based businesses long before they became a trend. We invented flextime (as we shaped our own routines) and job-sharing (in the sense that many freelancers together do the work of a single full-time staffer).

We were recognizing the challenge and the satisfaction of determining our own course well ahead of headlines about corporate executives leaving their perks behind to take the plunge into individualistic business.

It was exciting then, and for a variety of reasons (including encouraging trends in both publishing and business) it's even more exciting now. But in ten years I've learned that there's even more to successful freelancing than taking the plunge and living—well—to tell your tale.

First and foremost, there's the long-term opportunity to grow, to mature, and to tailor your career goals to changes in your life and inclinations. It may not matter to you now as you weigh the option of independence and survey the somewhat-daunting field that lies in front of you. In the final assessment, though, that may be the most precious asset you can gain from your decision to freelance: the chance to alter course mid-stream.

I've discovered that now, in my mid-30s, different parts of the profession please me. Where once I thrived on the everlasting promise of new beginnings, today I seek out stable writing relationships with fewer, better editors and clients—informal partnerships that allow me to channel my energy into harder thinking and better writing rather than brighter salesmanship.

Some of freelance writing's necessities once grated on my nerves. Now they give me pleasure. For example, I pay more attention to rigorous craftsmanship rather than journalistic snap, crackle, and pop. I've come to prefer polished luster to dazzle and flash.

I'm drawn to opportunities to learn more about subjects I've already explored in print and to gain real depth. The younger me would have longed to get on with it—explore new terrain, tackle new mountains.

I place a more realistic value on my own time—higher, that is. The joy of learning to do everything myself has become an expensive pleasure; I'm willing to call on others' talents and knowledge to supplement my own, and I try to invest my own hours in what I can genuinely do best.

At the heart of freelancing's appeal lies the issue of freshness. Maintaining that creative edge is a problem (at least from time to time) for every experienced writer I've ever known, salaried or self-employed. The continual round of new ideas, new editors or clients, and new topics helps beginners sail across their first years of freelancing. With more experience, though, I've learned that there's another way—that it can be maintained not only by continually courting new experiences and new media, but also by developing more expertise and credibility in those with the most promise. Depth, as well as breadth, has its satisfactions.

Consider this your chance to try on new identities and to finally establish, with genuine confidence, a sense of your own voice. It can be one step in your lifetime progress as a writer, or—in its infinite variety—the framework for that career itself. Either way, you survey the choices and pick those that suit you best.

Freelancing is not a goal in itself. It's a process of learning more about your world, your strengths, and yourself as a writer. It offers you the rarest opportunity most of us will ever earn: the chance to truly write your own script, and then see how it plays.

1

You, Entrepreneur

Like yours, my attitude toward freelancing was formed of equal parts of the sheer magnetism of adventure, the long to write clear, fine prose about non-mundane subjects, and the nasty nagging suspicion that—given its economic prospects—it might be the greatest weight-loss method in history.

Which is normal . . . not only for writers on the verge of making the leap to full-time freelancing, but for anyone in any profession who stands at the brink of launching a new venture.

And apprehensiveness is apt. Small Business Administration studies suggest that a minimum of 85 of every 100 new businesses that open their doors this year will have disappeared five years from now. (Such figures may actually be on the conservative side. A substantial number never see it beyond their first anniversary.)

Being your own boss is clearly risky business. That's as true of freelance writing as it is of shoe stores and lawn-care services and quaint little restaurants.

But . . . and here's the important part . . . every Main Street in America is lined with those who have succeeded in precisely the same fields where the SBA's 85 sadder-but-wiser folks failed to make their mark (outside of random lumps and bruises). The nature of their businesses was not at fault in most of those cases. More likely the decisive factor was the nature of the man or woman at the helm.

The same cosmic rules that govern auto mechanics and stockbrokers apply to writers as well. The risks you take are generally commensurate with what you stand to gain. You invest your money in hopes of making a profit. Why would investing your time be any different?

Plenty of self-informed experts will always turn up to tell you that professional writing is a jungle enlivened by dogs eating dogs . . . that rates are low, editors slow to pay, assignments hard to come by. In many cases their observations are certainly correct. But that's only part of the story.

More than nearly anyone short of worm ranchers, self-employed writers as a group are dominated by low expectations. Why do we all but plan for poverty even as we aim for excellence?

Perhaps it's our society's conviction that you ought to suffer for your art. Perhaps it's the pernicious notion that creative people are, per se, poor players in business's hard-nosed games. Or maybe it's simply because we often use the dismal popular prognosis as one more excuse for routinely selling the same old work to the same old markets in the same old ways in lieu of honestly reviewing our methods and testing new ground.

It doesn't take Lee Iaccoca to tell you that's no way to run a business. But you should listen to him, because you're siblings under the skin.

You, as a freelance writer, are an entrepreneur. The same realities that govern Chrysler have bearing on the outcome of your adventure.

Except for one. Don't expect the government to underwrite loans to get your business up and running. Writing and publishing are categories that the SBA, which loses fortunes every year on balloon stores and frozen-yogurt shops, refuses to consider.

The ambivalence surrounding the matter of writing-as-business is natural, I suppose, when you weigh the degree of commitment and personal exposure it inevitably entails.

Few people devote their free time to fitting eyeglasses and dream of polishing glorious lenses when their ship comes in. But an eon's worth of weekends, late nights, and early mornings, is invested in fulfilling sporadic freelance assignments by those encumbered with ordinary 8-to-5 jobs.

Grinding spectacles is not frequently seen as an antidote for the dullness of the workaday routine. Freelance writing is. Moreover, conceiving and selling magazine articles is ideal for dabblers; it requires no start-up capital, absorbs the odd free afternoon, and—when successful—adds nicely to your store of self-esteem. You can get your feet wet with one sale a month, or a year, or a decade . . . or even no sales at all, but lots of honest trying.

Freelance writing is a hobby for the vast majority of its practitioners. They may learn a good deal about querying, interviewing, and writing, not to mention patience in waiting for their checks, but their experience provides a weak and deceptive frame of reference when you weigh the pluses and minuses of the rarer full-time variety.

Occasional freelancers are tourists on safari. No, please don't be insulted if you fall into this category at the moment. I'm doubting neither the quality of your work nor your commitment to make it even better. But those who earn their real livings by day and write by moonlight can afford to relax by hunting on the veldt, taking aim at only the fleetest and most elusive prey.

The key is this: They can afford to miss those big bucks. Either way, they win. Their reward is in the novelty of exploring territory altogether different from their normal setting, in the thrill of the hunt, and in acquiring exciting tales to be traded 'round the campfire.

Your approach must change when you depend on words to bring home the bacon to a family that has to eat. A nice fat bird in the hand can be worth any number of trophy specimens—especially when the big ones are still in the bush, and halfway around the world to boot.

The pursuit will still excite you. The thrill will still be waiting when you hit your mark. But mark my words. As a full-timer, you'll choose your targets with vastly different goals in mind. You'll husband your ammunition, perfect your aim, and learn to bring the bylines down with frequency and a lot less effort.

Why am I so sure? I dabbled, too, long before diving into this business. The difference reminds me of easing into a swimming pool in June. You always shiver when you get your toes wet. Take a deep breath and plunge in up to your neck, and the water will turn out to be just fine.

I earned my early stripes in the kind of freelancing that's always most accessible to part-timers—magazines, of course, starting with the children's page of *The Dakota Farmer* (where my 35-word essays on wild animals and poems about my mother's brownies earned 35 cents per six acceptances—about the same rates certain minor markets still offer today).

A freelance submission to *The Fargo Forum*, a prominent daily newspaper, won me $15 and a job offer at 17. And there I learned that reasonable men and women really did look at freelancing as a pursuit somewhat less iffy than entering the regionally popular Crystal sugar's "Name the Lake Cottage" sweepstakes.

Approximately 95 percent of my colleagues mentioned freelance writing on their top ten list of dreams. (The other one planned to run for governor.) We talked about it endlessly throughout my eight years in the newsroom, resurrecting the vision whenever editors carped or county commission meetings ran overlong.

And we all dabbled. I sold a few record reviews to *Rolling Stone*, a pet-lovers' fantasy to *Cats*, a handful of breezy items to *New Times*, several short reports to *The Lutheran Standard*—you get the picture. The going rate seemed to hover just under the price of a decent pair of shoes—when I got it at all. In a harbinger of things to come, several publications were cancelled before issuing me a check so I could do the same.

At that moment, and with good reason, I subscribed in full to the myth that freelancing could never work on the prairie. My dabbling had cost me a dream, it seemed, just as yours may have left you today.

I was wrong.

Several years with the North Dakota tourism promotion department taught me a number of lessons—among them, that government service is more fun as an episode than as a career. More important, my position gave me a vantage point that most writers in my part of the world lack. Suddenly I was meeting freelance writers—real travel writers willing to travel thousands of miles to write stories about my own backyard.

And their addresses! Des Moines. Charlotte. Lincoln. Billings.

Billings? Montana happens to be the only state that makes us North Dakotans feel metropolitan and urbane. Moreover, while some of these freelancers were retired from lucrative careers or freelanced on their vacation time, a few—an *inspiring* few—really wrote nonfiction for a living. They all looked well fed.

I considered and dawdled, thought it over and dawdled some more ... coping as we all do when the dream of freelancing suddenly begins to vacillate between remotely possible and impossibly remote. I spent days making lists of magazine stories and markets, and nights awaking from nightmares of rejection and defeat.

I took long coffee breaks and bedeviled my friends for advice. None knew a whit more than I did; naturally they told me I was inevitably doomed to fail unless I moved to the Big City to try throwing my pearls before the really big swine.

Yet others hinted at possible work for their businesses or hometown publications, and leads turned up to several more potentially intriguing contacts.

My husband hates indecision. Finally he announced, "I can't stand anymore of this. Turn in your resignation and give it a try. At worst we'll live on tuna fish hotdish for awhile."

My mother was horrified. I'd given up a good job, a secure job, for this nonsense.

My employed writing friends envied me, and privately wagered that I'd last six months.

Other acquaintances concluded I must be pregnant. For all I know they're still waiting with the booties.

I was as scared as I'd ever been in my whole timid life, and as thrilled as the first time *The Dakota Farmer* said "yes."

The fear goes away.

The delight doesn't.

All veterans of self-employment treasure their own ideas about what it takes to succeed as an entrepreneur, from an MBA and the energy to work fourteen hours a day to a sizeable inheritance. The U.S. Department of Commerce has sketched out a list of qualities that can help you get to "yes":

- Do you get a kick out of independence?
- Do you genuinely like working with people? (After all, writing is a service industry, pure and simple.)
- Do you thrive on responsibility?
- Can you accept the inevitability of good and bad breaks and take them in stride?
- Do you generally learn from your mistakes?
- Are you able to juggle myriad projects and details all at once?
- Do you manage your time efficiently?

Freelancers tease themselves with other, more specific doubts as well.

Will you earn enough assignments to keep you busy? If you must, I think you will. That's why self-supporting freelancers learn to be flexible about the kinds of writing they prefer and alert to new opportunities as they occur to them.

To a great extent you create your own workload. It depends on the volume of queries you send out, the zeal with which you approach editors to sell your ideas, and the enthusiasm with which you pursue alternative writing jobs like video scripts and commercial work. Despite vagaries inherent in the business, you determine what happens to you next. Your energy and salesmanship are the critical factors.

Will you run dry? That's always been a terror of mine, but history has proven to me that it's unlikely. Ideas breed more ideas. The only time in my life when I was in danger of truly running out of fresh ideas was when, as an employee of multiple bureaucratic hierarchies, I didn't really have to set goals for improvements to hold on to my job.

Too much security dries you up and saps your energy. There's nothing like the challenge of making a new living every month to keep the curious, creative voltage flowing.

Will you have the self-discipline to work without supervision? That's a universal question. Back on the eve of my own freelance initiation, it inspired all kinds of veiled speculation among my friends, familiar as they were with my history of unfinished Christmas projects, unanswered letters, and innumerable diets gone awry.

Believe me if you can: you will almost surely discover all the discipline you need if your writing keeps the wolves away from the door. If you don't really need the income to survive, you may have to struggle against a million temptations, from researching endlessly to avoid the keyboard to sneaking off to watch the soaps on a lazy afternoon.

But if you threw away your only visible means of support when you bid your last job goodbye, and if you're stubborn enough to believe in your great adventure, you'll probably do just fine. Self-discipline as a freelancer is quite different from the kind you've struggled with when your job has left you listless, or a New Year's resolution that pales quickly on January 2. Self-discipline thrives in the atmosphere of intense interest in your income generated by the bank that holds your mortgage and the tough-minded folks that supply your power.

In other words, when you have to keep working to survive, the choice of whether or not to work becomes quite easy.

But are you talented enough? Is your writing stylistically dazzling?

Listen. It truly is a myth that only those who write like angels can find success as freelancers. Far more to the point, you're going to have to work like hell.

My experience as a member of several writers' organizations reminds me, time and again, that the most successful names on their roster are seldom the best-known and most widely acclaimed. Instead, they're usually the solid (though sometimes unsensational) craftspersons who have applied the most dedication to mastering their trade.

Finally, the darkest fear of all: can you—really, now—convince others to believe in you and your abilities? Do you believe, as well? Of all your fears, this is probably the most critical. It's a question you must answer for yourself, and perhaps only after trial and error.

You need something of the salesperson's flair to convince editors who've never seen you that you can come through with a manuscript that they will want to buy, or to persuade an executive with the State Association for the Very Short that you, at five foot ten, can empathize and edit their newsletter as well as any candidate.

Unless you're one of the few who are genuinely reluctant to talk about your good points to total strangers (and not just patiently waiting for your chance), I do think you can "sell" yourself. When I say "sell," I mean it in its gentler but just as persuasive forms: demonstrating your qualities shamelessly rather than modestly shuffling your feet. Instilling trust among those you've never met. Appearing to be the kind of person who ought to be given a chance.

It's nothing like hawking those packets of overpriced garden seeds around your neighborhood as a kid, or peddling raffle tickets for the church men's group, or strong-arming political contributions from reluctant acquaintances. This is real life. This is you. Rather than fearing this aspect of freelancing, at times I've noticed myself beginning to enjoy it. After all, who else gets to reel off her accomplishments and background without the slightest blush of shame?

Your real problem is whether you're willing to promote yourself to editors and clients, not whether you have some brash, innate ability to do so. I'd never sold so much as a glass of nickel lemonade when I began. Now, on good days, I approach the promotional side of my business with as much enthusiasm as I bring to the writing of a story that entrances me; sometimes I have to fight myself to settle back down to the typewriter, in fact, instead of endlessly promoting new projects while leaving current assignments waiting.

Marketing yourself and your abilities is going to be as important to your survival as a freelancer in the boonies as your polished interviews, your clever turns of phrase, and your self-correcting typewriter. You can learn it through any number of self-help books, through evening or college courses on salesmanship, and through experience. But not everyone can learn to like it. If you cannot or will not sell your ideas on the open market, freelancing is as unlikely a career for you as real estate.

Selling writing, of course, is vastly different from real estate in other ways. For one thing, there's no such thing as true market value; the value that markets place on writing of the same quality requiring an equivalent amount of effort veers wildly from next to nothing to a handsome sum.

Freelance salesmanship is a matter of weighing your worth to a preferred publication or client, and then working to make sure they understand your figures. Their last words will not always be "yes, of course." But it gives you something to aim for.

Effective selling requires the constant practice of the art they call "prospecting"—searching out new potential customers to expand their client base and insure a good supply of candidates to replace their present clientele as it shifts and shrinks, as it inevitably will.

Will you be rejected? Sure. But neither salespeople nor freelance writers need to equate "no" with failure. Some avenues will always turn out to be less lucrative or rewarding than others. The range of choices before you, however, is limited only by your own ambition and imagination.

Salespersons are avid consumers of motivational literature full of experts who encourage them to aim ever higher as they offer tips on how to close sales. Oddly, many sources to which writers turn for advice do quite the opposite. While offering all the guidance in the world on how to write and who to write for, they reinforce the notion that even successful practitioners are likely to have income equivalent to burger-flippers and domestic help.

Does money matter in a creative profession? Yes, I think it does— and for more than the minimum necessities of paying bills and buying groceries. Financial rewards play a subtle but perceptible role in maintaining your self-respect and self-confidence, even when self-expression is a primary motive. Income affirms the skill you've brought to your life's work. It endorses the importance of what you create. It carries the choice of writing far beyond the self-indulgence with which scoffers occasionally dismiss it, and puts you on a par with other professions.

Money can't buy a writer self-respect, any more than it can fulfill any other artist whose standards are deep, exacting, and inborn.

But, then, neither can the lack thereof. Given a choice of writing well and starving, or writing well in relative comfort, only masochists knowingly choose to limit themselves to earning less.

A survey conducted several years ago by the American Society of Journalists and Authors suggests that the median income for writers—established writers, not dilettantes—remains in the low 'teens, only slightly more than it was ten years ago.

Somehow during that same decade I've earned no less than nearly three times that figure and often four times or more. I've met dozens of my far-flung counterparts who can say the same—or considerably better.

Why the difference? Two statements from a *Time* article about the so-called freelance ghetto provide the answer:

Author Gay Talese: "There is no way you can prosper writing for magazines alone."

Literary agent Scott Meredith: "There are no writers left who can make a living just by articles."

And that's precisely what I've figured out here in North Dakota, as friends have simultaneously confirmed it one by one across the forests, mountains, lakeshores, and concrete badlands—wherever New York City isn't peeking in their windows.

How could we be so smart when some big-name national writers are apparently rationing soap and toothpaste? We had an initial advantage over the poor, toiling metropolitan writers whose bylines we envied on the pages of the so-called major markets. We'd never really expected to live by magazines alone.

Flexibility. If you're going to write to eat, you can never, never afford to limit yourself to only one kind of writing. Not just major markets, though their fee scales look so tempting from a distance. Not just travel or women's or sports magazines. Not just newspapers, or regional publications, or even just one facet of the many commercial freelance assignments open to you in your own locale.

When you live in a place where no freelance writer's lived before, you carry fewer preconceptions about what freelancing means. We struggle and scheme simply to make our mark as writers, not as "writers for the top dozen major magazine markets" or bust.

If the only writing you think can give you pleasure is that packed between slick, full-color covers of magazines stocked in even the tiniest drugstore, you're not ready to burn your salaried bridges and become a freelancer where you live today.

The same's true if you harbor a little hierarchy of markets: all-out effort for Class A, half-hearted effort for Class B, and, for Class C, work that's slapped out on a hot, uninspired afternoon between cold cans of Coors.

If you're ready to meet the challenges of freelancing, you accept that every assignment is worth your best efforts. You accept that your classiest work is never "too good" for the clients who'll enable you to pay your rent. You acknowledge that Betty Friedan and Norman Mailer might not be impressed by some of the jobs you invite: the annual reports, the brochures, the monthly Elks Club newsletter. You also get used to the fact that they're not even looking.

One more thing. If you're serious about making a living by your writing in the community where you live, you seldom can afford to nurture the old news media prejudice that only work for magazine and book publishers "counts." You need to be willing to look at a client as a client, whether editor or association director or marketing manager for a local bank.

That doesn't mean you'll have to compromise your ethics by accepting assignments that involve lies or deception, or undermine and negate every value you hold dear. As a freelancer, you're in the best position of all to turn down those requests. You simply explain why you won't take them on in a civil tone of voice, and walk away.

But you may discover that commercial assignments are no more compromising per se than those given out by newspapers or magazines, who for equally commercial reasons you may never know find a certain query or manuscript exactly right for their readers . . . and their advertisers.

This may not sound like the kind of freelancing you expected to read about. There's a reason for that. Most freelancers I've met share a quirk that I think explains the contradiction.

Asked about our work, we first tell about the top magazines we've sold to. Then the best medium markets. Then every other that's ever carried our bylines—right down to the time we were quoted in the *Reader's Digest's* "Toward More Picturesque Speech" column. Only if pressed do we volunteer the other half of the story—which is that survival on these apparent triumphs alone can be a mite thin at times, no matter what address we call home.

Most freelancers who write magazine nonfiction have greatly expanded from their preconceptions about writing markets. I don't know one who'd turn down an invitation to write a lucrative, honest but anonymous annual report. Or sell reprint rights to a minor, minor publication market. Or who'd say no to the chance to edit the right newsletter, write for a good house organ, or develop publicity plans for a new civic group that the writer believes in.

To flourish, they've explored all the possibilities of the written word. They write books, sometimes for trade publishers, sometimes self-published, sometimes for commerical clients. They make minor markets pay, selling the same story to several publications, or perhaps through self-syndication to low-paying newspaper buyers. They create opportunities to use their expertise in other media—radio and TV, maybe, or by teaching and putting together seminars. They sample the smorgasbord of commercial opportunities that lie just beneath the surface in the average community.

They are open to new assignments, whether they're jacks-of-all-trades or specialists in a few subject areas. Basically they found their careers on the principle that freelance writers in the wilds of America need to be as creative in their marketing and media as they are in the articles they write.

And you should be, too.

I've learned firsthand to stay open to new opportunities. But that wisdom came the hard way. Initially I set out to discover freelancing armed only with my tremulous confidence, lists of bright ideas to be pursued, and a secret fallback resolution (that come total disaster, I'd hunt up another job in six months).

Phase One of my freelance life was a heady time of endless cups of coffee beside my desk, carefully putting the dust cover back on the typewriter when I turned it off for the night, and fending off questions about whether I was pregnant.

I applied the principles that had worked for me in the past and helped sell my quarterly freelance manuscripts. I wrote brilliant query letters to the best and brightest markets. I took rejection in stride, and rejoiced over editorial go-aheads issued "on spec," with no guaranteed sale or kill fees.

No writer's block. No drought in the idea department, either. I wrote and polished half a dozen articles which editors had agreed to see. Typed error-free in perfect manuscript form (adopted from *Writer's Market*) and accompanied by immaculate self-addressed stamped envelopes, they fairly reeked of a newly minted freelancer's high hopes. I sent them away.

I waited.

And waited.

And waited. There's nothing more pitiful than a grown woman waiting on the sidewalk for the mailman in January in Bismarck, North Dakota.

It began to dawn on me that following the rules I'd memorized from writers' magazines was not going to, of itself, insure my half of the household budget. While I was still gaily receiving the congratulations of colleagues and basking in compliments about my courageous and industrious nature, I was noticing that something was lacking in this perfect life.

It was cash.

I reconsidered my approach.

During Phase Two of my freelance career, I began to do what I should have done while my daydreaming was still underwritten by someone else's salary budget. I took stock of my local assets, personal and professional. I began to seriously study every permutation of the printed word around me. I multiplied my potential skills, divided my monomaniacal attention to national markets, and came up with the conclusion that writers are as necessary here as they are in New York. Better yet, there were demonstrably fewer writers to fill those needs in North Dakota.

One major item on my inventory was my telephone file. I'd always thought of those men and women as friends or business acquaintances or highly placed sources. Now, as an independent, I knew they'd become something new and priceless: contacts.

They had for me an advantage not shared by the anonymous editors with whom I'd been corresponding. They already knew me, knew my work, and were accustomed to the far-out home addresses we generally had in common. They would know what I could do without query letters. All I had to do (all!) was convince them that they had an unrecognized need for outside writing help, and that I was conveniently available for their aid and comfort.

Also on my inventory were the local and regional publications and buyers of the written word most easily reachable from my home base. Like most casual freelancers-on-the-side, I'd disdained these easy markets in my attempts to crack *Redbook* and *Esquire*. I'd only occasionally looked at the handful of North Dakota magazines (two, actually) that buy the kind of writing I do best. I'd even less often stopped to reflect on how many nonwriters in business and government put words on paper every day, not because they want to, but because they have no facile writer to do it for them. Poor folks, they often loathe the whole idea of writing and would gladly turn it over to more willing and experienced hands.

While gazing at the top of the magazine mountain, that most remote of beginners' challenges, I seemed to have overlooked richer, sunnier valleys right here in the foothills.

During Phase Two, I mapped out that territory. Almost immediately I realized that here at home I could build a foundation that would support whatever writing challenges I'd eventually conquer.

In the words of the three-martini-lunchers, I began to send out feelers. I listened to the grapevine's news of who was doing what and needed help. I made no straightforward pitches to gain assignments during this period . . . but only because I wasn't to have enough time to get started before work began heading my way.

My telephone, which I'd previously had to dust to keep presentable, began to ring of its own volition. I was invited to offices for cups of coffee and casually loaded conversations. I bought a few coffees myself and had business cards designed to drop off as an afterthought.

The results? In six months my billings added up to exactly 150 percent of the salary—and it was respectable—I'd have received if I'd stayed employed. Most heartwarming of all was the speed with which my business was picking up; soon I didn't have time to count the minutes until the mailman's daily call.

Those six months included some assignments similar to ones I'd done on both my previous jobs, others I'd handled casually as a free-lancer or sometime-volunteer, and a couple that had never before occurred to me. At the end of the first year, my tally included the following undertakings:

■ A continuing assignment as humor columnist, book reviewer, and frequent contributor to *North Dakota Horizons*, the quarterly image magazine published by the state chamber of commerce.

■ Stories on energy development for the *North Dakota REC Magazine*, the other statewide magazine for a general audience, sponsored by an association of rural electric cooperatives.

■ A two-hundred page final report published in book form by a state historical commission which had finished its project and dispersed its own staff.

■ The first of many slide/tape productions, this one for the state's emergency radio network. It was accompanied by an illustrated booklet covering the same facts about a then-unique law enforcement communication system.

■ Planning and promotion of North Dakota's International Women's Year conference, a strictly part-time position including publications, publicity, and physical arrangements.

■ Several ghostwritten speeches for a highly placed state official whose office was too busy and too understaffed to handle them in-house.

■ And all the queries and articles I could keep up with. Between these other projects, which captured more and more of my interest, they were beginning to reward me with both encouraging successes and the foundations of my magnificent rejection slip collection.

Now, even as I was cashing checks and improving my outlook day by day, I felt an uneasy tingling. Something had to be wrong. Freelancing couldn't be this rewarding in far-off North Dakota . . . that's not how the books and articles said it would be. It wasn't bounded by sacrifice and desperate struggle.

In fact, it was fun.

2

Cutting Loose

Only one person in all the world is qualified to tell you when the time is right to launch your freelance adventure.

That person is you.

The pursuit of dreams is an inexact science. There are many signs that indicate direction, but no one signal to tell you, "Go!"

Those around you urge eternal caution, especially when they count on your paycheck for braces and piano lessons for the kids. They, at least, are sure when the time will be right to try—immediately after you've won the Illinois Lottery, for example, or you've landed a nice bequest but want to avoid the stigma of joining the idle rich.

You yourself may have an inkling, too, that the magic day is drawing nigh. You can't stand the thought of another year spent processing insurance claims, perhaps, or another interminable Monday management conference when the same people deliver the same endless reports about "compelling" issues that barely keep you awake through the meeting, much less through the night.

Or, on the up side, you've just made a major sale, have two go-aheads on your desk, and are feeling flush and prosperous. Your love of writing has finally begun to harvest some recognition, and that fruit seems juicy and ripe for the plucking.

Now?

You never know—but certainly not for any of these reasons.

Freelance writing is not a refuge. It's not a reward. It's a business, best approached like more conventional ventures: slowly, carefully, and with your eyes wide open.

Like the cautious founder of any kind of business, you know that the time to open your doors (or, in your case, close them and sit down at last to write) is when you've finished doing your homework. You must know the market before you begin, and you must have a plan of action.

By researching your market potential *before* you take the big plunge into self-employed writerdom, you can put many of your fears at bay. You can better afford to take a chance with your family's financial security (however briefly) and gamble a bit of your own peace of mind, all in pursuit of the freelance dream. It's the only logical alternative to the dramatic corporate departure that your heart may still long to stage—the grand tell-off-the-boss, thumb-your-nose gesture that's most akin to stepping off a cliff and expecting the Lord to catch you.

Of course you wouldn't try it that way, no matter whether you're mad as hell and determined not to take it anymore! Short of slamming doors and trusting fate, there are safer ways to cut loose from routine and sail away. The wisest is to chart your course and test-sail your trusty vessel long before your mates begin to wish you bon voyage.

Best of all, you can conduct this preliminary exploration right where you are, while you continue to discharge your daily duties and collect your salary (which you'll be squirreling away for the days to come).

Let's assume you've already searched your soul for honest personal qualifications—motivation, discipline, confidence. Next on your list of research projects is to examine the setting in which you'll star in your freelance drama. In the coldest, harshest light of day, explore the ways in which your location will affect your freelance potential.

Only a fool would leave a good job instantly to attempt freelancing in an untried, untested locale just because I've said it can work in North Dakota. You need to know your geographical destiny from the inside out before you can begin to plot the directions in which you'll stretch.

For geography, as much as your own abilities, does have a profound effect on your prospects far from Publishers Row. Every address has its own distinct strengths and weak points, assets and liabilities. Mark them well, for your challenge is to steer your own strategy among them.

With answers in hand, you can move ahead armed by genuine information. Hopes and fears aside, you can determine what's right for you: A) To turn in your key to the executive restroom and add freelancing to your calendar in the near future; B) to keep the dream but go slow on the launch date, gathering more contacts and writing credentials toward that day; or C) to look at your writing as a lovely hobby and aim no higher than making it pay its own way.

The essential difference between the first two choices and C lies in the results of the reconnaissance mission you conduct throughout your own community, region, and industry. On the one hand, you can undertake a thorough review of the publishing industry as it relates to your future. On the other, you can establish the market for commercial work in your own locale, from individual clients to agencies and production houses.

If you share the orientation of 99 percent of freelancers-in-the-making, you'll turn your attention first to publishing opportunities. You'll chronicle the ready buyers of your written words by identifying the publications most likely to welcome you (or at least offer the chance to prove yourself), both national and regional.

Your work may have already appeared in some of their pages. Those editors need to know that you'll be more available than ever soon. As for the others, start introducing yourself through query letters.

You'll begin to identify subjects and information resources that are both accessible to you and likely to catch an editor's eye. You'll initiate a network of contacts, those whose doors are open to you who can fuel your own imagination and share their expertise (even a bit offbeat).

You're probably familiar with your best source of this information—the library, with its treasure trove of reference material.

Library resources pick up where that classic reference guide to magazines, the annual edition of *Writer's Market*, leaves off. For example, even the smallest local libraries maintain back issues of a broad collection of regional and local magazines and newspapers. Among them you may find excellent and accessible markets that never make the national reports. One afternoon spent browsing among them should convince you of the encouraging fact that the thousands of listings in *Writer's Market* are only the tip of the iceberg. As a bonus, you'll also encounter among their contributors a virtual "Who's Who" of practicing writers in your corner of the world, each in himself (or herself) a potential source of guidance and advice.

Those close-at-hand markets are only the beginning of the resources the library can help you tap. Many maintain special reference rooms stocked with scores of trade periodicals, special professional publications on business and education subjects—more markets, and a ready source of background information not available in consumer publications.

The periodical indexes (*Readers' Guide* is the best-known among half a dozen to which your library may subscribe) hold data of another sort. They can help you pinpoint some of the subjects you may sell most easily to editors beyond your neck of the woods.

Let me explain. One of the handicaps of writing from an odd corner of the country is that it's almost impossible to envision how the nation sees you. How would a fish describe water? But you can hop outside your local fishbowl with a few minutes' research on what local topics have in the past appeared in national publications—almost always the context in which outsiders are likely to think of the geographical territory at your command.

Under my own state, for example, you'd see articles about farming and farmers, stories about severe weather, and topics that range from controversial western water projects to oddball politicians.

Farming, political mavericks, and rotten winters are all part of the scenery for those of us who live here. We take them for granted. The stories that seem to us to be worthy of coverage are those that are unusual, atypical—*not* farming, power, and blizzards.

What do you take for granted? In Utah, perhaps it's the Mormon Church or the preponderance of underpopulated national parks. In Hershey, Pennsylvania, it's chocolate; in Milwaukee, beer; in Missouri, the Ozarks. In every case, it's so much a part of local life that you think it's been done to death.

Yet familiarity makes the national editor's pencil tap. Totally new subjects are destined for the newspapers. Magazines prefer to examine the relatively familiar for new facets and in new depth. Those standard topics they already associate with your address may be exactly the ones on which they presume you to be most authoritative. They just make sense when considered in the shadow of your poor, maligned address.

While you won't, as a rule, concentrate on stories specifically about or limited to your own region, this kind of research provides some free insight into the image your geography imparts to you. It's somewhere to start, suggesting subject areas where you'll be moving with the current rather than battling your way upstream against outsiders' preconceptions and geographical prejudices.

While you're at the library performing these two pleasant exercises, introduce yourself to the reference librarian (or, in very small libraries, the head librarian). Share your intentions. Ask advice on publications, specialized local libraries for certain industries, or just about anything else on your scouting agenda which has been giving you trouble. Besides being generally great people, librarians can be as close to all-knowing about your community as anyone you're likely to find.

Your next step in this scout-out is right through the door into the territory where you plan to freelance. If you're in place already, it's as easy as making appointments to visit those who can fill you in on various facets of the writing outlook.

On the other hand, your chosen freelance location may be a region to which you hope to move. Scouting at a distance is far less effective than facing your sources across a desk or table in a coffee shop. What kind of excuse can you make to spend some time in your future locale before you lead moving vans there? You might combine your next vacation with a research trip. Besides the pleasure of exploring the destination's personality, you can spend weekday working hours calling on editors and potential clients. (Traveling to talk with them may even carry hidden benefits, since many people tend to be more candid with visiting strangers than with more familiar faces.)

Editors of nearby publications deserve a personal visit during your scouting days. More than any other group in your selected locale, they know about freelancing where you plan to live, at least as it's now being performed. They'll tell you far more in person about your genuine prospects of writing for them than they're likely to mention over the telephone or by letter. A visit is guaranteed to be a dozen times more helpful to you than even the best market listing. Editors will tell you outright what your chances for sales are and what they are looking for, and may even suggest some specific stories to try out your work.

Don't let your reticence prevent you from "bothering" these presumably busy individuals. For one thing, editors of local and state publications deal with far fewer freelancers than those whose circulation covers a larger part of the country. Many of those who write for them may not be professional writers at all, but hobbyists and sparetimers to whom deadlines and heavy research are a burden they don't care to shoulder.

For another, you can save both your own time and theirs by weeding out sure misses in person rather than sending in long-shot queries that require a written response. The protocol of dealing with editors on Publishers Row, as described in books and articles on magazine writing, is often suspended or greatly condensed when the office is in downtown Fargo.

Editors aren't the sole sources of valuable insights into your fiscal prospects as a freelancer, however. You can scout commercial clients as well, even before you're ready to announce your independent status.

But you need to be circumspect. While you can ethically stockpile magazine assignments and a backlog of promising material for queries, soliciting business accounts from the vantage point of someone else's payroll is a touchy matter. (We won't even discuss trying to lasso your employer's clients. While it's done, it's never talked about in polite company.)

Far better, then, to work around the subject nearest to your heart by gathering general data and sending out subtle feelers. If you're already in the information business, put your professional grapevine to work. If not, tap into those sources.

You need leads or outright answers in several areas.

Who has historically turned to freelancers for copy or other kinds of creative work? Are there particular times or specific projects coming up that are likely to require outside (non-staff) help?

Are independent writers already active in your community? Ten years ago the answer was almost surely "no." Today you may well find competition. If so, in what areas do they specialize? Is there service or expertise lacking that you could provide? (Investigate local writers' and editors' clubs or, perhaps, organizations like Women in Communications to locate others of your exclusive breed.)

Can you tie in now with those who might become sources of ongoing information? Your options might include service clubs or local chapters of the Public Relations Society of America, International Association of Business Communicators, or American Advertising Federation.

Professionals in the fields of advertising, public relations, and the printing industry are also close to what's being written and by whom in your community.

Public relations and advertising firms present a special case. The freelance writer occasionally competes with them on some kinds of copy-heavy jobs like annual reports or publicity campaigns. In general, though, the possibility exists that you might become allies or even coworkers.

Agencies may rank among your best local clients someday, once you get past the competition bugaboo. They often have writing overloads that back their own staff against imminent deadlines, and are generally accustomed to farming out assignments to independent contractors in other creative fields (notably photography). Once they've learned you're available, they may be interested in subcontracting writing jobs to you as well.

Advertising being the business it is, your own contacts may provide you with intelligence on their competitors' clients as well. It's a small professional world, and word travels fast; one or two contacts can keep you up-to-date on possible assignments in most of your community. As for keeping them up-to-date on *your* availability, consider providing them with samples of your work and reminders of your accomplishments. Regular contacts by mail or, preferably, telephone keep your services in mind. Remember, though, that these people earn their livings by selling their own time—don't waste it on frivolities.

Men and women employed full-time as writers for business, government, and industry also may prove to be useful allies. With information the core of their own business, is it any wonder they're so good at keeping up on developments in the public relations field? They can let you know whether their own employers are prospects for freelance writing as well as fill you in on leads in related offices.

But commercial writing isn't the only part of your freelance outlook that they can help improve. Getting coverage of consumer or trade stories for their companies or agencies is part of their own assignments; as a freelancer, you may be interested in developing their suggestions into salable, readable magazine articles. These same friends on the inside can help you line up interviews and background information for projects that touch their fields.

As if this weren't enough, there's a third area for cooperation. Many employers do not permit their own writers to moonlight. Yet these writers are sometimes asked by business associates if they'd be interested in taking on freelance work. If they know you're available, they may be able to refer some of these potential clients to you. The reference of a known professional can be a valuable foot-in-the-door, especially for beginners.

Printers provide a special category of scouting information. If you're serious about investigating all the kinds of potential writing jobs in your area—as I think you should be—they're among your very best allies.

I've suggested that editors and those who work in advertising and public relations have a strong grasp on the local writing grapevine. In my experience, printers have proven to know even more about what's going on—who's producing what, who needs editorial or writing help, who has a good budget for the printed word but lacks expertise in writing it.

Printers have a stake in the written word. They need words, after all, to set type, lay out publications, and print them up. The enormous range of customers who seek out their services includes nearly everyone who might be a potential client for your freelance writing. Their customers, too, sometimes mention the need for assistance. If the printers know you're available, they can pass the word on.

The third group your scouting expedition should introduce to you are the potential commercial clients themselves—the local government agencies, businesses, and associations who may contract with you for editorial and writing services.

Many of the best freelance commercial clients are far less than obvious to you as you begin your search. Some of my clients not only had never worked with a freelance writer themselves, they'd never even seen one. My availability in some cases changed their plans for spreading the work among reluctant in-house staffers. In other cases it's allowed them to take on projects their regular staff was too busy to handle. In nearly every case, I was worked into their normal information plans after they learned I was available. At the time I began freelancing, there was almost no one else locally who took on the kinds of assignments I've sometimes handled.

Who are your potential clients? Now, there's a good question. At one time I would have pinpointed the company or agency whose staff was too small to include a full-time public information person, for some that fit this description have been among my best clients. But in other instances, those who can't afford to add staffers also can't afford to hire outside help (unless you're working on grants or cooperative projects, which are another story).

Very large agencies and businesses at first seem to present just the opposite picture: Most have staff assigned full-time to writing duties. Again, first appearances can be deceptive. If they value the written word highly enough to hire their own writers, they often also value the variety and fresh viewpoint an outside contractor can bring to their projects. They're used to working with writers, and can be less surprised by the amount of time required to perform a "simple" assignment that demands extensive research and rechecking.

Nor is the vast middle ground a wasteland for freelancers. In a medium-sized community, they're the great majority of the clients you'll work for. Some have writers of their own; some don't, relying on ad agencies or reluctant executives to put together what few words normally need to be written.

But they have special projects. They have expansions and changes of direction. They have one-time or infrequent needs to reach the public with specific information. They sometimes long for fill-in help, due to staff changes or reassignments, and sometimes just need someone with different or more polished skills than their own staffers possess.

At any level, the best approach to finding out your prospects is to make an appointment and talk with the highest executive you can reach—the one who can decide to depart from tradition by engaging freelance help. During these scouting stages, you won't be really looking for assignments. You'll be testing the climate . . . and planting the seed of an idea that may come to fruition after you've actually quit your job and moved into your freelance career.

Those contacts may potentially be as good as money in the bank. But during the first months while you're turning the ideas you've scouted out into cash, you need a reserve to live on. Your scouting period is the ideal time to begin to cover your start-up financial obligations. You have two ways to do this: amass enough capital to pay your bills for several months (possibly through test freelance assignments handled by moonlight), and reduce your regular obligations to the absolute minimum you find feasible.

The need for savings doesn't indicate a lack of confidence on your part. No matter how wildly successful your first freelance efforts, you still need to plan for the worst: magazines that pay slowly or fold before they get your check made out; government clients for whom payment is an excruciating procession through one office after another; business clients who try to delay paying their bills for sixty days or longer to use your money interest-free as long as they can. And for that matter, typewriters that break down, bouts with the flu, and sudden midwinter crises of spirit that desperately demand a vacation.

Some experts advise all workers to keep three to six months' income on hand where it can be reached easily in case of emergency, recession, or sudden de-employment. I don't think their advice is too conservative for novice freelancers to follow. Six months' reserve will get you over the worrisome moments of starting your new venture; it'll relieve you of money anxieties long enough to concentrate on more important things, like writing.

I believe you need to try freelancing for at least a year before you can make a fair assessment of whether it's working for you. Six months' reserve should guarantee that, since even in the beginning you should be able to bring in at least half as much income as you want to make. (If not, you haven't researched your prospects as thoroughly as you should.)

Even after you've pared down your monthly expenses, the sum of six months' paychecks may seem like a lot. Your answer to how to acquire that financial stake must be as individual as your own writing dreams.

If you have investments that can be turned into cash, consider your writing a better investment and cash them in. A cache of solid stocks, a little real estate, the savings bonds your grandma has given you for every birthday—all can mean the cash security you need. A bonus is that since your initial freelance income may be lower than your salary for a time, your tax bracket will shrink and you'll minimize the tax to be paid on your profits.

If you have no such cashable cushions, you'll just have to find a way to save. Cut down your obligations now and continue on your job for another year. Test the waters by freelancing in your spare time, saving every cent toward the day you make your break. Cut back a little (or a lot). Take a temporary second job.

Building up your financial foundation is a necessary step toward freelancing. It may postpone your escape from your job or represent unwelcome belt-tightening for awhile. But it's worth the sacrifice for a shot at your dream.

You can limit the size of financial reserve you need by cutting down your regular bills. I was able to securely start with much less money in the bank because over a period of three months my husband and I applied extraordinary effort to paying off every credit card, every store charge account, and every other obligation due to come up during my first freelance months—regular insurance premiums, college loan repayments, and the like.

If you're already living the middle-class life, you may find—as I did—that it's virtually impossible to cut your obligations to zero. Home mortgage payments roll around like phases of the moon. Car payments continue. Utility and telephone bills can be counted on, and the expenses of freelancing require accounts at office supply stores, camera shops, and travel agencies.

A working spouse simplifies. Your cash reserve has to take care of the rest. It's up to you to find the level of financial backup, coupled with reduced expenses, that will free your mind to turn creative thought to your new career. If you feel real confusion about how much money you need to get started, talk with a good accountant accustomed to working with small businesses; his expertise will provide you with good guidelines and great peace of mind. (Warning: Accountants tend to err on the side of conservatism. Don't let a gloomy one talk you out of your freelance plans, because she probably doesn't know one thing about it.)

I don't think you'll really need the financial contingency plans you're laying out during this start-up period. Nor do I think it's necessary, or even prudent, to prune your expenses (and lifestyle) to the nub. If you've done your homework thoroughly and mastered your craft, you should see results much sooner than six months from when you start. I was out flexing my MasterCard within a month of cautiously resolving to pay cash forevermore.

Yet no matter how promising your prospects, it can never hurt to establish a financial course of action for your first days of freelancing. It eases your predictable doubts about the wisdom of your decision, the visions of your children going hungry or with cavities unfilled. And others who depend on your monthly paycheck won't agitate quite so vigorously on behalf of regular income instead of adventure.

You'll be freed to spend your hours, instead, weighing the options your scouting has shown are available for your initial freelance assignments. The issue of money will fall into place. But first you ought to examine all the background you've built up, and take a long, honest look at how this research has affected your own attitude toward freelancing.

There's some chance that your scouting project has already dampened your hopes. Oh, I don't mean that the leads you turned up aren't promising. They're almost certainly better than you—doubting Thomas that you are—really expected.

But this has been a blessed lot of work. It can be exhausting. It wears out shoes (and this has been only a foretaste). During at least your first few months on your own, you'll be spending as much time searching and selling as you will at your typewriter.

Which brings up another good point to consider now, while you still have time. Do you have the enthusiasm and vitality to dedicate yourself to digging up every opportunity your area can offer—not just now, but on a continuing, month-after-month basis? Freelancing is something you keep doing anew in your chosen part of the country, though after you've gotten started its demands may ease up a bit on the promotional end.

To keep up that level of energy, you need inner resources to maintain your buoyancy. You need as much confidence as you've ever summoned to be able to walk out your employer's door for the last time and eagerly embrace the unknown (whose terrors, of course, you've already cut down to size through astute scouting). You need to launch your freelancing venture on a mental high. It's not wise to try to take off from a low point of your psychological reserves.

We've all heard the one about the guy who gets fired by an unjust, insensitive boss and turns immediately to writing—he's next heard from when his best-selling manuscript endows him with income for life. (The boss then comes on bended knee to get him back again; the erstwhile employee spurns him, and the boss never forgives himself.)

While I'm not particularly qualified to pass judgment on fiction, I do know this one's a dilly. The post-pink slip period is about as rotten a time as you can pick to start yourself as a freelancer in your neck of the woods.

Two reasons: Your eagerness and energy are bound to be at a lifetime low after you've had that kind of blow to your vocational self-confidence. You may not notice it at first, and surge ahead powered by sheer spite. But sooner or later the adrenalin level is going to return to a flaccid norm, and your vitality will slip seriously.

And you're not going to be prepared for the challenge of getting started freelancing if you've suddenly found yourself tossed out on your ear. You haven't had the time to do your homework. You haven't made the important low-pressure contacts with those who can help you. You haven't got your business matters in order. If that's not enough, in the close-knit community where you're likely to live, you'll be starting out not only weak on hard data but shadowed by a suspicious little cloud—for people really do believe that where there's smoke, there's fire. In other words, no matter how much your boss is generally conceded to resemble Simon Legree, he must have had *some* solid reason to fire you. (Don't explain it to *me*. Explain it to all those good acquaintances and former colleagues who are whispering about the scandalous turn of events.)

I do know one gifted and prominent writer who started in this way, of hard necessity, and has gone on to greater income, visibility, and admiration. He wouldn't recommend his route to freelancing, though. It's unnecessarily traumatic and horribly destructive to the confidence you need to get started.

Confidence is a funny thing. Its absence is a lot more obvious than its presence. My father always warned me that large, ominous dogs could somehow smell if you were afraid of them; I've noticed his advice applies to editors and commercial clients as well. They may not go straight for your jugular like a nice, straightforward killer Doberman, but they do go straight for the door—and that can cut off your circulation just as quickly.

So if you have even the slightest element of choice, start freelancing at a high point in your life. Turn down some alluring promotion and set out on your own. Accept your coworkers' best wishes and have a grand time at your going-away party. Resist the impulse to tell your employer exactly what you've thought of her for the past thirteen long years. Smile and shake her hand instead.

There is a reason for all this good humor.

Who do you think your first writing client should be? How about someone who knows your work well, needs immediate help to fill an open position, and dreads having to train some upstart still wet behind the ears in all the intricacies of your former job?

Your just-barely-former boss, that's who. Consider discussing whether you can carry on some or all of your former duties on a freelance basis. You may be surprised at how well your full-time job can be transposed into a part-time contract as a freelancer. The chances of this will be substantially dimmed, however, if you've informed your boss of his resemblance to a snake in the grass or the wrong end of an equine.

You'll notice I assume your last job is one that includes writing duties. If it isn't, hold onto your paycheck a little longer. You're not going to savor what comes next.

If you do not already have professional experience in some aspect of writing, you're taking a foolhardy chance to try freelancing before you do.

You can get that experience through many kinds of salaried positions. You need to work somewhere where you're required to write often, accurately, and preferably quickly.

That's exactly what you'll master on a newspaper. Any kind of newspaper. The *New York Times* has certain advantages over the *Sioux Falls Argus-Leader*, but both provide commensurate gifts to freelancers intent on freelancing where they've ended up. At the *Times* you may rub shoulders with the famous and acquire a bit of notoriety yourself . . . especially if your writing tends to the truly spectacular and you're tough enough to elbow your way to the top.

But at the *Argus-Leader* you can accomplish the same thing on the scale of the place where you've chosen to live. You'll learn to write—and meet the local movers and shakers. You'll have the fear of the Lord of Deadlines pounded into you—and develop a readership which recognizes your name and knows that you're a bona fide writer. You might not excite quite so much envy from your peers, but your prospects may be just as bright and ultimately satisfying as your counterpart the megalopolis marvel's.

There are other places to hone your craftsmanship, of course. Public information, public relations, and advertising jobs involving copywriting all offer the same basic lessons in writing style and precision. They provide some visibility which you can build upon after you go out on your own. And the casual contacts you make on your job every day can lead to potential freelance assignments in the future.

Work for which you've been paid counts here . . . but so does volunteering. Especially as you begin, you're likely to donate your time to gain experience as well as contacts and a track record. Some of the most innovative PR campaigns have stemmed from contributed services: Witness the Advertising Council's often-memorable work on behalf of public-spirited issues.

You can take college courses in writing, too—even courses specifically in freelancing. They may be great for helping polish your work or teaching the rudiments of manuscript marketing. (Or they can be lousy.) But by themselves, they almost certainly will not make a self-supporting freelancer out of you.

Why not? Those who teach, for one thing, have seldom earned a freelance living themselves. They may urge grammatical, philosophical, and creative perfection, but their idea of how to write to earn money can be pretty fuzzy.

The courses can't teach you to hustle. They can't teach you to get out and meet people, to sell yourself, to scramble in all the ways the self-supporting freelance life requires. In fact, some that I've known actually work against the kind of enterprise demanded by serious freelancing, giving students a taste instead for the smoking-jacketed, brandy-sniftering, literary-salonish, writers' lifestyle that exists only in dated movies and fifty-year-old short stories.

(And while courses in fiction and poetry may be an enlightening pastime, they're virtually worthless when it comes to preparing yourself for serious self-supporting freelancing. Your chances of living on income from fiction are slim indeed, unless you write erotic historical romances by the dozen; from poetry, they're virtually zero. Yet even these areas can represent at least a fractional element of your income, as you'll see in Chapter 7.)

Of course, there are classes that differ from this mold, notably those special few taught by real live working freelancers. Maybe you'll teach one yourself someday. In the meantime, they can be at best just one block in the working foundation that'll enable you to freelance successfully.

You must write to get jobs as a writer. The more visible that writing, the better your freelance prospects become. Far-off editors will want to see solid samples of published work. Commercial clients will want printed proof that you can tailor your work to their special requirements before they hand out assignments.

Newspaper writers have this item checked off early. If your writing experience is in less visible channels, there are still steps you can take before you leave your job to get your name recognized by the public in your part of the world.

One way to build up your reputation as a writer is to make use of the most closely read publications in your city, state, or region. In later chapters I'll preach to you about the cardinal rule of the freelance business: Get paid what your work is worth. But in this single case—the quest for reputation—we'll push that rule to the back burner and concentrate instead on how to use low-paying local publications as a source of inexpensive self-advertising.

Those who live in urban areas served by all kinds of publications will never know how seriously we who are less advantaged take the few publications which serve us. In North Dakota there's one general-circulation magazine that reaches the bulk of the decision makers, the socially prominent, and the just-plain-people in the state all at the same time. (It falters badly with the *Rolling Stone* crowd, but they buy only 25 to 50 percent of their articles from freelancers anyway.) *North Dakota Horizons* has contributed an utterly disproportionate share to my visibility here. Though it's published only a tiny fraction of my total work in any given year, and though its circulation is a small percentage of that of other magazines I've written for . . . still, it's the one that strangers mention when they say they've heard of me. Publication between its scenic covers is a good entrée to just about any kind of writing assignment in the state. (That name recognition is especially handy when you try to cash checks out of town.)

Every community has its version of *Horizons*: if not the county seat weekly, then a city magazine, a business publication, an entertainment guide, a magazine for outdoorsmen, or some other kind of periodical that finds its way into lots of homes and gets taken seriously.

These articles may not pay very well, but they're a good investment just the same. Writers are an unusual and interesting species over almost all of the country, New York publishing circles aside. In North Dakota and states like yours, perhaps, your vocation—once recognized by enough people—can make you genuinely memorable.

Writing, however, isn't the only good way to make yourself known in your community. Don't look at freelancing as your chance to escape all the pressures of dealing with people. Actually, it's an invitation to get more involved than you've ever been before. As a freelancer in your part of the world, you need people. They're clients. Sources. Inspiration. They're your instant, handy antidote to the loneliness that comes with facing no one but your typewriter.

Back when I was employed, I was never a joiner. I treasured every minute of time to myself—for writing, for reading, for watching soap operas, napping, whatever happened to recharge my batteries. So when I began saying yes to invitations to join groups or serve on committees, I was as surprised myself as the members I took by surprise.

People are partly recreation. But getting involved with as many as you can manage to meet is a good sound business decision as well. The contacts you make as part of a group or public project can be the very best kind. You have interests in common. You get to know one another in a tension-free atmosphere. You become *friends*—not just cordial business acquaintances. You see each other as allies.

If you're new in town, these groups can help you learn all you need to know about your new home. They're a source of introductions, of referrals, of writing leads. Whether your own tastes run to the Sierra Club or the Lions, the Audubon Society or the Elks, Zonta or NOW, you'll almost certainly enhance both your social life and your freelance career by being an involved part of a group working toward a mutual goal, not merely a passive, anonymous observer.

You've scouted out your area (or the spot where you want to live) now and have some notion of the pluses and minuses it's endowed with. You've identified some potential clients to work on locally; you're getting your first batch of magazine queries in the mail. You're building your reputation, your file of contacts, your confidence.

So are you ready to freelance yet? There's still a little groundwork left to lay. A creative approach to finding freelance assignments is only one of the two laws of successful freelancing.

You still have to go into business.

3

Look Like a Winner

Freelance writing is often singled out as the kind of business in which you can engage with little or no up-front expense outside of what it takes to keep your body warm and your fingers moving across the typewriter keys. If not a jug of wine, a loaf of bread, and the will to write poesy, then it would seem to require a minumum of a yellow legal tablet, a couple of felt-tip pens, and your junker of a portable typewriter set up on the kitchen table.

Yes . . . and no. Part-time writers have made do with little more than that and still scored solid successes. If you're devoting your full energy to your writing, though, you need to do much better.

True, clients and editors are not at all likely to make surprise inspections of your habitat. Your setting, though, is going to be experienced in intimate detail by the one person most important to your success. Your chief executive officer. Your employer. That is, you.

We're talking investment here—overhead, the business expenses that include not only start-up costs but a bit from your income every single month.

At first these steps may seem like an extravagance for a profession reputed to flourish on time and inspiration. Nothing could be farther from the truth.

Think of the comparatively modest sum that such preparations require as an investment. It's venture capital, not gambled but thoughtfully invested in a business venture that you've researched well.

That business is built on filling a demonstrated need. It's guided by a researched game plan. It revolves around a top-quality product—your words—and is guided by an entrepreneur who is willing to risk everything that he or she has accomplished in methodical pursuit of a practical and attainable dream.

What more could you ask?

If writing is to be your business, your boss owes you a decent, well-equipped working environment. Moreover, that chief executive (you, of course) realizes that the persuasive scent of success begins with self-respect.

It is precious hard to respect yourself as a professional communicator when you're composing deathless verbiage among the crumbs from your daughter's breakfast. Whether it can be done is not the point. It should not need to be.

Confidence in your professionalism begins with the way you present yourself. You have a choice. You can lean toward the familiar stereotype of the absent-minded dreamer in musty jeans and bedroom slippers, or you can play the part of the successful businessperson whom you avidly hope to become—a minor contender for the chamber of commerce.

There are two elements to the way you "package" yourself as a writer. One is the behind-the-scenes matter of office and business procedures. The other is enacted stage center in front of a paying audience, the men and women whose business you solicit. Included here are the ways in which you identify yourself as a serious writer, both in face-to-face encounters and when your query letter lies in someone's "in" box.

Though quite different, both elements have a bearing on the impression you make on your clientele—editors, agencies, commercial customers and the like. On the one hand, you are dealing with first impressions. On the other, you're equipping yourself to deliver everything you promise, and more.

First, let's peek behind the curtain where your customers will never go: your office.

Whether in a closet or a country home, you'll be spending the lion's share of your working hours in it. It needs to be convenient, yes, and well-lighted. It needs a door to close out distractions. It needs all the typical accoutrements that encourage production, from desk and decent posture-supporting chair to telephone, reference library, files, and typewriter (or, better yet, computer—more on that later). And if you're lucky, you'll be able to add another near-essential to the list in the interest of maintaining sanity . . . a window.

But your office demands something else, too. It should reek of commitment to this new direction for your career. It should fairly shout "Permanence!" in a most assertive voice.

A full-time freelancer deserves an office as conducive to steady accomplishment as any outside workplace. Part of its function is symbolic. A card table in the laundry room might keep your papers off the no-wax vinyl floor. But will it encourage your self-confidence? Help keep your motivation on course? Suffice as evidence of your intent if a doubting mother-in-law demands to take a peek?

I'm not talking about cozy comfort. I'm talking about tough realities.

Consider the way you'd prepare for an interview with the governor of your state. You'd do your homework, of course, in thoroughly researching the matters at hand. But you'd also groom yourself for the encounter; to be taken seriously is the first hurdle in collecting the incisive comments you intend to bring away with you.

Levi 501s may be "you," along with flannel shirts and Nikes. But that's not the sort of ensemble a hard-headed governor-interviewing journalist would choose. It's ten-to-one that you'd pull the pinstripes from the back of your closet.

We're raised to speak the nonverbal language of clothing so well that we seldom question such choices (though in front of the mirror we continue to agonize—Lord, do we agonize).

The environment in which we work, though, has something equally important to say. Setting up the first office intended solely for your personal use presents challenges that have equally little to do with fine interior decor and creature comforts. At its heart, it's a practical investment in your image of yourself, a concept you convey in everything you do.

Take your setting seriously. When you do interview your governor, he won't glimpse the setting in which you work. But he'll see its effects in the way you regard yourself as surely as he'd notice spots on your tie.

This is where you'll arrive for work every morning and prepare to depart at night, the scene where local clients will picture you at work and perhaps occasionally visit on business, and the place to which you'll casually refer when talking to editors who call and friends who think you're unemployed. It's a sanctuary.

It's also a practical convenience. Shoeboxes full of notes, correspondence on the kitchen cupboard and a portable Smith-Corona reached by sitting on a bar stool are depressing and fairly shout that your freelancing is merely an aberration so temporary it's not even worth rearranging the furniture.

Trust me: I spent my own first month in a spare bedroom pecking away at an ancient Royal standard with sticky m's and e's. All that kept me going was the sound of hammers pounding down below, as my husband finished enough of the lower level of the house to give me space to call my own. And I stayed there for the next ten years until the changing nature of my business made an outside office absolutely imperative.

That brings up another oft-discussed issue. Should you elect to work at home in the first place?

During the days of your freelance business launching, your answer will almost certainly be "yes," contingent only on the availability of a modest amount of space to accommodate you. It's bound to be desirable, if only because working in a portion of the place you live substantially reduces the business overhead (expenses) subtracted each month from your income. If you choose to claim a home office deduction when you file with the I.R.S., it may even cut your taxes. (Warning: Deducting a home office is a ploy not without distinct pitfalls, the likelihood of audit being only one among several. This is a question to discuss with your accountant.)

Convenience is another point in favor of home sweet home. Working there reduces your morning commute to about twenty seconds, the length of time it takes to pour a cup of coffee, walk down the hall, and pull the chair out from your desk. Too, you can easily incorporate evenings and weekends into your writing schedule without the guilt of abandoning your family. And it takes more discipline than you should have to muster to re-board a cold, cranky automobile on a frigid night for going back to a darkened downtown office.

Yet the home office has liabilities as well. Most obvious is the dilemma of how to squeeze it into an apartment or house where space is already at a premium. (If there's not even a corner to call your own, you may have to consider alternatives.) That's closely followed by the complexities of shutting out a rowdy cast of household characters. A door, a lock, and dire threats may help, but beware the pressures to backslide!

Self-discipline may be a bit harder to come by. Your personal favorite distractions are only part of the problem. By working at home, you bear an all-too-close resemblance to someone with time on your hands. It's harder to train friends and relatives to respect your work schedule. You'll collect endless midday United Parcel Service deliveries for your neighbors (both spouses are absent at "real" jobs) and perhaps host visits by Jehovah's Witnesses and Mormon missionaries who'd love to share a few moments of your time.

Women in particular face a challenge here. A male freelancer working at home may be a curiosity, but a female faces all-knowing nods. We look a lot like full-time housewives. The fact that anyone can with impunity label herself (men, too) a freelancer further compounds the problem. Taking extra pains to look professional is clearly in order.

Finally, some people who are leaving salaried positions as writers find that years in a frantic newsroom or public relations bull pen has left its insidious mark: they can't concentrate when it's too quiet!

Strange but true. Two different freelancers of my acquaintance have claimed this to be the major stumbling block to working in their homes. One eventually got used to comparative tranquility, cranking up his favorite FM jazz when withdrawal became too terrible.

The other worked out a deal with friends in a real estate firm. For a minimal monthly rent she occupies a tiny back office formerly used for storage and takes breaks in their staff coffee room for free.

How you view yourself and your own enterprise does depend in part on the investment you've made in yourself—time, space and setting. Subtly but surely, your working environment has an effect on the confidence with which you present your work (and yourself) to others.

Your self-confidence shows even more clearly in the second category of essential elements that help you present yourself as a professional writer—the printed materials that provide a showcase for your experience, abilities and commitment to your work.

There's no mistaking the ground that stands to be gained or lost here. Editors, commercial clients, and other potential supporters of your quest for success will judge you by what they see in their mailboxes, read at their desks, or slip into their briefcases as you shake hands in greeting—your letterhead and business cards, your summary of your credentials, and your portfolio or file of samples of published work.

These go beyond the most basic packaging of all: the clean, correct and confident manuscripts with which you finally fulfill your end of the bargain. Yes, queries typed dimly with a defeated ribbon on plain copier paper do undoubtedly turn into published stories on occasion. Even when they arrive wedged into little lick'em envelopes lined with a madras pattern.

Yes, those in the publishing world do recognize the truism that you can't judge a book by its cover. Why, though, would you risk the good impression you're trying to make by presenting yourself in anything less than the most professional light possible? The freelance life is challenging enough without playing fast and loose with the easy stuff.

None of these staples requires a major investment. But each is worth some specific attention to insure that it represents you well.

Take your stationery, for example. It's your first line of defense against being mistaken for an amateur. It provides a frame of reference for showing off the article or book query it bears—a subtle reinforcement of the highly professional image you're trying so hard to convey. At the same time, it is Exhibit A in an editor's review of whether you're a writer to be trusted. Correctly done, it at least shows that you're stable.

The quest for an aura of stability disqualifies many of the more gimmicky examples observed in my letters from beginning freelancers. Quill pens and little typewriters (or even worse, tiny computers) have probably exhausted their useful life as symbols of the writing business. Mouth-watering colored papers are out, especially when accessorized with a message typed in a coordinated hue of mauve or fire-engine red. (Drooling aside, queries are simply more difficult to read in living color.)

What works most efficiently is a design that provides the information it's intended to convey in a clear, direct and rather conservative manner—your name, your address, your telephone number. Adding "freelance writer" or "professional writer" rarely makes much sense, since that should be abundantly clear from the context.

A logo (or graphic emblem) can take you one step further, providing consistency throughout your materials and a dollop of extra recognition in repeat contact with editors and clients.

You can dash down to the corner rapid-print shot for a slapdash letterhead, envelopes, business cards, and any other official-looking permutations that might fit your situation (mailing labels, billing statements, postcards or whatever). You can count on it being speedy and inexpensive. Yet I'd counsel against this particular bargain.

Instead, consider taking on the one-time expense of conferring with a good, creative graphic designer whose work you admire. Practicing designers usually have a superior grasp of styles that are current, tasteful, and effective. The sure hand of a graphics professional can protect you against costly mistakes . . . costly, that is, in terms of lost opportunities to reinforce the competent image your stationery is intended to promote.

Audition designers before choosing one to deal with your graphic identity. Let them educate you. Request to see samples of their work. Ask which they feel is most effective, and why. Don't hang back from talking money, either. Like most creative professionals', their fees are almost certainly negotiable. A reasonable estimate is important to establish before you permit work to begin.

What you'll pay depends in part on whom you hire. In my part of the country, a logo or well-chosen typographical design generally involves a fee from two to five hundred dollars. The lower figure is more representative of a freelance designer or small studio, while larger production firms and advertising agencies might charge on the higher end.

Don't scrimp by hiring your neighbor's artistic cousin at four bucks an hour. Good design is like good writing: it takes time and experience to do it right, and you'll generally get what you pay for. Nothing smacks of a freelance dabbler quite as clearly as shaky hand-drawn calligraphy or excessively precious illustrations in the corner of the page. Over-ambitious work that doesn't quite come off is far worse than no fancy stuff at all.

Your designer can recommend printers who do good work, and you can audition them as well. If your letterhead design is simple and the paper stock widely available (as it should be), you may want to investigate both full-service printers and well-equipped rapid-print operations. One caution: request an estimate up front and expect your firm to live up to it. Like graphic artists, like writers—in fact, like just about everyone you'll be dealing with as a professional freelancer—printers have no hard-and-fast price lists.

While your stationery is being produced, you can turn your attention to a related bit of ammunition in your campaign for clients. Review your professional credentials, useful to quote in query letters and worth producing as a separate piece if you plan to approach business clients. Then assemble samples of your most successful work to be used in gaining clients.

When you're fishing for assignments from distant editors, your ideas and enthusiasm are always the hook . . . and your credentials and samples the bait. They provide a reason to take a chance on those juicy proposals. They can reassure the wary blue-pencil-pusher that you have been tested by others and that you passed with flying colors.

The biographical data that counts are pertinent qualifications and experiences. The typical sort of résumé is poorly suited to offer this kind of proof-of-purchase. Editors are less than fascinated by your education, marital history, personal statistics, and hobbies (unless these somehow have direct bearing on the story you propose). Instead, they're looking for a track record that demonstrates any of the following: A) dependability; B) flexibility with a range of topics; C) dependability; D) credibility with the subject at hand, or E) dependability.

Published credits are best, along with past employment in relevant fields. Those published words belong among your samples to be mailed along with your queries to new markets and to be shown in portfolio form to your potential commercial clients.

It should go without saying that you'll include your finest work—but is it equally obvious that even less-impressive finished articles should be included if they appeared in high-quality, high-profile publications? As a general rule, anything published is better than anything in manuscript form; illustrated pieces are usually a more apt choice than words-only, and nicely designed pages take priority over hectic, confused spreads.

Why lean toward choosing form over content when your true goal is to sell content, period? Your editor or client-to-be is inevitably rushed and likely to do little more than flip through the examples you provide. The editor will recognize the names of familiar publications or businesses and judge the quality of others by their attractive presentation.

You need not send original samples along with your queries. Good-quality copies can by obtained from that rapid-printer who bid on your letterhead. They're inexpensive, less messy to handle, and need not be returned—a small relief to whoever reviews them, and a boon to your postage budget.

Avoid overkill; two or three polished examples are more powerful than a dozen ditsy ones. One tidy format is to reproduce the cover of the magazine in the month an article appeared with the story on the back. If it's a long one, use $11'' \times 17''$ paper folded to four $8\frac{1}{2}'' \times 11''$ pages; position the cover on page one and the story on pages two, three, and four.

Newspaper samples in particular benefit from being copied, since newsprint deteriorates so quickly when it's folded. If the layout is cramped and invaded by ads and adjacent stories, as it's likely to be in this field, then take matters into your own hands: cut apart the columns and realign them neatly beneath the original headline along with whatever photos or illustrations accompanied the story. It's tidier and more appealing. Besides, do you want your chosen editor to concentrate on your article or the grocery ads on the back of a smudgy clipping?

Printed samples are also useful when you're calling on new local clients, providing you something to leave behind as a reminder. (Package them neatly in a pocketed folder with your business card clipped inside.)

However, the key prop for your face-to-face presentation is the professional-style portfolio. Traditionally a tool of photographers and graphic designers, it offers similar advantages to writers. It showcases your best work in an organized manner, guaranteeing you the prospect's attention and demonstrating a variety of areas in which you may be able to assist him or her. (Maybe you'll give the editor ideas.) Moreover, if you're nervous in these confrontations, the act of turning its pages will give you something to do with your hands.

The usual portfolio is housed in an 11" × 14" or larger zippered case toted by handles. Inside are ring-bound acetate pages that enclose samples permanently mounted on light mat board. These are available in a broad range of prices in any art and office supply store.

As you did for your copied samples, select samples for your portfolio not only on the basis of the writing, but also for illustrations, graphics, and the medium in which it appeared. Commercial presentations call for not only magazine or newspaper credits but whatever other forms you've worked in—booklets, brochures, news releases, speeches, scripts. Your goal is to establish the impression not only of high-quality writing, but of versatility and competence in initiating new kinds of assignments.

Stationery is important to your freelance presentations. What's even more important, though, the essential tool on which you compose the queries and manuscripts it's destined to carry—your typewriter or computer, the key tool of your trade.

Ancient Underwoods work. So do portable typewriters left over from college days. But as writing professionals deserve an office and proper business stationery, they absolutely require excellence in the machine with which they spend their days (and nights, sometimes—weekends too).

I spent many fruitful years in partnership with an IBM Selectric II typewriter, the Cadillac of the industry with its dished-out keys, its spacious keyboard, and its array of type styles. If you are adamantly devoted to simply typing and can find a reconditioned model, I'd endorse it still.

If, however, you're willing to rethink your approach to writing—no less than that—an investment comparable to a new top-of-the-line model can get you into the computer age.

Computerized writing is a shock for the traditionalist. In practice as well as in its deplorable plastic-coated name, word processing demands a period of days or weeks to learn and often months more to establish the same comfort and fluency that you achieved with the dear old Selectric. Add to that computers' fairly chunky list prices, and you've got a serious decision on your hands.

I reached my own decision half a dozen years ago. Once I'd laid my fingers on a showroom model's keys, the answer could have been nothing less than "yes." And though I've made missteps (buying a CPM model exactly two weeks before the debut of the incompatible IBM PC, to name just one), not to mention five years of payments, I've never regretted adding my own high-tech invader to my decidedly low-tech lifestyle.

That's the worst stumbling block for those of us who aren't electronically gifted, I think—the thought of pounding too much technological know-how into an unyielding brain. Here's what I have learned about using micros: All you really need to know is how to turn it on, boot up the program (don't get excited—you only type "B" and let the software do the rest) and apply a few dozen simple commands to make words jump around the screen.

You can go much, much farther. But why? I've baked chocolate chip cookies for twenty-five years without knowing a whit about wiring my kitchen stove. Turn a dial and the oven gets hot; that's why it's known as an appliance. Likewise, I've written millions of words without reading my computer's secret silicon mind. As long as green blips appear on the screen when I push the "on" button, it's doing all I'd ever ask of it.

If you hate the notion of spending a few weeks in alien territory as you learn to apply word-processing commands, hang on to your typewriter. (You might look into the electronic variety, though, with its store of crossbred computer-like abilities). But if you want to write far more quickly, edit with genuine ease, and print out clean final manuscripts as nearly perfect as you can make them, here's your golden opportunity.

Do you harbor some doubt of whether you can master this new art by yourself? Then browse in well-staffed computer stores rather than discount houses, and chalk the price differential up to adult education. A knowledgeable salesperson can guide you through the maze of models and functions from which you must choose.

Ask about software first. You'll need a word-processing program to start with. (I've always used one of the more powerful, Wordstar; other newer varieties also deserve consideration.) If your technical skills are shaky, you can employ additional programs to check your spelling, grammar, and even punctuation. You may also want to look into a financial spreadsheet, great for business records and balancing your checkbook.

Another option to keep in mind is that certain kinds of computers, especially Apple's MacIntosh and some IBMs, also support publishing programs capable of producing professional-looking copy and layouts. You don't need those features for basic freelancing; someday, however, you might become involved in commercial work or self-publishing and find them invaluable. By choosing the right model now, you reserve the right to upgrade its capabilities at a later date.

Don't skimp on the printer. These come in two basic varieties, dot matrix and letter-quality. The dot-matrix style spits out your manuscript in letters composed of up to thirty-two separate dots, while the latter use a type wheel and produce printed copies equal to—in fact, indistinguishable from—a good typewriter.

The professional choice, and naturally the more expensive, is letter-quality. Its advantage is summed up in a single word, readability. Those who deal with many, many letters and manuscripts a day generally despise plowing through dot-matrix submissions. They make their eyes jump, and that raises blood pressure and the likelihood of "no."

A third component of your computer armory is the modem, a simple-looking device that permits your microcomputer to talk on the telephone to another computer or a typesetter far away. This is what market listings mean by the cryptic phrase, "electronic submissions OK."

Does your computer need to perform this technological trick? In certain specialized cases, maybe. Mine doesn't, and it's never been an obstacle to me. This may change as more publishers join the revolution-in-progress. For now, I'd counsel you to go slow. Someone will always be happy to sell you the necessary equipment and program later.

So far we've considered start-up investments that basically occur only once. Another element of your overhead, however, is the continuing expenses that go on as long as you're in the writing business. These include telephone service, postage and shipping expenses, and travel and entertainment—all vital, all relatively costly, and all capable of being held in check only by on-going review and conscious effort.

What would an office be without a phone? Heaven, that's what—but it's not feasible. You need to be consistently within the reach of editors, commercial clients, and your sources and subjects. Not only is your telephone critical, the way you handle it speaks volumes about your degree of commitment to your business.

Arranging local phone service is the easy part. You already are wired for it, albeit as a residential customer. I see no need for a second business line; that only provides two separate phones to interrupt your concentration. Instead, you may want to change the status of your present line to a business account.

Technically you're obliged to do so, though you can find hordes of self-employed people who work at home who never bother. There is one advantage to a business listing, which comes at a price (here, about twelve dollars more per month for single-line commercial service). And no matter what route you select, there's also a complication.

Yellow Page listings are available to you only if you switch from residential. Are they worth it? I've experimented. You get one very plain listing free under the category of your choice. I tried the next step up, or a bold-face line under "Public Relations Counselors." It cost me about ten dollars extra per month and elicited only a dribble of inquiries from potential users of my services, along with a fair number of truly bizarre encounters with very confused people, perhaps from outer space. It did, however, more than pay for itself with the few good jobs that eventually turned up. In the meantime, it may have served to remind those who knew me simply as "writer" that I could in fact offer services in that area.

I use the past tense because I no longer maintain a listing beyond the single line that's free. It's fine as a place-holder, but I seldom take walk-in (I should say "call-in") business.

If I were starting out, however, I would consider trying a small display ad (the kind in a box of its own) delineating services. I'd also weigh the benefits of additional simple listings under headings like "advertising agencies/counselors," "audiovisual production services," or "commercial photography" if those were areas in which I was equipped to deliver. But beware: Any mention of your name whatsoever in a photo or video context is going to result in calls from youngsters wanting to know if you do weddings. (It took me two baffled years to figure out where they were coming from.)

The second and more complex factor in choosing between business and residential service is the new format introduced into Bell System directories. It segregates business and residential listings rather than letting them mingle as they once did. (Directory Assistance also uses these categories.)

You may encounter problems here no matter what you do. Your phone will undoubtedly be listed under your proper name. That's the only feasible alternative for self-employed writers, since few inquiring contacts can be expected to be armed with anything but your monicker. If editors or customers are looking through the directory for business purposes, they'll likely turn to the business section; thus, you ought to have a commercial listing. But if they're calling long-distance assistance to find your number and neglect to emphasize that you're a business—which they certainly will—the operator will look for a residential listing and report that you don't exist.

The telephone company says this cannot happen. It can. After moving to a new address, I spent two years trying to straighten out my telephone existence, an annoying period enlivened by occasional run-ins with friends and former clients who'd tried to find my number and deduced that I must have skipped town.

What to do, what to do? Take nothing for granted. Especially if you plan to work with commercial clients, a business listing is likely to be necessary. But ask your phone representative about cross-listing to residential . . . and then call Directory Assistance yourself to check what they really have accomplished on your behalf.

In the meantime, look into arranging for a second listing under your name in the directory's residential section. It will cost a dollar or so extra per month but save you untold aggravation.

The monthly fee, of course, is only the beginning of what telephone service will cost you. Its use can save you enormous amounts of time in interviews and research; it can also help you clarify assignments, negotiate prices, and incidentally develop personal relationships with your publishing contacts.

The phrase "long-distance charges" could have been invented expressly for us long-distance writers. The telephone is too useful to curtail; instead, look for ways to get more for your money.

Federal deregulation has been more of a bomb than a boon for many of us nonmetropolitan Americans, but the trials of AT&T have provided one bright spot. Rates are falling; discount and premium packages abound. Not only that: competitive long-distance services like Republic Telcom and Sprint offer their own cost-efficient services. Take time to research your local options.

Even in a time of moderating rates, several other penny-pinching strategies can be employed to get the maximum from our legacy of Ma and all the little Bells.

It isn't really cheap to call anywhere from North Dakota except to other places in North Dakota. I've found there are ways, however, to cut twenty-dollar phone interviews down to size, and to avoid paying for your subject's "hmmms" and "let me sees." You may find it unavoidable to first contact your sources during normal working hours, the exact period during which the telephone company, in its wisdom, charges its most businesslike rates. It's easiest to contact many people at work—also most courteous, unless your questions are of a specifically personal nature.

But to phone someone unannounced is to reach her far from the peak of her answering powers. I've found it more effective to first make a concise daytime (full-rate) call to explain my project and how I hope the subject will fit in. Then I arrange to call her back at a mutually agreeable time, after she's had a chance to gather her thoughts and take care of the impatient salesperson waiting in her office. One important element that makes the call-back time agreeable on my end of the line is that it be after 5 p.m., when rates go down, or otherwise avoids peak rate periods.

Now, 5 p.m. in North Dakota isn't necessarily 5 p.m. where my subject answers the phone. If I'm calling west to Rocky Mountain or Pacific standard time zones, I'll reach him at 4 p.m. or 3 p.m.—still in the office, and at a less hectic time of the day. Yet since the call is placed from Bismarck, I get to take advantage of a 20 percent after-5 discount (larger perhaps where you live). On a long call, that quickly amounts to real savings.

Calling people in the eastern standard time zone eliminates my advantage after lunch. But we get up early here in North Dakota. Since the time you *start* your call determines the rate you're charged, I can call eastward any time before 8 a.m. and qualify for a discount. But after that, into prime-time work hours, the rates go up.

Writers farther west have an even better situation. While 7:30 a.m. in Bismarck is 8:30 a.m. in New York—just a little early to catch many editors or agents at the job—the mountain and Pacific time zones add additional hours to the differential. That breakfast-time call from Cheyenne, Wyoming, is 9:30 a.m. in Manhattan; the same call from Portland, Oregon, would reach the editor at 10:30 a.m. All this finagling results in savings worth the computations: Calls placed between 11 p.m. and 8 a.m. your time are discounted 60 percent.

If you can arrange to call your interviewee back when he really has more time and leisure to talk—say on Saturday, or before 5 p.m. Sunday—you'll get the same discount of more than half the usual rate. And even on Sunday evenings, when all America calls dear Mother back home, you qualify for 35 percent less than the going price.

What are you going to do with all these savings? One good place to apply them is to your other telephone problem: what to do when you're away from home and the client or editor finally calls you back.

You have two options short of a full-time receptionist's services. One is those telephone answering machines. The other is a live answering service.

The machine has its advantages. I started out with one, a good model which cost several hundred dollars. It was clearly superior to cheaper models simply because it was voice activated. That is, I didn't have to listen to my own voice saying "Nancy is not home," and so on, before every message when I retrieved my calls.

I hated it. I dreaded taking messages off the tape, partly because about two-thirds of them were preceded by a comment about how the caller despised talking into tape recorders over the telephone.

I did not research whether they preferred no answer at all because I can't afford to miss calls, not even once in a while. Instead, I invested in one of Bismarck's big-city luxuries, a hookup with the single local telephone answering service.

The service picks up my calls on the fourth ring. Three rings gives me time to grab for the phone no matter where I am or just long enough to finish typing the sentence I'm composing. If I really can't be interrupted, I let the service catch the call and phone later for the message.

(If you've got suspicious friends or in-laws, they may begin to wonder if you're really gone when the service tells them you're out . . . or if you're just avoiding them.) Though a certain percentage of callers don't like my service any better than my former machine, the majority tell me they much prefer talking to a live human.

There are drawbacks. Once in a great while I return a call to a mystified person who left a message for the plumber—who uses the same service. The other negative is the cost. I pay forty-five dollars a month for the privilege of having my calls covered from 8 a.m. to 6 p.m. six days a week; costs are sometimes higher in larger cities, but this seems to be about average. Just one important call that I would have otherwise missed makes up for that monthly billing, however. I count it as one of my best business investments.

If no commercial answering service serves your area, you might consider setting up your own by enlisting the help of a reliable family member or neighbor who spends the day at home. Unless the person lives with you, you'll have to invest in a second phone line to his or her home plus a monthly service charge for this extension; it will cost you no more than the installation fee you'd pay for hooking up with a professional service.

My answering service also has secretarial help available for typing, transcribing tapes, and mailings. Their cost for transcription is now about ten dollars an hour—the transcriber's hour, not per hour of recorded tape. The going rate for typing manuscripts is about $1.50 per completed page.

Your telephone costs are only a portion of the regular monthly expenses you must plan for. Another is postage. Steadily rising costs insure that this item will inexorably increase, 22 cents by 22 cents—small nibbles that ultimately take a healthy bite out of your income.

Your best defense is to become a knowledgeable consumer of this service which, griping aside, is one of the best gifts with which the government could endow us. The U.S. Postal Service and its private competitors, from United Parcel Service to Purolator and Federal Express, can save you from missing a deadline, insure your valuable manuscripts and photos against loss, and provide incontrovertible proof that a publisher did indeed receive what you sent, no matter what.

Don't take a chance. Put your work into the hands of first-class mail, no matter how attractive alternatives like the fourth-class book rate might seem for bulky shipments. First-class and its one-pound-plus partner, Priority Mail, offer reasonable speed at a reasonable price.

Insurance is a good investment only for mailings that include photographs. (Of course you'd never send off a manuscript without retaining a copy yourself—would you?)

The other services vary in their effectiveness. Here in North Dakota, UPS shipment is often equally fast and less expensive than the post office for large envelopes and packages for distant publications. My husband, a photographer, frequently uses the service for packets of photo transparencies which would cost plenty to mail. As a bonus UPS packages are automatically insured for the first hundred dollars of value, are always delivered to the addressee's doorstep, and require a signature upon receipt.

The biggest drawback is that UPS collection centers are invariably in the most inconvenient outer margin of your town. Trucks pick up packages from regular shippers, but charge extra for only occasional service. Try finding a regular UPS customer whom you can reimburse for including your material along with his or her own. Some businesses, too, are beginning to serve their customers as UPS shipping stations.

If you've squeezed the very last drop of blood out of your deadline, however, express delivery services may be the only way to save the day. Several may be available in your area—or may not, depending on just how rural your address really is.

Being a devotee of the last-minute rush, I've tried four different private services. Each has been more or less reluctant to serve a customer generating as small a shipping volume as I do, especially one whose packages must be picked up in such an out-of-the-way residential location. They're geared to heavy users in the central business districts. Their service is costly. And if your local air service is spotty, they may even save less time than you expect; your shipment might travel by surface transportation to the nearest transshipment point.

My conclusion: Go back to the post office and enlist the superlative aid of Express Mail. You're unlikely to do better than its overnight service at any cost. The price is one-fourth to one-third of private air express rates, and it offers all the same benefits to occasional and small-business customers that it does to the biggies. That's a promise that other high-speed delivery services simply cannot match.

Are you getting the impression that your letters and manuscripts are going to be a great deal more well traveled than you are? It's true! Nevertheless, your personal travel and entertainment expenses possess the potential to become a big part of your monthly budget. Fortunately they're also the ones most easily controlled . . . and definitely the most fun.

By business entertainment, I don't mean taking clients to Las Vegas or buying them fifty-dollar-a-plate dinners . . . although there might be reasons for you to splurge on either one someday. I'm more concerned with fifty-cent cups of coffee, occasional lunches, perhaps a drink together after hours.

The government recognizes these treats as a legitimate expense of doing business, though current law may permit you to deduct only a portion of unreimbursed expenditures. You might as well go along with them. Since I prefer to meet clients on neutral territory—neither their office nor mine—I practically live at a pancake house a few blocks away, where the pots of coffee I've purchased could fill one of the smaller Great Lakes. (This is one way to minimize the liability of working out of a home office, by the way. I could do my writing in the runway of our local airport and they'd never know.)

You need to keep track of these expenses for your own budgeting and for the Internal Revenue Service at tax time. Jot down your expenditure in a daybook along with who you coffeed or lunched with, their business, the date, and the matters you talked over.

Impressing people with lavish lunches is not necessary to establishing yourself as a professional. Picking up the bill for coffee definitely is. You ought to expect to spend a modest amount each month for entertaining clients, sources, and editors (if you're so lucky as to nab one when he or she is in your part of the world).

As a rule of thumb, I try to hold expenses down to no more than my usual weekly lunch money—thirty-five dollars or less. In pricey urban areas you'll obviously have to budget more generously. I let clients whom I meet with frequently set the pace for expenditures; it's not unreasonable to expect them to reciprocate. Sources and those whom you're courting for business are another story. Still, it's best to hold cost to a modest level. You don't want your entertaining to interfere with the serious purpose of these occasions, which is to exchange business information.

Travel is the flip side of the coin.

Yet you can't play the host to all of your sources and editors; you have to go to many of them. Telephone calls and letters won't always preclude travel expenses, either. Some things must be done in person. It's almost impossible to obtain photographs in some situations, for example, unless you're on the spot to take them yourself.

But travel can break your budget in no time. Take it from the North Dakotan: Distance makes travel costly in both money and the time it takes to get there and back. You can tame the monster of travel costs. The secret is good planning.

I never go anywhere on business with only one objective in mind. Flying only from Bismarck to Minneapolis can cost over $150 per round trip, and two nights' lodging and meals can swallow another hundred even on the cheap.

It takes a very good story to justify two hundred fifty dollars in extra expenses, along with several days' nonwriting time during which I can't count on earning a nickel. But if that same trip results in material used for three or four or half a dozen other projects as well, it becomes a bargain in terms of both money and hours.

Time that you'd squander watching situation comedies in your hotel at night can just as well be spent pursuing an interesting new article idea, collecting quotes, and case histories for another story, checking the local university for experts who might lead to other sales, or digging through museums and cultural centers for new perspectives or more depth on accepted ones. You can use spare hours to make fresh contacts with editors of publications whom you've already met, or new acquaintances who may one day buy material from you. And if you really do have an extra hour or two before your plane leaves or while you wait to make connections, the most fascinating coffee companion in a strange city is always a reporter for one of its leading newspapers.

Average out the cost of your trip over the number of waking hours it allows you to spend in a new locale. You'll see that you can't afford to sleep late and call it quits at the cocktail hour. If you need a break, take a nap when you get home.

If you really can't get that much material in Oshkosh, you can explore flight layovers in cities along the route. They're usually available at no extra cost or for a very modest boarding fee. And alternate routings by air may hold some benefits, too. You can fly from Bismarck to Chicago, if you so desire, nonstop; by way of Minneapolis; or via several milk runs that put you within shouting distance of nearly everywhere in eastern South Dakota, southern Minnesota, Iowa, and southeastern Wisconsin. If you don't fly, the bus and in rare cases the train may allow you similar flexibility with routes and stopovers. Your plans are even more adaptable if you drive.

Need I mention that *any* travel and entertainment expenses must be meticulously recorded in your daybook? Keep receipts for all meals, cabs, and other incidentals, and you'll definitely need your hotel receipts at tax time. (As a general rule, your conscientious daybook is all the proof the law requires on individual expenditures of twenty-five dollars or less. Receipts are always required for larger amounts.)

The tax law introduced in 1987 has made it even more imperative to keep track of these little bits of business expense, since only 80 percent of the total is deductible. The same rules should give you added impetus for negotiating with editors and clients to pay your expenses.

Travel and entertainment minutiae are only some of the details you need to keep track of. At the minimum, you need to instantly begin a good filing system to preserve every receipt and bill related to your business.

You need an accountant—not next April 14, but *now*. The changing tax structure has in one broad sweep outdated much of the conventional wisdom about taxation and deductions for the self-employed, writers included. Twenty percent of your entertainment expenses are only one casualty. Depreciation standards for vehicles used for business have been altered. Some formerly deductible categories are gone forever; others survive in limited form; and some, like the opportunity to deduct 25 percent of your health insurance premiums (if you're not eligible for coverage under an employer package), have actually been added.

Full-time freelancing adds other issues to your relationship with your government. You'll have to prepay income taxes to the feds and, perhaps to your city and/or your state. You'll shoulder a Social Security obligation twice that of on-staff workers, whose boss pays an amount equal to what's deducted from their paychecks. You may be expected to file for a federal tax number, provide Form 1099s for other independent contractors whose services you engage, and jump through a variety of hoops—all vaguely baffling and bearing penalties of law.

Under these circumstances, shared by all American businesses, you clearly owe it to yourself to take the choice of an accountant seriously. Try to find a certified public accountant or firm which deals with other self-employed individuals; if you're not satisfied with your first choice, don't be reluctant to move on.

Of all your professional relationships, this could be the most important you've ever established. When your investment and your income are at stake, the best advice that you can find is barely good enough.

4

The Bottom Line Says More Than "The End"

Money.

Of all of Webster's verbiage, this may be the hardest word for a shy new writer to pronounce.

Yet no single noun is more central to the subject of freelance writing . . . not only for those of us who create a living at the typewriter, but for the entire vast cast of editors and intermediaries who stand between us and our readers.

The love of writing has brought you to your typewriter, but it's the money that permits you to stay there. By the same token, respect and affection for the written word may lie at the heart of the publishing business, and the need to inform motivates the commercial realm; but profit guarantees their survival, too.

Freelancers are welcome in their domains for one reason over all. It's not our brilliance. It's not our charm. It's not even our dogged persistence, though that comes close.

We freelance writers are a bargain.

Adrift in the fresh, exciting possibilities that your own writing business offers you, you're forgiven if you've overlooked this fact. Yet the same advantages that attracted you to freelancing bring sparkle to the eyes of those who'll pay cash for your well-crafted sentences. The freedom, the flexibility, the potential for fame and fortune . . .

The **freedom**—to honestly criticize a piece of work to their hearts' content without having to reconcile their attitude with the office goals for realizing employees' human potential (and face their all-too-human urge for revenge).

The **flexibility**—of calling in someone new to take a crack at a job that's had the regular staff stymied or which, no matter how they try, still sounds a tad stale or bound by the same old company line.

The **fame**—the ability to take advantage of a writer's reputation and

experience without having to pay the hefty salary he or she would undoubtedly demand (if you could snare the writer) as a full-timer.

The **fortune**—or the financial advantage, at least, of giving nary a
thought to the freelancer's Social Security, unemployment taxes, pension fund, health insurance, profit-sharing plan, or multiple state,
federal, and local tax withholding programs.

Freelancers present a whole range of benefits to clients beyond
their glorious way with words, their wit, and their delivery of finished
manuscripts by deadline. Why else would so many successful magazines rely heavily on freelancers' contributions when a quarter of the
writers in America would gladly die for a chance at any staff position
they cared to create?

Working with freelancers can be neat and clean from a client's point
of view: They do the assignment, you pay their bill, your bookkeeper
enters it under "miscellaneous fees and services," and you're home
free, with no ties to bind you.

Working with freelancers holds obvious advantages to those who
already know their many good points. But what do you say to the guy
in Muncie who's never even seen a freelancer, or who once paid his
sister-in-law five bucks an hour to write an awful brochure and thinks
of professional writers in terms of gratitude for loose change?

He's used to working with freelancers in other areas of his life. His
doctor and dentist in private practice are freelancers of a sort. So's the
man who remodeled the kitchen, the photographer who shot his
daughter's wedding pictures, and the accountant who comes in to
handle his taxes.

But all those people have an advantage. He knows exactly what to
expect of them, and has some idea—from years of personal experience—what to be prepared to pay them.

You're almost certainly a new factor for him. He's wondering what
he'll pay an hour . . . and for an hour of what?

So it's up to you to initiate those novices, your clients (and a few editors of smaller publications, to boot), into the mysteries of how a
freelance writer can brighten their lives.

Consider these points:

Your fresh, unjaded viewpoint. You are, after all, an outsider to his
publication, his agency, or his firm. Matters that are more of the same
old grind to him and his employees are almost sure to be new ground
for you. As an outsider, you bring your own set of experiences and
prejudices and your own perceptions to his subject, whether you're
doing a story on the home applications for the minicomputers he
manufactures or an annual report explaining higher-than-usual research costs and lower-than-usual profits to consumers as skeptical as
you.

Editors value the variety of viewpoints they gain by assigning stories to freelancers. Staff writers sooner or later develop a certain uni-

formity of attitude and style, whether by official decree or habit. After my own years with a newspaper, I saw the world around me in pretty much the same way as the reporters who sat beside me, behind me, in front of me, and over by the water fountain in our city room. That uniformity, conscious or not, has its drawbacks: For one, staffers are likely to perceive new developments in the ways they've understood the old. They sometimes miss striking new angles and story elements.

The same is true for commercial clients, with added implications. Someone who knows her business inside out but can't write a sentence without sweating is not likely to instinctively know what she wants in the way of written communications . . . or, if she's sure, she just may turn out to be wrong.

Witness all the thousands of brochures handed out across our country that promote businesses and agencies with a picture of the whole staff, a chronological history of the concern (year by year! no omissions!), a line or two about why you should call on them, and their phone number. All that may be of great interest to the one who makes out salary checks for all those smiling faces and who struggled for twenty-five years to get the company off the ground. It does not make one whit of difference to the average recipient of that dull but costly presentation. Unless one's own face or that of a highly desirable stranger of the opposite sex is in the photo, the whole thing is sure of a short trip to File Thirteen.

Only a freelancer cowed by too many years within the salaried fold would ever allow that internal perspective to be presented with a flourish to a cold, uncaring public. You know, as an outsider, that it bores you to depression and does nothing to communicate a real message to those it's meant to reach.

The same fresh viewpoint goes for writing investigative stories involving publications' sacred cows (admitted or unacknowledged) and handling stories outside an editor's usual frame of reference. Why shouldn't it apply to commercial clients in identical ways? As a freelancer, you're closer to the public than the average editor or client who hires you. You're in a position to know what's going on outside the ivory or pre-stressed-concrete tower in which they're doomed to work.

Here's another way freelancers are worth their fees, no question asked: *As translators.*

Never thought you'd make your living as a professional translator, did you? But don't head for the United Nations yet. Your services are badly needed at home, wherever you find home to be, as a communicator who takes a maze of technical gobbledygook and turns it into clean, clear, meaningful English.

Translators are prominent in every variation of the freelance trade. Science writers take scientific research, as understandable to you and me as lines and dots chipped in rock by prehistoric savages, and turn it into readable, yes, fascinating verbiage. Writers with other "hard" specialties such as economics, medicine, and legal matters perform the same sleight of hand through the medium of their own backgrounds and their typewriters.

Commercial clients need your translation services just as badly (and sometimes much, much worse). The person whose business correspondence begins "We are in receipt of your letter of the thirteenth" (and commits further horrors from there on) may actually be a warm and wonderful human being, eager to say what's on his or her executive mind—but unaware of what a stuffy and inaccessible front that suit of verbal armor presents. Or perhaps communication is neatly avoided through the traditional jargon of the trade. Letters from lawyers are the classics of the genre, where even the stiff, formal salutation creates despair in its reader.

I've translated sets of form letters into English for state agencies; a ninety-six-page commitment law into brochures with a fifth-grade reading level for the Mental Health Association; and tons of hyperbolic travel literature into simple what-to-see-and-do stories for travel magazines. You might find yourself translating user guides for computer software, research studies on disposal of hazardous waste, or violent environmental objections to a billion-dollar dam project. In any case, the task is essentially the same—to turn meaningless verbal meanders into a message that can touch the public. No one does it better than a freelance writer.

Besides your ability to refresh old information and to translate technicalese, you have a third advantage that makes sense even to potential clients who have never worked with freelancers before.

You are available for temporary or special assignments. While a publication may hesitate to hire new staff to work on an intense yet finite project, they should have no such concerns about "renting" a day, week, or a month of your writing time. That is, after all, the essence of the freelance business deal: the knowledge that when you're done, you'll say goodbye, shake hands, and walk off into the sunset.

From the employer's point of view, your short-term availability is an extra plus. It enables him to contract for a share of your working time and take advantage of your strengths without paying the full annual upkeep on your expertise. He doesn't have to commit himself to keeping a specialist busy when the current project is finished.

Neither does he have to love you. He doesn't have to worry about whipping you into the ideal Corporation X automaton. Nor do you, in turn, have to resign yourself to working forever for someone who's not your idea of perfection.

The temporary nature of your freelance assignment is part of the reason for this low-pressure interaction. But there's another factor I think you'll like, especially if the strictures of serving as an employee have gotten on your nerves. As a freelancer, you're the peer of the people for whom you do assignments—not a subordinate. Your special qualities get a little more respect than they did when you worked within the system. And you yourself are free to savor the vagaries of individual clients' personalities and work habits while respecting the value of each other's achievements. The happy ending for your freelance jobs is that there's no forever after to be endured.

The fourth selling point for freelancers is that your clients don't pay for your coffee breaks. Nor do they sponsor hours you spend interviewing for stories that never work out, making out your personal invoices, scanning the morning paper for story ideas, or dreaming of the day you crack the major markets.

When they hire a freelancer, they pay only for what ultimately benefits them—researching, interviewing, writing, presenting the assignment. Since it's pure working time unadulterated in the thousand ways employees are kept (or keep themselves) artificially busy, you can justify charging considerably more per hour for the work you perform than you'd ask or receive on the forty-hour week.

Most clients grasp this advantage immediately. Though your fee can sound high to someone paying staffers seven or eight dollars an hour, most editors and clients realize the volume of time their workers spend accomplishing nothing during the average day.

They appreciate, too, the other kinds of genuine savings you represent—savings the novice freelancer may not even understand clearly on his own home ground.

By contracting for your services, they avoid paying the employer's contribution to your Social Security benefits. (Employers match the big bite taken out of workers' paychecks with an equal contribution of their own. That's 6½ percent of gross pay at this publishing.)

They avoid the expense of health insurance, life insurance, or any similar benefits that go to their employees. The cost varies; on our family policy, my husband's employer kicks in the better part of two hundred dollars a month.

They don't contribute to a pension fund for your golden years. They don't pay unemployment tax to cover your possible claims. (That's where unemployment checks come from for the formerly employed, in case you didn't know, and why freelancers almost never qualify for unemployment.)

They don't worry about including you in the company profit-sharing plan, guarding your occupational safety a la OSHA, or even finding you a desk and a typewriter in a semiprivate cubicle. You don't load up the secretaries' workday. And they never, never owe you a paid vacation.

Finally, as a freelance contractor, you don't show up on their employment rosters. In some businesses and public positions, this is a genuine asset. Some business owners wish to remain in the small business category, since employing more than a certain number of people can bring them under the scrutiny of more government regulators and necessitate compliance with additional reporting requirements.

Government agencies, too, on occasion appreciate a solution to their manpower needs that doesn't require another entry on the payroll to be justified to legislators. In North Dakota, it can be a political liability to have employees on staff whose function is clearly labeled "public relations." Political opponents rhetorically suspect (sometimes with cause) that the offending party is actually doing political work. In such situations and their parallels in your own area, freelance writers on contract can be an ideal and economical solution to the public's genuine need for understandable information from government.

These pluses for your clients add up to the reasons your income goal is within your grasp. Whether it's $25,000 or whatever you set for yourself, it represents good value all around—a respectable level of payment for what you do best, and a bargain for your cost-conscious clients.

Which is fine, good, and encouraging. What you want now is a way to translate these neatly dovetailed needs into dollars: specifically, the number of dollars which you must earn to make your freelance writing self-supporting.

You must establish two figures to use as tools for carving out that living. One is the minimum total annual income that will justify leaving your salaried job. The other is the hourly sum you have to recover from every kind of work to reach that goal.

Twenty-five thousand dollars is not an arbitrary amount for me. It represents approximately what I'd earn in a comparable salaried position—somewhat less, perhaps, than in some kinds of work, like corporate relations; a bit more than in government information; quite a bit more than I might expect to earn as a reporter for most of the dailies in my part of the country.

All things considered, it's a minimum amount that someone with my experience and skills can reasonably expect.

Perhaps it's not the most justifiable figure for you. Look honestly at your own professional writing level and investigate the going rate for similar salaried employees in your own area before you select some number out of the blue.

If you have a decade of news media experience or have worked as a writer in public relations or advertising for more than a few years, you clearly are justified in expecting to earn at least the equivalent of your present salary. Your skills are established. Your background has contributed to a certain stature in your community (or can be translated into that kind of reputation in the new community you're planning to move to). You've proven over the years that you can work on schedule, that your writing is purposeful and to the point, and that you're familiar with the kinds of assignments which you'll be proposing to take on as a self-employed writer. If this picture is you, you can confidently count on rapidly reaching the $25,000 level or much higher.

If, on the other hand, you're just beginning to work as a writer, your first year's goal should be more in line with the paychecks you'd earn at the salaried jobs for which you qualify. You can count on steadily increasing your rates to achieve a substantial living as you gain experience and credentials, and as word of your writing spreads. But you clearly cannot hope to equal from day one the income potential of one who has exercised skills for years that you just now are hoping to demonstrate.

Your goal is a private matter, so set it at a level you can live with. Both over- and underestimating carry dangers. If you expect too much, you may not reach it and become discouraged; you may also have to charge rates out of line with what your work is really worth, and thus cripple yourself by limiting the number of clients willing to pay that much to hire you. Underestimating your worth simply results in less income than you should be bringing home. Your clients will never pay more than you ask; you'll be giving them an unexpected bargain.

Arriving at your goal is the most difficult part of setting up your business. Modesty and high hopes clash, and—if you're like me—you vacillate between valuing your worth too highly and much too little. I can only advise you to look at how much you must make to keep your obligations covered, and then at the kind of background you bring to freelancing. Then take a leap of faith to establish a level which sounds reasonable. You can revise the figure as you go along by taking on more jobs, by working more hours, or by adjusting your hourly rate. But do remember that it's much more pleasant and psychologically rewarding to revise your expectations upward than to have to trim them down, so a conservative figure is a wiser choice than the sum of your wildest dreams.

To me, setting an income goal is the first and perhaps most important step toward achieving it. That magical number, however tentative, lifts your thinking out of the passive realm in which many freelancers function. It lifts you beyond the practical but ultimately self-defeating notion that the only way to increase your earnings is to write more, sell more, spend less, and keep your fingers crossed that someday you'll receive that Big Assignment just off the end of the rainbow.

An annual goal is the tangible standard with which you establish the value of your time—not only in the long run, but by smaller chunks with which you accomplish real-life tasks. It gives you a gauge for judging whether any given assignment in the topsy-turvy realm of publishing is truly worth your time, and gives you a starting point for preparing estimates in other writing situations.

Your annual goal is the foundation for setting an hourly rate—the best ammunition you'll ever have in scoring a bull's eye on your income target. It's an intensely private figure. You need not post it on your office door or share it with a soul. But heed it well. If, on the average, you receive that amount for the projects you take on, and if you are productive within the guidelines you set for yourself, you'll come a lot closer to wrapping up the year in solvency.

Figuring out that hourly amount is fairly simple. Project your overhead—your office and travel expenses plus benefits—for the first year, then divide it by twelve for a monthly amount. (By benefits I mean the necessities that apply in your own case, especially health insurance premiums. To be really businesslike, you should include the sum you'll pay for Social Security, though of course that will depend on the year's outcome.)

Let's set an arbitrary figure of $400 per month for overhead. Add it to your monthly goal—again, let's say one-twelfth of that annual figure of $25,000, or roughly $2,100. That means that, on the average, your monthly goal is $2,500.

Your hourly value is determined a little differently. Divide the total annual projection—roughly $30,000—by fifty weeks. (You do want a vacation, don't you?) Then factor in the number of hours you reasonably expect to spend working on assignments during a given week, and you've got the magic number.

Using this example, the weekly goal comes out at $600. If you presume you'll be working forty hours a week, you can see that you're shooting for $15 per productive hour.

That's not bad, is it? I've found it's easily achievable, even by beginners. This rose has thorns, however, based on the peculiarities of the writing trade.

You can count on spending many, many hours (especially at first) in necessary tasks from which you can't directly recover a cent: researching ideas and writing query letters; calling on potential clients in your locale; sending bills and collecting what's due you; and generally performing all the other duties required of any fledgling business. Those hours are really part of your overhead, too, and must be covered by income from real writing time.

So add a margin into your price structure to cover the expense represented by these vital tasks. Go back to your weekly goal and divide it again, this time by a more reasonable estimate of the hours in which you'll directly earn income—thirty, perhaps, a believable number once your business is rolling. The hourly rate goes up to $20.

Naturally these figures are all hypothetical. You may well find yourself working longer weeks—and occasionally shorter ones—once you've caught the rhythm of your own freelance business, and you can always adjust your target figures to reflect these realities.

At last, though, you have a measuring stick for judging the relative value of different kinds of writing jobs. It will demonstrate its pre-

cious value to you the first time a commercial client says, "Fine—
what will it cost me?" But it will also prove itself as an implicit standard for judging editorial assignments in the baffling Wonderland of
publishing economics—magazine articles, books, copyediting,
ghostwriting and the rest.

The crazy economics of freelance writing are based on no common
standards. No government agency monitors the worth of the commodity we produce, the written word; not even the most empire-hungry
bureaucrat would dare to try. And so it's up to you, and you alone, to
place a value on your work and scramble to achieve it.

Writers can find it confoundingly difficult to separate profitable assignments from those ultimately less rewarding. My first instinct as a
beginner was the normal one—the bigger the check that finally
popped into my mailbox, the better. It didn't take too many experiences, though, to shoot holes in that theory.

Time and energy must be balanced against the final outcome. A series of smaller jobs accomplished with a minimum of ferocious all-out
effort can be far less demanding than one larger project that pays the
same in a single lump. Editors or clients who explain their needs
clearly and answer questions along the way can be worth a great deal
more in the long run than those who are vague, who demand endless
rewrites because of their own vacillations, and who turn your life into
a puddle of mental anguish whenever they call.

So, too, must you consider the manner in which you're paid. Did
you receive the fee you expected on acceptance? On publication?
On a cold day in Hell? Were directly related expenses handled
separately from your fee, and reimbursed promptly? (Carrying them
for five months on MasterCard means you've been assessed a 19.8
percent interest penalty.)

Not every assignment is going to meet your hourly goal. Nor is every
single one going to elicit a long string of pluses when it comes to these
other matters. Armed with your numbers, though, you can move on to
the next step before you refuse those that aren't blue-chip investments.

That step is honest, direct, and damnably hard for almost every
writer whom I know. It is to negotiate for what you need from the assignment. Based on the outcome, it may ultimately mean saying "no."

Call it "assertive freelancing" if you will. I've discussed it at a host
of writers' conferences and come to expect the shudder that sweeps
across the room. The mere mention of haggling seems to violate whatever standards are left after I've explored the concept of an hourly rate.

Writers somehow expect to be above such gritty matters. Yet in an
industry where standard rates are absolutely absent and where assess-
ments of quality are absolutely subjective, it's folly to expect to survive—much less prosper—without speaking up on behalf of your
work.

If there is one common tragedy most likely to befall beginning free-lancers, it's not what you think . . . not the agony of rejection. We all get used to that, after all, and we live through it. No, it's more subtle and more deadly. It's mistaking the sum that nice editor suggests as the last word rather than a first offer. That guarantees you'll sell top-rate work for a minimum price forever.

Bargaining is an accepted part of freelancing, though those who bargain with freelancers are loath to let you know it. Most publications' payment schedules are tentative at best; they'll pay more for work they really want, that's in demand, or that's produced by a writer whom they want to work with. But neither an editor nor a local client will tell you this, and if they know their business, they seldom make a first offer of more than the minimum they could conscionably expect to pay.

You won't offend editors or clients by probing the situation if the proffered payment is far beneath your income guidelines, and if you've set those guidelines in a realistic manner. You may not always receive an increase, though I've found you usually do. But you'll almost never be thrown out of the office on your ear, branded an ingrate, and told never to darken their hallowed doors again. (If you are, forget them: They clearly don't deserve you.)

Many writers have found that it's quite possible to be both very busy and very poor. If you're taking on freelancing as a business, it's part of your job—not your editors' or your clients'—to see that you make a fair living from the assignments you complete.

Negotiating payment sounds like daunting business. Get your feet wet, however, and I believe you'll find you can get through it with dry palms and no more than a small slip knot in the pit of your stomach. Once you've seen how well it works, you may even come to actively enjoy it.

The key is to quell your fear of talking about money. Bring it up first. That has double value: It indicates you're not cowed by the prospect of negotiating, and it avoids the nerve-twanging experience of being asked to name your price first.

Does this sound odd, given all I've said about setting an hourly fee for use in moments just like this one? You might be right. After more than ten years on the front lines, though, I've picked up one, and only one, helpful hint for use when bargaining with the wily client.

Try to get your customer to put the price on the table first. Why? This puts you—not the editor—in the position of accepting or rejecting the offer. You can quickly calculate how well it matches the figure that—be honest, now!—you already have in mind. You're positioned to accept or reject the amount. You're poised to bring up other critical matters like the timing of that payment and reimbursement for expenses (don't count on it unless it's spelled out).

If you're anxious for the assignment and even the least bit shaky in

your firm resolve to get what you're worth, this ploy has another benefit. Believe it or not . . . that offer, once it's spelled out, may actually be
higher than you'd ask if pressed to name your own figure. Haggle it
upward a bit more and you'll gain a surge of confidence in your savvy
that's good for the rest of the week. Even if it's less than you expected
you've established the general range in which you're bargaining; your
counter offer is less likely to swamp the boat altogether.

Of course, not all situations warrant—or permit—this kind of strategy. Nor will you always be in the ideal position of responding to someone's offer, no matter how much you might wish to be. Commercial
clients in particular expect you to be able to develop a reasonable estimate of what your services might cost for a project under discussion.
You'll bless your hourly rate every time you find yourself playing this
tension-packed guessing game, "What's It Worth To You?"

In my beginning days I was invariably stumped for an answer. I
could no more produce a dependable estimate than resign myself to
accepting whatever minimum might be offered me. (That's an especially bleak prospect when you're the first freelancer your proto-cli-
ent has considered hiring, and the client is still stuck on the notion
that a writer's predominant motive is the sheer delight of creating annual reports.)

To this day the question makes me shudder. But experience allows
me to narrow the answer down to one of two options. Each works in its
own circumstances.

Occasionally the best reply is to simply state your hourly figure:
"My rate is twenty (or thirty, or forty or more) dollars per hour." Some
clients do prefer this, particularly those in business or government
who are accustomed to dealing with outside suppliers of services.
This is how advertising agencies will approach you, for example,
since their own charges are generally based on units of time.

But many others may clutch their chest and feign (we hope)
heart attacks when you name your numbers in this straightforward
manner. Face it: The all-too-human response is to compare your
pay-per-hour with their own nearest and dearest yardstick, what
they themselves make for every sixty minutes of service. Don't
expect them to automatically factor in the vast and awesome differences between their guaranteed salary and your entrepreneurial risk.
Just expect them to gasp for breath.

Instead, offer a lump-sum estimate—the number of hours you
expect the job to take, multiplied by that now-secret rate. It is likely
to sound more manageable, placing as it does an upper limit on the
total cost of the work you're proposing.

Whether or not an estimate ought to be guaranteed is a thorny matter. I'm perfectly willing to hold to mine, given a set of ground rules to
keep the project within the agreed-upon bounds. But some commercial jobs have a tendency to creep out in every direction with changes

of mind, changes of heart, changes of personnel, and other upheavals in the familiar terrain on which you based your projections. Do you leave an escape clause in your negotiations to cover these incidents of slippage by clearly defining terms and adding, "Of course, if additional work is required, that will be billed at the same rate."

Another thought may occasionally cross your mind during these financial discussions. How can you guarantee that you, a tiny one-person business, will be paid by the tough-minded customer with whom you're dealing?

Creative work is generally performed on a handshake. It usually works, but you can count on some variations based directly on the kind of person whose hand you're gripping.

Some writers have turned to contracts in an attempt to circumvent the very rare but very real possibility of being taken for a ride. To me, though, the legal paper has never been worth the trouble, since I'd be unlikely to pursue a solution through the courts anyway because of the cost and trouble. Nor does the existence of a contract guarantee a ruling in the writer's favor. Creative standards are ephemeral and subjective; the client who firmly intends not to pay has a thousand ways to go about it.

Your best defense against these disasters is your own good judgment. If a project sounds odd from the start, trust your sixth sense. Get out while it still costs you nothing. In the words of a long line of wise mothers, remember that if something sounds too good to be true, it probably is.

Instead of a contract, I use an informal letter of agreement. After we've shaken hands on project parameters and a price, I send my clients a letter restating our conversation as I understand it from my notes. If they have different ideas, they're provided with a clear-cut opportunity to let me know; in the meantime, my files acquire a copy of a document no more legally binding than a handshake, but a great deal clearer. If the relationship gets sticky farther down the road, the document helps to redefine it.

One final issue you may wish to consider with larger projects is the timing of payments. It is perfectly normal and utterly sane to require a third of your estimate up front before work has begun. An additional third is payable when you reach some identifiable milestone, with the balance due on completion and acceptance.

This is quite standard in business. It reassures you of two things. Your own start-up costs are covered. Two, you have a subtle check on whether your client is financially qualified and as serious about the project as you are.

Finally, there is one last category of undertaking that barely fits under the heading of business, but comes up so regularly that it deserves to be addressed. It's the donation of your writing services in service of a cause, presumably a good one—professional work you do for love, not money.

After you've become established, I'll bet you have the same experience that I've encountered with charity and volunteer organizations. Everybody in town seems to have some modest proposal they're waiting to ask me to write for them . . . as a donation, because their cause is so just and noble.

The nerve of some of these perfectly nice people can be astonishing. Men and women whom you've never met and will never see again call at unpredictable hours to ask you to chair publicity committees and perform all your regular professional routines—for free. Youth groups, churches, candidates for everything from PTA president to political office—all have approached me at one time or another to do for free what I do for a living.

Practice the word: No. But don't apply it heedlessly to every plea that comes your way as automatically as the dog next door howls at the sound of a police siren.

I do take on a certain number of these requests. But I don't do as many as I did before I became wiser and more cynical about their motivations. I apply a true-false test to them.

True or false—I really care about this cause.

True or false—I want to make a contribution toward their goals.

True or false—I owe the person making the request a favor, or I admire what they're doing, or I just feel benevolent today.

True or false—I can handle this request with a minimum investment of time, and it won't interfere with work for my paying clients.

I do not do for free what an agency or group normally pays to have done . . . by others. Ever. I do not take on even simple projects just because it's easier to do than to turn them down, or to get a particularly persistent recruiter off my back. If I'm only mildly interested in the cause, I give what my civic-minded neighbors give: money.

Part of the reason you'd better feel good about causes to which you donate your writing time is that good feelings are just about all you'll get out of your work. In some few cases you'll make contacts or stumble across information that can be translated into articles or commercial work. For the most part, though, the worthiest causes come equipped with no such promising connections.

You can't take a donation of your services off your income tax, either, even though writing free for a worthy cause takes time away from your income-earning pursuits, and time is money. The best you can do is deduct out-of-pocket expenses run up while doing good works, like car mileage, office supplies, and postage. This makes you one of the very few persons to donate to the cause who does it solely and demonstrably for love, not money. Even the guy who digs down to give them a dollar can take it off his taxes.

So choose your causes and favors carefully. Your mission in your community is to help it learn to appreciate, work with, and remunerate freelance writers. You'll do nothing to establish this praiseworthy principle if you undercut the value of your own profession by helping bystanders associate the written word with casual and cost-free efforts by volunteer publicity chairpersons.

When you do give, give freely and with enthusiasm. That's the spirit you want people to remember when they think of the only freelancer in their part of the world.

Ultimately you'll work out a balanced diet of writing assignments that meets your income goal and provides you with the kind of variety you need to mature as a writer and maintain your own enthusiasm. Some work naturally excites and challenges you more than other kinds. Magazines and books, for example, may cause your writing juices to start flowing. Yet, because they sometimes pay beginners a limited hourly rate of return compared with other assignments, you'll want to balance them with more lucrative but sometimes less exciting commercial projects, local editing jobs, or forays into the world of public speaking, teaching, or writing for broadcast media.

Likewise, local commercial work demands balance. While it can, at times, pay higher rates for work of relatively less intensity, it also can be stultifying to limit your efforts solely to brochures or publicity or radio ad copy. You might reach your income goal with somewhat less effort, but you'd lose the invigorating challenge and variety that add up to the joy of freelancing.

The need to earn income to support your household doesn't have to limit your spirit of adventure. Quite the opposite. Use it as an incentive to try new topics and techniques, expand your writing horizons, and keep in touch with the spirit of discovery that accompanies so many newly mastered skills.

Freelancing is one long voyage of discovery . . . not only now as you begin, but as you go along from year to year. Your horizons are limited only by the vigor with which you explore possibilities waiting for a writer in your corner of the world.

5

Magazine Writing: Think Like a Farmer

When employed writers dream of freelancing, they think first of national magazines. A roll of stamps, a hot idea, a polished query letter sent to an address in New York City ... and then they're on their way to discovering the truth about this most obvious of targets for their prose:

Magazine writing as it's generally approached is more of a sport than an occupation. To enter the field as a hunter in search of game requires the sure hand of a marksman, the stoic patience to stalk a canny deer ten miles through icy drizzle, and blind faith that the trophy of a lifetime will be yours if you prove yourself stouthearted.

The sportsman's vision of the magazine game has vivid appeal to nine-to-fivers, representing as it does a break from their tame climate-controlled work lives. They adore the joy of matching themselves against the most ferociously competitive big-name writers in the nation. They savor the intense concentration of stalking that elusive quarry, the editor who wants to see their work. They revel in bringing deft salesmanship into play as they take aim on a distant, unsuspecting market.

They take pride in forever practicing the steady hand required to bring down a target that's changing shape and moving fast among the shadows. And they have the luxury afforded by vacation time and a secure income to trade late-night stories around the campfire about the Big Ones that got away ... taking almost as much satisfaction from picturesque near-misses and outrageously miscalculated shots as they might from actually hitting their goal. Rejection can be a badge of honor when you've been turned down by the very best.

As a test of stamina and savvy, hunter-style magazine writing ranks near the top. The prospect of a trophy-sized byline in a handsome periodical can make many a day slogging through the mud seem worthwhile. Yet even the pros can come back empty-handed. The success of yesterday's hunt never guarantees tomorrow's.

Great sport. But can a writer live decently by sport alone?

When your bank balance hangs on connecting with the target most every time, you can no longer afford too many long shots. But that need not rule out writing for magazines as a part of your freelance strategy.

The trick is to give up hunting and think like a farmer.

For certain, farming is not a glamour occupation. Yet the world needs to eat, and so do freelance writers. Plant a seed in fertile ground, tend your field, and the chances are good that you'll reap your reward when the time is right.

I like comparing magazine writing to farming—and that's not only because I live where John Deere is a good deal more familiar than John Irving. It implies sweat and digging. Neither appears too often on lists of tips for magazine byline hunters, but both are key ingredients in the success of any writer who aspires to earn an honest living toiling in the publishing vineyards.

A good farmer always keeps his eye on the weather. Here's your long-range forecast as an aspiring magazine journalist far from Manhattan's concrete canyons: The outlook is neither as wonderful as you wish it were, nor as dark as those who boast of papering whole rooms with rejection slips would have you believe. Simply put, it's partly cloudy. (Make that "partly sunny" if you're the type who sees a glass as half-full rather than half-empty. You'll find few farmers, though, who fall into that frame of mind.)

You may indeed succeed in cultivating sales among the mass-circulation magazines that circulate millions of copies from coast to coast. While top-name writers are fang-to-fang in that fiercely competitive environment, it is never accurate to say the door is closed. You can sometimes crack these top-paying markets by studying places where their needs intersect your own homegrown material—first-person stories, like *Redbook*'s "Young Mother's Story," for example; reader contributions like the pithy homespun anecdotes which *Reader's Digest* devours, or even provocative opinion essays featured in all kinds of magazines from *Newsweek* to *Cosmopolitan*.

More likely, you can turn up opportunities in publications that circulate across just as many miles but serve more specialized groups of readers. The mania for reaching a targeted audience has spawned a promising profusion of newsstand publications directed toward certain advertisers' specific needs, from *Big Beautiful Woman* and *Muscle and Fitness* to *Chocolatier* and *Walking*.

Regional publications provide the best odds of all. Here, too, the news is good. Targeted marketing has reached all the way down into medium-sized cities with a profusion of lifestyle and business publications invading territory dominated no more than a decade ago by a daily newspaper or two and the broadcast media. You'll find a comprehensive list of regional publications (nonfiction, fiction, and poetry) in the *International Directory of Little Magazines and Small Press-es* (Dustbooks).

No matter what your objective, however, think like a farmer. Consider where you're planted. Diversify—broaden your idea of the markets that are worth your while—and narrow your sights to the assets with which geography has blessed you.

That's so basic that it seems obvious. Yet it bears repeating. There are writers in nearly every U.S. state and Canadian province who are supporting themselves today on just that principle. They—and I, here in good old North Dakota—have learned something from their experiences with editors which few books have stated in explicit terms before:

Certain stories are inherently easier to write and to sell from an address that's thousands of miles away from an editor's office.

Certain resources you may find close to home are so valuable to some types of publications that they all but insist you specialize in them.

And some stories are so incredibly hard to sell, or so horrendously expensive to research and write from a distance that they really deserve to be left to our mega-urban counterparts. Our time is simply better spent fishing in more productive waters.

We who write from out-of-the-way addresses have also learned that, for us, magazines of certain stripes make better markets than others . . . that particular editors (working in a variety of settings) are more likely than most to keep an eye cocked for talented beginners . . . and that others still, whom we locate by trial and error, are actually willing to guide newcomers through the myth-shrouded learning process that master writers sentimentally recall as their "apprenticeship."

Remote writers apply patience and steady research to finding these congenial markets. They rejoice and take note when they locate the good ones where competition (for one reason or another) is less ridiculous than in the top offices that are besieged with hundreds of submissions every day of the year.

To produce a decent yield from your magazine marketing efforts, in short, you need to make the best of your unorthodox location and learn to minimize or avoid the practical issues and prejudices which might keep an editor from taking you on.

Right now, before you add to their daily workload with more eye-popping query letters and flawless manuscripts, let's spare a moment of sympathy for the devil—those editors who'll someday field your mail and pass judgment on your proposals.

It's nothing personal, but two things about you make them nervous. Will an unknown from the back roads of America actually turn out to be experienced and disciplined enough to turn out the kind of articulate, entertaining, erudite articles they so desire? And are you just too far away to reasonably take a chance on testing?

Digging through one day's addition to the slush pile in any magazine office in the land opens your eyes to the prudence that lies behind their suspicious natures. I've had the opportunity to read other people's mail on several occasions; to my amazement, I found myself all but awestruck with sympathy.

Frankly, editors do get enormous amounts of absurd junk. I'd always suspected warnings against this stuff in books on writing were inserted mostly for comic relief! But no. I've witnessed tons of poetry, mostly bad and all of it directed toward publications that have never used so much as a couplet; clichéd nostalgia; syrupy tributes and forced guffaws in the category loosely defined these days as "women's humor"; half-baked politics and half-poached metaphysics; and—yes!—astonishing manuscripts actually written in longhand with No. 2 pencils on perfumed paper emblazoned with perky little buttercups.

We may assume that you and I are not responsible for any of these mortal sins, having studied guides like Lisa Collier Cool's *How to Write Irresistible Query Letters* and other advice in writers' magazines. But tucked among them were others—heartbreakers—that did strike a chord. They're the queries that almost fit the bill, but belied their promise upon closer scrutiny. Too bland, too stale, too much like something already on the boards for next month. Or they're perfect for an audience—someone else's, readers who are wealthier, or older, or more family-oriented, or more avidly consumed by the urge to learn everything there is to know about widgets.

Multiply my personal sampling by the volume of mail received daily in the editorial offices of America's periodicals, and you realize how this torrent of near-misses enlivened by outright disasters is bound to dull the hopes (and senses) of the man or woman who must read it all. Unfortunately for us, the great bulk of this miscreant deluge carries a return address far, far from the Big Apple . . . if for no other reason that there are more of us than there are of them, and we're forced to use the mail.

If you have ever identified in any way with Pavlov's unfortunate dogs, you can surely identify with the despair of these editors. The U.S. Post Office has conditioned them to associate postmarks from weird-sounding cities like Fargo, North Dakota, with material that's hopelessly unusable. No matter how badly they long to find the occasional jewel buried in the slush, they're bound to view your tidy envelope with a bit less than pounding pulse and rising expectations.

Let's assume that an astute eye does get beyond the cancelled stamp to your well-crafted query letter. Our editor still must recognize—as should you—that some stories are more easily written far from downtown Manhattan than are others.

"Others" are those that require editorial input in detail or in depth. From the editor's standpoint, that means more tactful negotiation and cooperative effort with the new-found writer. If your query falls into these tricky categories, a genuine handicapping factor has entered the scene: distance, sheer distance.

It's more convenient for an editor I know in Minneapolis to work with fellow Minneapolitans, and for one in Fargo to use compatriots than even the most promising comer in Grassy Butte. It's easier—at least, it *seems* easier and faster—for a New York editor to knock heads with writers conveniently sharing the same telephone area code. It's cheaper, too, considering long-distance calls and breathless periods of waiting for replies by express mail.

One step further down the path to publication, the editor finds similar advantages in writers of familiar address when it comes to communicating second thoughts, additional suggestions, and anxious requests for an article's immediate appearance. A rewrite that never leaves the boroughs of New York can often be accomplished in mere days. Contrast that with the iffy delivery of transcontinental mail from New York to Nevada and back.

Face it. We all prefer the simplest route to reaching our objectives. Can you really blame an editor for relying on a stable of nearby proven professionals instead of taking chance after long-shot chance on us deserving outlanders? She has only a few sheets of paper and our word to go on when she judges whether we're up to producing the irrefutable, amazing, world-class copy she feels her publication demands. All the SASEs in the world can't make her life easier at that point. (Okay, go ahead and accuse her of Manhattan myopia if you want to. But you know now there are other, better causes than the big-city provincialism to which we love to ascribe our rejections.)

You need to be aware of these odds against your brainstorm when it lands on an editor's desk. Yet you need not be intimidated by them. You can provide your own editorial insurance of the kind that's worked for other writers equally isolated from editors' acquaintance, who do manage to sell consistently to every magazine you can imagine.

The most obvious insurance is to be meticulous about tailoring your queries or unsolicited manuscripts for the markets you submit them to. The editor's first question is whether your article fits her readers' interests and needs, and whether it fits into the issues she's currently at work on. If she can immediately answer a tentative yes, you've crossed Hurdle One.

Do check back issues as thoroughly as you memorize a magazine's requirements in the current *Writer's Market* or other directories. Read the competition as well to get a feel for each magazine's subtle differences and the topics that are currently hot. (If the competition has a story on your idea this month, don't expect your editor to buy it just to keep up appearances.)

Once your idea passes that first test, other questions present themselves because of your unknown address. One is whether you—an untested writer from somewhere the editor may not have heard of or even be able to pronounce—are capable of carrying out the assignment you propose.

The editor's tool for digging the truth out of you is the "on spec" go-ahead. He's agreed to take a look at it, period. No money is committed; no title is added to that issue's article budget in ink. If your work doesn't meet his standards, or even if unrelated factors, like a similar story in a competing magazine, ruin your chance of a sale, you receive nothing in return for your effort.

Unknown writers or those with only minor publishing credits usually can't avoid being told to pursue an idea on speculation. (Avoid it? As a beginner, you'll nearly raise the roof with excitement when you get your first such conditional "Yes, maybe.") But one way to minimize the problem that the tentative go-ahead is meant to counter is to tell the editor enough about yourself to give him some degree of confidence in your ability to deliver.

You don't need to recount your life story—unless it's a dilly and you want to peddle it to *People*. However, there's no sense in not mentioning your very best credits, whether local or regional publications, salaried writing experience, or published articles in minor and medium markets.

Writing credits aren't all that counts in your favor. If you have special expertise or background that qualifies you for the topic you wish to tackle, by all means detail it. Especially be sure to bring it in if your query covers a complex subject you might otherwise seem unlikely to match up to—technical or medical topics, for example, or subjects requiring a highly informed opinion. Your source material and the authority to handle it well are the heart of your query. In fact, these stories for which you're unusually well qualified may be your strongest bets. Writing style can be patched up if the material is good; but if the subject's clearly over your head, the story can't be saved by any brand of editorial grace.

Editors wonder whether you can dig up needed data from your out-of-the-way location. I've found them easier to convince if I casually suggest my sources up front. A story on overseas travel to the American West became more salable when backed up with discussions with the European-based travel marketing director for the Old West region, who works every day with cowboy-happy Germans and Scandinavians seeking help with travel plans. Another story on "the new museums" was surely received more thoughtfully in light of behind-the-scenes access to half a dozen of the very best new-style centers on the West Coast and across Canada.

You do have to sell a little harder to get queries accepted from afar. Forget the advice to be brief if brevity hurts your case. Often all you're doing is allowing the busy editor to rule you out more quickly. I don't, of course, mean two-thousand-word queries. But tell your own story well enough to sound professional. A breezy fifty-word note from the boonies suggesting an idea to an editor who's never heard of you is as inappropriate as overalls and work boots at Windows on the World, and will create a like impression. Again, study *How to Write Irresistible Query Letters*, an invaluable guide to not only connecting with receptive editors, but getting your relationship off on the right foot.

You do face limited alternatives when selling yourself on paper to an editor you've never met. But that's not all bad. The query system saves time and money by weeding out the stories that will never work, and it does make use of your good points—for isn't writing prose that persuades what you do best?

You needn't remain an invisible person known only by your postmark forever, though. Becoming established as a distinct individual is vitally important for those of us at a distance who can't drop in to remind editors we exist. And it *can* be done.

Your own professionally designed letterhead and envelope help promote this distinction. In lieu of the sight of your face, they're a way to help an editor recognize you. Granted, they're superficial and tell nothing about your many good qualities besides taste in stationery. But they're a visual cue. An editor who debated over my query a few months ago or remembers the cover letter on a purchased manuscript is likely to recognize, however vaguely, my simple black and gold logo when it comes back carrying another proposal. The advantage is slight but cracks the ice ever so gently.

You know how hard it is to visualize a person you've never met—how hard it can be to remember that this invisible person is really out there in a spot that's no more real to you. I try to take steps to become three-dimensional to editors who have (or should have) already bought stories from me.

Once someone has accepted that first fateful manuscript, she's not likely to get rid of me. Badgering her of course, is probably suicide. But I do try to keep my name and letterhead before her with additional queries, compliments on an issue I particularly admired, and updates on stories she may have considered but rejected "for the time being."

Your objective is to remind the editor you're a real person. Since she may be a little uncomfortable working out of arm's reach of your developing manuscript, ease her worries. Don't be afraid to pick up the telephone and call to clarify suggestions you're unsure of or to warn her of new developments that may change your premise. And if unforeseen circumstances delay your story past its deadline, by all means let her know! Don't let her wonder if you're still out there.

You can use the phone to half-sell articles to editors who already know your work. Though they'll probably want a written query on the subject anyway, the call can let you know whether the coast is clear before you research a new topic. One editor whom I've not yet managed to sell has even asked me to call him before submitting new proposals, since both of my previous near-misses were scuttled not for themselves, but because they were too close to other assignments that beat them to his desk.

By calling, of course, you not only find out if your query would be in vain—you add the sound of your voice to the one-dimensional portrait you present by mail. A person you've talked to is that much more real.

When making those calls, though, observe the courtesies of all good business contacts. Have a definite proposal or question, not a fishing expedition ("How about a story on North Dakota? Or something maybe on teenagers?" Guaranteed failure!). Have a solid reason for butting into her working day. Any less genuine a motive is immediately obvious to the busy person on the other end of the line.

Telephone conversations help. You aren't really fleshed out in a stranger's mind until she's met you and traded comments in person. All the writers I've talked to agree that editors who know them are more likely to purchase their work, given a basically sound proposal in the first place. Meeting editors is not as easily accomplished as finding their phone numbers, but it can be done.

The editors of top national magazines, as well as the entire spectrum of specialty publications, turn up en masse at writers' conferences. Solo appearances are not unheard of, even in remote locales; many hit the lecture circuit as experts in their own fields.

Sponsors of these conferences and lectures can be useful people to keep in touch with. Their speakers usually have extra time in town— more now than ever, given the present state of airline service in America's hinterland. Those who booked their appearance—someone, perhaps, from a college English department, a women's club, or an organization for writers—may be able and willing to schedule a rendezvous for you during a lull in the headliner's schedule. If the coordinator is especially cramped for time, you may even end up taking the visitor to lunch or showing him around town; the harried overseer's gratitude for your help would certainly be gild on the lily.

I'm not suggesting you ambush an editor when he least expects it. That's boorish. By appointment, though, you can talk over your common interest in writing and casually suggest several ideas which spring from the local landscape and tradition that may be of interest to your guest: an outstanding local solution to a common social problem, perhaps, that could inspire similar remedies elsewhere, or a historic site with a long, colorful history buried beneath its dry stones and dull inscriptions.

If you've chosen your brainstorms well, you may hope for the editor's noncommittal cure-all reply. He'll suggest you forward a query, either to his desk or that of another staffer who handles the pertinent department. Either way, you've won a valuable foot-in-the-door prize,

though one without guarantees. If he's suggested you query his colleague, you can certainly mention that by way of introduction. On
the other hand, if your letter wings its way to your visitor's mailbox,
he'll probably remember the interesting discussion that took place in
your charming town.

If you're a writer from North Dakota or Mississippi or an equally unlikely spot, you're more memorable than you suspect. Once met,
you're not one of any crowd, but a curious and interesting exception.

Make the most of this geographical edge by becoming a three-dimensional human being to those whom you want to sell. The best antidote to distance and geography may just be fighting fire with fire—
highlighting your exotic location as a positive and memorable charac-
teristic rather than a fateful misfortune.

The best prospects for not-in-New-York writers

Your address is much more than a source of amusement to metropolitan magazine editors.

It can be a handicapping factor if you misjudge its impact on the
kinds of stories you're trying to sell ... or, if you use it for all it's worth,
it can have a neutral or even a pleasantly positive effect.

If you are really serious about making a living as a writer where
you've chosen to live, you owe it to yourself to be realistic about what
you can and can just barely sell. I am sure that someone, somewhere,
is selling exactly the kinds of stories I'm going to tell you to avoid, for
sooner or later you can accomplish anything you set your mind on.
But as a self-supporting writer, you need to keep an eye on your own
cost—in time and money—in selling a longshot as compared to selling a story that's accepted quickly, easily, and with less exorbitant out-
of-pocket expense to you.

For our purposes, there are only three categories of stories to be
written for nationally circulated magazines: Those that virtually demand the peculiar New York viewpoint or access to that singular
city's resources; those that could be written almost anywhere and
your living in San Francisco or Tulsa or Tacoma influences only your
final telephone and postage bills or has no effect at all; and those
where your own location, for one reason or another, is a tangible advantage.

The first category is, fortunately, the smallest. Some magazines use
this type of story almost exclusively—*New York* magazine, of course,
being an excellent example. The stories in this group range from high
sophistication to the depths of urban crime. Fashion, home furnishings on the trendiest levels, gourmet dining, the foibles of the jetset—
all are out of reach to most of us, unless we invest unusual effort and
expense. So are exposés of gang life, subway safety menaces, and the
urban drug culture. Just as national politics is tough to cover from anywhere but Washington, D.C., so the purely New York piece is not a

likely winner from the Texas Panhandle.

But your stories don't touch the very heights or depths of city society? An urban location can still make a difference in the salability of your article if it's of a certain type. Some medical and self-help stories simply sound more believable with big-city experts quoted than they do from the mouths of sources elsewhere in the country; it's conditioning, but a fact nevertheless. A psychiatrist in Bismarck can be every bit as accomplished as one practicing in Manhattan, but her pronouncements won't have the same ring of authority—unless she's talking about the effect of deep winter on sanity, or the psychological problems of farmers, or unless she's fresh from a New York practice.

Stories related to industries headquartered in metropoli are also best written (or, more precisely, best sold) from those locales. That's fashion's advantage in New York, or movie gossip's edge in Los Angeles. Those appropriate addresses for freelancers reassure editors that they have access to the best information of its kind—that they have absorbed their subject, by some process of osmosis if nothing else.

Even if you've absorbed the city's sophistication during long years spent working there, you can't expect to take more than nostalgic memories when you move to Montana. Your degree of authority depends on current access.

Any of us could hop a plane and be in New York for dinner tonight, so it's unfair to say that we are totally without access. But the cost-benefit ratio is too low, when you count air fare, living expenses, and the time it takes away from your typewriter. City stories are a bad investment for those of us living and writing elsewhere. They cost us far, far more to write than they do our metropolitan counterparts.

Fortunately, the vast majority of magazines don't concentrate exclusively on the highly localized metropolitan viewpoint. Read any major women's magazine this month and you can't miss the wide range of authors' addresses that give hometown credibility to every kind of article, from food to family problems. This nationwide angle is so important that editors actively seek outside viewpoints. An editor on *Redbook* who spoke recently at a writers' conference in Michigan said her nonmetropolitan origins provide her with that edge. "I've always thought I had an advantage in not being from New York myself," she told the gathered writers. "I was one of 'us' rather than one of 'them.' "

Many of these location-neutral stories, once an editor's decided to look at them, can be written as well from one city as another, and require fairly equal amounts of travel and other expense for most writers wherever they live.

For location-neutral stories, you have three excellent sources of information on which stories have the best prospects of piquing an editor's interest—short of managing to meet the editor in person or having any sort of inside help.

First you'll consult the annual edition of *Writer's Market* or one of the other market directories. In regularly updated entries, the staffs of thousands of magazines lay before you exactly what they think they want (and don't want) to see. Many mention free sample copies and writers' guidelines. I request these whenever they're available, especially for publications not stocked in our local library nor listed in any of the periodical indexes. I've found the sample copies most helpful. The guidelines tend to be little more than an extended version of listings in the market directories, but may offer clues about whom queries should be addressed to, annual special editions, and specific needs or not-needs which space prevents from inclusion in the annual directories.

In *Writers' Market*, as well as in monthly market reports in *Writer's Digest* and other writing publications, editors stress time after time that freelancers should study their market listings closely. It's such obvious advice that it's taken for granted; yet overlooking this one unmistakable step can be very costly for the remote freelancer.

Sending gun control stories to hunting magazines and sophisticated sexual humor to the women's supermarket periodicals is clearly a waste of postage. But worse, it's wasting an opportunity to lay groundwork with an editor who could come to respect your judgment. Your very sharpest observations on what fits into a given publication are none too good for any market you approach. Misfit queries only confirm some editors' preconceptions that distant writers aren't likely to understand and satisfy their needs.

The price of a few stamps may seem worth investing in a shaky query on the off chance that it'll strike someone's fancy. But add to it the hour or so it takes to put together even a casual idea and the ill will garnered by wasting an editor's time, and you'll probably conclude that the attempt to sell a magazine its first prose poem in two decades is too expensive an experiment to indulge in. Selling well-tailored ideas and articles at a distance is risk enough for most of us.

Your second source of pre-query information is the familiar *Reader's Guide to Periodical Literature* and the more specialized indexes at your library. You can learn in a few minutes whether the topic you're working on has been used where you hope to place it or in similar markets in recent years.

Current and recent issues of the magazine are your third available clue to what sells and what doesn't. Review advertisements for clues to the age, interests and income level—the demographics—of its readers. Study its masthead, which lists editors and senior staff of the magazine. What subjects are handled by staffed departments? (In a women's magazine these may include food, fashion, interiors, and health. A men's magazine has its own established set of staple topics covered in-house, as does almost every category of periodical you study.) While selling stories in these areas is not impossible if your angle and information are just right, suggestions for subjects the magazine desires but which aren't handled by full-time staff are more likely to be chosen.

The table of contents offers other hints. Look not only at the topics but at who has written them. Eliminate those that are regular features with the byline of a known staff member or contributing editor. Scrutinize the writers' biographies often included at the end of articles or near the bottom of the first page. You can learn quite a bit about the writers' locations, experiences, and the qualifications you hope to match. Travel stories, for example, have always encouraged me with their mention of writers' home bases in Iowa or Wyoming.

References to the writer's years on staff with the magazine you're reading offer less hope. If all those familiar faces are now out in the field competing for the present editor's consideration, an outsider's chances are significantly weakened. Also note whether author credits are listed. The line you're looking for is: "This is his/her first appearance in our pages"!

The articles written by writers most like yourself suggest the most fertile areas for your own efforts. There are sure to be exceptions galore. But as a beginning, try applying this technique to weed out the weak areas from those where your chances are strongest at the moment. Don't try to duplicate published stories—X-ray them to see how they're joined together. How are comparable themes slanted and approached? What form do they take most often—essay, anecdotes, interviews? What kinds of anecdotes, what quotes, what expert opinions have been included to make the author's case? Even the editor may not have considered her needs and preferences in this kind of detail before. Yet she's provided you with a neat and clean model to demonstrate exactly what she's deemed relevant and suitable in months gone by.

At the same time, your research provides a short course in how topics can be recycled by slanting them for a variety of noncompeting markets. (For more insights, try Duane Newcomb's *How to Sell and Resell Your Writing.*)

You don't have to be in New York to come up with ideas for the kinds of stories that remain. What you will do is listen closely to the people around you—your family, neighbors, and business associates—for indications of the kinds of joys or problems that concern them most. TV and newspaper headlines will provoke other thoughts; so can a trip to a trade show, a random overheard comment, and any number of other everyday stimuli.

No matter where you live, you'll find certain kinds of stories that are not place-specific but which are easier for you to research and write with a voice of authority. That same sensed authority in your writing makes these stories easier to sell to editors than other ones, just as fascinating, that are beyond your (reasonable) reach out there in the boonies. It's up to you to find out what your authoritative subjects are.

That good old *Reader's Guide to Periodical Literature*, dog-eared by now, is the source book for finding how the nation's eyes (and editors) see your part of the world, if they glance your way at all. The topics already associated with your address are the ones you'll sell with the greatest ease—for me, rural life, climate extremes, and the burgeoning western energy industry; for you, whatever editors associate with your part of the world: agribusiness in the Midwest, ecology in the Pacific Northwest, gambling in Las Vegas and Atlantic City, country music in Nashville.

Strangely enough, I've found that editors of even the most innovative, forward-looking, groundbreaking publications are more likely to buy ideas they half-expected when they looked at your address than they are to pick out the really exciting, entirely new topics that catch your own eye. Baldly stated, what you take for granted may be of more interest to them. What's been written about most often is the more, not less, valuable for this past exposure.

Leave shockingly atypical newsbreaks to the newspapers, who still subscribe to the "man bites dog" school of journalism. Modern magazines are more interested in an analysis of the more familiar "dog bites man" that adds new insights to man-dog relations.

Another difference between newspapers and magazines is the way articles are built. This was an important realization for me, resulting partly, no doubt, from my own newspaper experience and partly from my reliance on papers for information that leads to article ideas and stories.

A newspaper story stresses the local side of any subject. It often starts with a general observation—that elderly people are having a hard time living on Social Security checks, for example, then immediately narrows it to a specific local case—that half a dozen widows in a run-down part of town admitted to reporters they stretch their meatloaf with Alpo.

Most magazine stories, on the other hand, use specific anecdotes and statistics to build up their general themes. That's where your local sources come in. Your neighbor may tell you about a problem her family has met and conquered, and it may suggest a possible article. But unless you aim for one of the first-person departments, such as "Neighbors" in *Woman's Day*, or plan to turn out a confession piece, this one family's story is of limited interest to most magazines' wide readerships.

But it can be the stimulus to start gathering supporting data to identify a widespread problem and indicate how readers everywhere can solve it. Your local material has value, for it's the basic building block. But you'll need anecdotes and quotes from other locations, research among authorities who can back up your observations with facts, and enough material to flesh out your originally local subject into an article that those who never will meet your neighbor can appreciate.

You can accumulate your supporting data without traveling all over the country cross-examining total strangers. Your starting point is— surprise!—the information resources you have at home.

Remember my suggestion that you get to know your librarian while you're scouting out your community? Buy him or her a cup of coffee and talk about what you're working on these days. (With librarians' interest in writing and writers' in libraries, you have the makings of a natural alliance.) Ask for suggestions on sources. Get a tour of the stacks. Even a small library can usually be counted on to contain some titles relevant to your subject. Better yet, an alerted librarian will keep your interest in mind when reading book trade publications for news of new issues and even when deciding which new books to add to the collection.

Most community libraries are now connected, some by computer and others by Teletype, with larger libraries in their states. You can greatly expand the number of books at your fingertips by using this free service. In North Dakota, I can get almost any title issued by a national publishing house within a day or two through the libraries' computer hookups with each other and the state library itself. It's not only far less expensive than ordering needed reference materials through a bookstore: I've found the libraries to be ten times as fast in securing what I need.

The second stop in gathering data is to talk to local experts in the field. If my story involved the juvenile justice system, I'd talk with police assigned to young offenders, to the state reform school staff, the Law Enforcement Assistance Administration in the state, local mental health workers, schoolteachers, and so on.

Few of these people are likely to have the deep, solid voice of authority that a national magazine article requires. But they do each have something that can lead to that authority—connections and background in their own professional fields.

I have had fine results with this borrowed range of contacts. Since most public workers and executives in private industry now take part in professional associations, national training workshops, and regular conventions, they may be acquainted with the national authorities you want to locate. I have never been refused when I've asked a local expert for an introduction to a prominent national figure whom he or she knows personally. Most are glad to do it, since having such high-powered friends in their own professions enhances their reputations.

These local experts have another resource—their subscriptions to national publications and journals in their fields. Smaller libraries like Bismarck's seldom subscribe to specialized trade publications and you'll never find them on newsstands. Yet people have a habit of saving back issues of periodicals that relate to their work. You'll probably find someone, in the course of your hometown interviews, who has complete collections of several different publications which you can borrow for background information and insight into new developments in your subject area. Review the trade chapters in *Writer's Market* for broader listings organized by industry. Then cross-reference with your contacts to develop appropriate story ideas.

Your local experts can also help fill you in on the meaning and implications of technical material you turn up elsewhere. While your time with a prominent national authority, even with the benefit of an introduction, may be short, your friends back home will be glad to discuss the facts you've gathered and explain them in your subject's context.

When we think of interviews, we usually picture a face-to-face question-and-answer session. When the face you want to interview is a thousand miles away, you can use two cost-effective interview methods at your disposal and never enter an airport: your post office and your telephone.

You can get the information you need by courteous use of these two conveniences, often more easily than you could book a personal interview even if you were willing to spend the money to travel.

Despite all the complaints we heap on it, the U.S. Postal Service really is the remote writer's best friend. Use it to send a letter outlining your project and your questions to the experts whose opinions will help you most. You might want to pose your questions in questionnaire form for easy reply. Or you might ask your subject to call you collect at his or her convenience—a quicker and sometimes easier way to get answers to involved questions.

Or you can use your letter as an introduction and follow it up with a phone call. In either case, keep your questions to the point and the time required to answer them brief. Those that can be answered by yes or no won't get you the explanatory, quotable answers you need for your story. But those that can't be answered halfway adequately in two or three sentences won't often be returned at all.

Stamps and phone calls cost money—they're part of your writing overhead. Don't be afraid to use them enough to get the best of what they can offer. Supporting quotes that you didn't get so you could save ten dollars in long-distance charges might cost you the sale of a story worth hundreds, and in which you've invested hours and hours of time.

But sometimes even the smartest use of phone and mailbox can't get you what you need, and you have no alternative but to go to your sources in person. Under such circumstances, travel costs can be a good investment. Like all good investments, business trips should be made to pay.

We've already considered the multipurpose travel expedition that offers you time to explore more than one project while at your destination. To get the very best returns on your primary purpose from your travel investment, however, be intent on gathering all the impressions that you'd never get by letter or telephone: your subject's surroundings (sight, smell, taste—in decorating, perhaps, or via sips or samples), relationships with others you meet, habits, pastimes, emotional pitch. Then use these clues in your article to enhance its color and credibility.

When you have solid, firsthand knowledge that you've paid good money to assemble, use it as fully and vividly as you can. Those details are the evidence that you've really done your away-from-home-work.

So far I've mentioned stories in which your location is a drawback and stories in which it's a neutral factor. But there's a whole Santa's bag of surprises left that are your location's gifts to you—the stories in which where you live or want to live is a positive asset.

I've sifted out five kinds of stories that are easiest to sell from the boonies. I've sold articles in each category with what I've come to believe is greater ease and far less risk than is involved in trying to crack the general-interest topics. They include:

- Travel and history.
- The outdoors.
- Personal experience.
- Religion and inspiration.
- Rural living and suburban living.

Besides these, there's an enormous sixth category that we'll consider in a bit. But first, let's look at the possibilities these present.

Travel and history: What could be more perfect for writers living hither and yon? What counts in travel writing is not where you call home, but where you call home from. Your location puts you near a range of travel destinations, no matter where you live, that makes up an automatic low-cost list of salable topics.

History often fits into this category because so much travel is historically oriented. Together, travel and its historical sidelights can have a market nearly as broad as the whole range of national magazines.

Besides those directly connected with travel—*National Geographic Traveler, Travel and Leisure, Travel/Holiday,* for example—general consumer magazines like *Better Homes and Gardens, Esquire* and *The Saturday Evening Post* offer regular vacation articles slanted toward their particular readerships. A variety of customer publications also concentrate on travel topics, from the airlines' in-flight magazines (*Delta Sky, US Air*) to motor club magazines (*Discovery,* or any

of the state Automobile Association of America magazines and tabloids) and those mailed to owners of makes of vehicles, from VW's
Volkswagens World to *Ford Times*.

During my years as assistant travel director for the state of North Dakota, I was engaged in a pursuit that I've since learned was headed in
exactly the wrong direction. Our staff attempted to attract travel writers to cover our state by touting little-known historical landmarks and
well-hidden meadow bowers. Oddly enough (we thought), they seldom snapped up these fresh, never-before-covered stories that we
practically filleted before their eyes.

A principle already mentioned, that what you take for granted in
your locale may be just what turns an editor on, goes double for travel
and history articles. Those writers knew—and I finally learned myself—that our almost-secret tips wouldn't distract an editor from a
three-day-old Danish. What travel editors prefer, instead, is application of the fresh-but-familiar principle to places that people really visit. A new slant on Mount Rushmore still sells, though that hand-
carved mountain may be the only travel illustration in the country
that has graced a few hundred thousand license plates as well as every
self-respecting publication in the field. Overemphasized or not, people still want to go there. If you can hang a new angle on the trip, you'll
sell the story.

National park stories usually sell. Stories on absolutely breathtak-
ing parks minimally maintained by county government and located
two hundred miles from the nearest transcontinental highway do not,
not unless there's something mighty special you've dug up out there.

Teddy Roosevelt, Calamity Jane, various mountain men with peaks
named in their honor, and General Custer help sell travel stories to
major markets. Brave but obscure cavalry second lieutenants, lyrical
but little-known Indian chiefs, anonymous sodbusters and missionaries who founded Protestant splinter sects in the middle of corn-
fields do not. Those stories can be sold, of course, if you dig up the
drama and pathos and humor in them. But you won't sell them to the
big travel markets. They've got bigger fish to feature.

Historical monuments marked today by only a pile of stones and a
plaque will not sell (unless possibly accompanied by a luxurious re-
sort-style RV park). Virtually anything in Hawaii or Alaska, however,
probably will, as will Mexico, Texas, and Florida in winter, lakes
where either the fish or the resorts are spectacular, and annually superlative fall color descriptions.

A surefire way to deduce which destinations may capture the editor's interest is to study the tourism ads in the publication for which
you hope to write. As with an enormous percentage of cosmetic, auto-
motive, and fashion articles, what you read about travel in a magazine's editorial content has ever so much to do with the advertisements that surround those stories.

Some magazines are entirely obvious about this connection. When the Old West Trail tourism group bought a major block of full-color advertising from the *Saturday Evening Post* several years ago, a Wyoming writer who knew of the purchase offered—and sold—an equally imposing travel story on the region. The copy ran amongst the paid advertising; though the story wasn't exactly bought and paid for by those lucrative ads, its content was certainly suggested by them. Likewise, some magazines—*Glamour* among the most obvious—carry tourism copy only to please travel advertisers; a certain amount of favorable editorial comment is virtually a part of advertisers' agreement with the magazine. (Like other commercially wise publications' travel departments, the *Glamour* travel column is staff-written.)

Other publications, especially those focusing sharply on travel, have much less of a direct cause-and-effect relationship between advertisers and editorial content. But I can assure you that none of them would be adverse to a good, legitimate story that happens to concern a major advertiser. Look to the ads for clues on immediately salable topics.

I can mark the beginning of my own sales in the travel and history field very precisely. It was when I realized what I should have known back when I marketed tourism—that prominent, accessible regions make the best proposals, especially when captured with a new slant that makes them come alive again. A good share of readers peruse your articles because they've already been there and want to relive those good times in an untrite way, not because they're currently planning to go or just expanding their horizons.

So what has your location equipped you to make fresh, exciting, and intriguing to this mixed bag of past and future travelers? Your best starting places are the ones you deem most obvious. If they're near an interstate highway, you're in luck. Research by my former agency demonstrated that travelers seldom take side trips more than an hour from the four-lane, and the energy crisis makes that even more credible. If you can fly to your destination and use mass transit or rental vehicles to get around, you may have spotted one of the travel hot spots of the 1990s: work it for all it's worth.

Keep seasons in mind as you ferret out travel tips and historical yarns. Several editors I work with assure me that summer-oriented stories are a glut on the market, especially in the RV-camping field. Winter stories, on the other hand, are prized, since many of us in the northern states just don't write them (and southern writers apparently get very tired of them). Unfortunately, the North Dakota travel story set in winter does not exist; no editor in his right mind expects readers to be fascinated by a trip to the land of thirty below zero. Similarly, Phoenix in summer is a bit iffy, as is Fairbanks in February.

The outdoors: Travel pieces segue neatly into the outdoor field as well—a distinct category which not only includes some adventure travel but also all the outdoor sports, from hunting and fishing to mushroom hunting, running river rapids and just about anything one can do where Nature's at its best or simply its most obvious.

Outdoor stories find their way into the Big Three—*Outdoor Life, Sports Afield*, and *Field & Stream*—right on down to dozens of state and regional publications including my state's own *North Dakota Outdoors* and *Dakota Country*. As with travel, material in the outdoor field has appeal for editors of general-interest publications, from conservationist periodicals to fraternal publications of the Elks and other orders to the glossy major markets.

Your address confers a special benefit here as it does with travel. The wilder and woollier your surroundings are presumed to be, the better you may be presumed to know your field (and stream). Stories sold specifically from my own area include how to fish the state's great river reservoirs (where one of the best fishing holes is above a flooded former cemetery from which coffins were long ago removed), hunting waterfowl in the prairie pothole country, and canoeing on the seasonally boisterous Little Missouri River through the badlands.

If New Yorkers can be expected to know Greenwich Village, Broadway, and how to hail a cab in a rainstorm, you can associate yourself with prairies or lakes or mountains. There is a thriving handful of outdoor writers in Minnesota who know those lakes and the woods that surround them as well as they know their markets. Another small group of successful writers (and photographers) live around Jackson, Wyoming, in the Tetons close by Yellowstone National Park; they're first with elk herds and geysers. All across the country, as you identify an area rich in outdoor writing possibilities, you spot another collection of writers who've made that ground their own.

Your geography is ready to equip you, as theirs has staked them, with its own varieties of the wilds. Even if you live amid the smokestacks of the Ohio Valley, there's something waiting for you. Hike out and look it over.

Personal experience: If your geographic angle is full of possibilities, consider your own experience. It's portable. It's inalienably your own, yet can touch the hearts of complete strangers and illuminate universal truths. And nearly every category of magazine in the country uses personal experience stories in one form or another.

You can explore a multitude of applications for your experiences—first-person tales of drama and homely tensions, major magazine articles that use your own experience as a springboard for stories of broader scope, inspirational articles, juvenile nonfiction, a variety of fiction markets, and more.

One of the reasons that personal experience articles are universally popular among editors is that they appeal universally to readers, who see their own lives reflected in another's story. An advantage that your location bestows upon these manuscripts is the not-from-New-York writer's experience may be considerably closer to universal in the United States than that of the urbanite who frequents Bloomingdale's, The Metropolitan Museum of Art, and Lincoln Center. Non-New York experiences, whether they transpire in Kansas City or Nephi, Utah, are perhaps more applicable to the majority of readers across the country. Why else do all those New Yorkers write about their childhoods in the hinterlands?

Your locale colors your kinds of experiences, too. I've published stories on polka festivals and church lutefisk suppers. My mid-America upbringing, which occurred not so long ago, has provided other material: recollections of hot summer days spent in "prairie air conditioning," the damp coolness of a pre-recreation room stone-walled cellar; and reflections on the best good old days of all, which were of course in 1969.

You have your own savings account of experiences, whether hunting agates in Montana or landscaping with cactus in the Southwest. The place you start from adds flavor to your experiences; your insights provide the nutritional value that makes these stories so meaty to nearly every kind of magazine.

There's almost no way you can avoid having salable experiences happen in your life unless you sit very still and breathe evenly—and even then you can become a spokesman for meditators or catatonics. Survey your own life and that teeming around you. You're carrying some of your best stories around with you and may not even know it!

Religion and inspiration: As travel stories blur into articles on the outdoors, personal experience moves neatly into the religious and inspirational field. These stories in their most internal form can be a subcategory of personal experience—or strong, hard-hitting journalism in other applications.

Spiritual stories await you in almost every community in the land. Nonmetropolitan America, we're told again and again, is closer to its churchgoing roots; that affinity literally extends the Bible belt from coast to coast.

Religious stories can be moving little essays of personal awakenings or hard-edged news of churches facing and solving problems. The evolution of church bodies, like the creation of the Evangelical Lutheran Church in America by the merger of three Lutheran denominations, provides real newsbreaks and thoughtful interpretation. Cults like the Moonies (eminently visible in small towns all over the country, and unavoidable in most cities) provide more possibilities, as do the big-money evangelical crusades that move through communities such as Bismarck; the struggles of small churches facing extinction due to rural population loss; and crusading Christians (and followers of other faiths) applying their religious principles to social ills.

The myriad publications offered by every religious denomination and not a few sects are an accessible market that nearly everyone can sell. But the religious market doesn't stop there. General consumer magazines, recognizing that churches and religion are a vital, familiar part of readers' lives, often publish stories of an inspirational nature. *The Saturday Evening Post* and *Newsweek* or *Time*, for example, carry stories of religious impact—the *Post* in a generally devout tone of voice, the news magazines more interested in the televangelists' varying fortunes.

The religious markets have a reputation for poor rates of pay, somewhat offset by their willingness to consider simultaneous publication with their counterparts serving other denominations. (A Catholic who reads your story in one of her publications is unlikely to encounter it later in a magazine that serves only Presbyterians.) Four sales of the same $25 story add up to $100 just as surely as one for a hundred bucks does.

Some of the religious markets, however, do better than this stereotype suggests. *Guideposts*, a nondenominational publication, pays up to $300 for full-length manuscripts and $100 for shorter works. *Christian Life* pays up to $200. General-interest publications that purchase inspirational material pay the same for the privilege of publishing it as they do for secular stories.

Rural and suburban living: As religion is an accepted part of nonmetropolitan life, so are a variety of other topics that range from the homey to hard-nosed economic issues.

The percentage of Americans who make their living from farming has been decreasing for years, from an estimate of over 90 percent in colonial times to less than a third of Americans today. But don't let this fool you. The back-to-the-land movement of a few years ago, supplemented by hundreds of thousands of new food and hobby gardeners, wood-burning-stove stokers, ex-urbanites fleeing city tensions for the supposed rewards of their own pieces of land—all have combined to make farm and country living stories a better bet today than they have been for years.

You needn't be a farmer to write for this market. *Sunset* has demonstrated that even sophisticated Californians have an avid interest (as writers and readers) in gardening, backyard living, appreciating nature, and other bucolic pastimes.

As with each of our five special categories, rural living stories meet their markets in magazines designed specifically for these interests, but also overlap generously into other categories of general- and special-interest publications.

Farm and rural markets run from the agricultural trade magazines—which use general-interest as well as highly technical stories on how to raise more oats—to family life (*Farm Woman, Farm and Ranch Living*) and more specific topics, like gardening, crafts, and avocations.

Rural living queries also tend to take root in the new wave of magazines that focus on the allure of living in the country: *Mid-Atlantic*

Country, of course, but also *Mother Earth News, Ideals,* and many more. General-interest magazines, too, use rural stories that fit their own special concepts of who their readers are—female activists in small towns and on farms for the women's magazines, country readers sick of a steady diet of crime-ridden urban bad news (*Grit*), and members of religious denominations who share the small-town or country viewpoint and range of problems and experience.

Rural life reflects the roots of a majority of Americans, whether their bumpers sport "Big Apple" stickers or their barns are ads for chewing tobacco. There's another bounty waiting in your area—from personal reminiscences of pioneers to ethnic traditions still kept alive, from small-town-neighbor ethics to the fine arts of schottische. Blame it on the anniversary of The Statue of Liberty . . . or *Roots,* or city insolvency, or all the TV commercials that feature a front porch, a rocker, and Granddad savoring a frosty glass of a chemical-based calorie-free drink mix with his grandchildren at his knee. "Just like your Grandma used to make."

Whatever the reason, you're now in precisely the right place for these kinds of stories. It's about time, isn't it?

These five big, fat categories have something else in common in addition to being the most congenial to us outlanders.

The magazines that specialize in these subject areas are almost without exception published in the kinds of places where we ourselves live. Tennessee. Ohio. California. Wisconsin. The New York-centered offices are a minority in company like this. Is it coincidence? However so, let it be a lesson to you not to overlook pastures close to home, where the grass just might be greener than you think.

Most of the magazines that use stories from the sixth group of geographically gifted topics aren't published in New York, either. They're trade magazines, which, though never seen by the public at large, outnumber all others by a hefty margin.

They won't win you a lot of fame. But they will serve as steady, dependable markets for many of the close-to-home stories that cost you least in travel and research time. Payment ranges from puny to excellent; an average story, in my experience, earns between $75 and $400.

Trade magazine editors are honestly fun to work with. They talk to you. They take time to explain why one idea works and another doesn't. They are glad to hear from you. They really want you to succeed in selling them something. And those with whom I've worked pay regularly, dependably, and a lot faster than some of the glossier publications.

Finding these markets is half the challenge. *Writer's Market* lists hundreds, but that's just the top of the barrel. A foolproof way of finding out which trade magazines serve members of industry in your part of the country is to ask. Drop in on an acquaintance who works in the field you're interested in covering; ask to see his trade journals.

The average businessperson has them stacked all over his or her office, creating guilt as they accumulate faster than anyone could keep up with them. Every industry is served by more than one trade publication, some by a roster that seems overwhelming, many of which are published weekly instead of monthly.

These magazines exist to bring helpful, specialized information to readers working within their fields, and also to provide an advertising vehicle for all the companies that want their readers to stock, sell, or consume their products. Some are house organs for dealers in a particular network—owners of Standard Oil service stations, Rexall drugstores, Mercruiser boat dealerships. Others address all members of a profession in a geographic area—*Commercial West* for banks in the Ninth Federal Reserve district, *TravelAge MidAmerica* for travel agency ticketers in the thirteen Midwestern states and corresponding provinces of Canada.

Your business friend will be happy to lend you as many copies as you can carry away, possibly only if you agree never to return them. If you can't locate a business contact in an area that appeals to you, try the library of your community college or post-secondary vocational school. Since they educate people for the local job market, they usually have relevant trade magazines on the racks.

There are two ways to sell to trade magazines. One is to try to become a regular contributor, or stringer (which we will consider in a later chapter). The other is to query and sell articles of interest to them just as you sell articles to the consumer magazines.

You absolutely have to research trade magazines' needs and policies before trying to sell to them. Those borrowed back issues are your best way; or write the editor, explain your interest, and request several recent issues to study.

I've found that most writers I've talked with have a somewhat outdated idea of what these magazines buy. They're still hoping to sell the universal story—on cutting employee theft, perhaps—to noncompeting publications that go to dentists, plumbers, grocers, hardware store owners. Or they have a local success story in the field whom they propose to interview, photograph, and make a star in the magazines his colleagues and competition read.

Most of the trade magazines I've worked for look down their noses at these approaches. They've grown vastly more sophisticated—in layout and story content—in the past ten years than the rough-edged publications uninitiated writers picture them to be. Why not: Some of the trades have profit potential that consumer magazines only dream of achieving.

One reason why you might underestimate the trade markets is the books about writing for them that are stocked by libraries like mine were written fifteen or twenty years ago, before these trends began. So do your homework.

What trade magazines look for are stories that can inform, aid, or occasionally amuse their readers. One shop's experience can be useful if it presents ideas that can help other readers improve their businesses or illuminate new trends within the field. Horatio Alger these stories are not—they're hardheaded, well-informed explorations of current practices.

Don't overlook them. They can keep you afloat and teach you the freelancing ropes in a way that very few other markets ever will. Competition is less fierce, though standards are just as high. They may be just the markets you've been searching for.

How national magazines fit into your income potential

You *can* sell stories to national magazines consistently if you apply these suggestions and your common sense to marketing them—especially if you first escape the long-shot psychology of writers who don't believe they've got much of a chance of hitting their target.

I know writers in diverse locations who make all of their income from magazine sales, who make much of it this way, or who supplement occasional sales with one or more of the many additional writing markets we're going to look at next. Those who are making substantial incomes from their writing share a viewpoint toward magazine work that you'll have to adopt if you're to reach your income goal.

Being published in a magazine isn't an honor for you. It is how you make your living—the sale of a handcrafted product for a predictable sum of money. As such, it deserves your serious attention.

Nor are an agent's services the all-purpose panacea that remote writers long for them to be. No agent is going to take on an aspiring writer of magazine articles. On the other hand, an agent who's successfully placed your book might agree to handle occasional articles. The key is a track record. Those likeliest to find agents are writers who don't really need them to catch an editor's attention—Catch 22.

As a full-time freelancer, you'll no longer have the luxury of languid sales efforts, of feeling out doubtful markets through optimistic trial and error. Nor can you continue the part-timer's standard sales tactic—writing articles strictly on spec or sending them in cold, to sit out their indeterminate terms in unknown editors' slush piles.

You can learn how the income-earning imperative changes your viewpoint simply by quitting your job to experience freelance stress firsthand. Or you can save your fingernails from being bitten to the quick by looking at magazine writing from the most rational vantage point: how those editors whom you court so attentively can do their part to satisfy your own needs.

There are two pitfalls I've learned to avoid. One is pay-on-publication markets. The other is markets whose payment sounds good until you figure in how much it really costs you to write for them.

Either situation costs you hard money—the first through iffy, unspecified future dates of payment that might never come or might amount to far less than you'd expect in buoyantly inflated dollars; the second in time and research costs that you'll never recover when the check finally comes through.

I sold six stories during my first month of freelancing, totalling $1,500. It sounded good when I gloated to friends and acquaintances. I'm glad I got at least that much reward out of it, for the reality was somewhat less impressive.

Two paid within weeks of acceptance.

Two paid, as promised, on publication . . . but publication came thirteen and twenty-four months after the stories were sold.

Two met tragic fates. One was published just before the magazine went down the drain, and I was never to hear from it again. Not, you may be sure, because I didn't try.

The sixth story has been in limbo for years. The magazine has gone through three editorial staff purges to date, after each of which I've been assured my story will be scheduled soon. The story is so outdated by now it's as good as dead. In the meantime, it's provided me an education in how some editors work. The head of one of the new regimes actually called me to ask why they had the manuscript, whether they'd accepted it, and what they were going to pay me for it.

The moral of this sob story is this: Don't be so eager to sell that you overlook your own best interests. If you're living on what you make as a writer, you probably cannot afford to balance someone else's budget by taking payment in inflated dollars two years down the road. This habit is entirely reprehensible; try it on your own creditors someday, offering to pay for what they've sold you after you've finally used it up. Regrettably, the practice of paying only after a story appears in print is commonplace, especially among smaller markets.

I don't mean to paint all P-O-P markets with the same broad brush. Some are truly conscientious about it, scheduling stories within reasonable times and paying promptly after those issues appear.

But why let an editor fatten files with your copy for an unspecified portion of infinity? If you're just getting started and need the credits, perhaps these markets are worth selling. I speak from sad experience when I suggest that, under almost any other circumstances, you avoid them like the plague.

To avoid putting more time and money into a story than you'll be paid for it can be more difficult than spotting P-O-P's. It can be just as damaging to your cash flow, however, since it leaves you with a negative balance.

Keep track of the actual hours you put in on every story. That means not only at the typewriter, but research and reading time, hours spent getting to and from interviews as well as conducting them, out-of-pocket expenses for office supplies, travel, telephone and postage, and any other costs that you can trace directly to the assignment.

Oddly, an assignment that carries a payment that sounds unusually good sometimes proves to be the costliest; major market assignments sometimes set this trap. They may pay two or three times what you're accustomed to earning from smaller markets. If they require four or five times the effort and expense that the smaller market demands, the bargain becomes less impressive.

The potential value of a byline does sometimes outweigh the immediate bucks. A major magazine credit really can improve your sales record to some degree. In that sense, an assignment that costs rather than pays can be viewed as an investment in your career.

Once, it's an investment. More than once, it becomes a case of pricing yourself too cheaply. You are not a beginner petitioning the big time from an unlikely locale forever. At some point you bring experience and well-developed talent into play on every assignment you accept, and your time is worth more than it was before. When you sense that this is true, let the world know. You're not a beginner forever; nor should you receive beginner's rates.

Some magazines automatically increase the rates they pay after you've sold several stories to them. Some—beware—do not. They count on writers' natural resistance to talking about dollars to keep their work priced low. If you gulp down your embarrassment and say, "I think this is worth more money," you may be as surprised as I have been. Every single time that I've stammered that I would not accept what was offered, I have gotten an increase with hardly a murmur of protest. (That worries me too. If they accepted my demand so easily, I should have made it sooner or asked for even more.)

You can write for magazines for the thrill of it while someone else is underwriting the cost of your bread and butter. When you're really on your own and depend on your writing for a living, you'll realize that thrills don't keep the lights burning.

Writing for magazines as a full-timer is a business. A freelancer is a businessperson. Treat your work with all the respect of a mason pricing a fireplace or a utility company making its case for a rate increase, and market it as well as any salesman who sizes up a customer before beginning the pitch.

The difference is that you pursue your special business for both love and money. Unless you can live on love, keep an unblinking eye on the money.

6

The Markets Next Door

Be they ever so humble at casual glance, there are no markets quite like those closest to your home. You may have taken them for granted as you've grown up together. But once you've opened your eyes to their stellar qualities, you just may learn to love them best.

They don't represent the exotic: In many ways, their voices echo your own, or perhaps your parents'. They speak for and to the people whom you know best.

Take them for granted, do you? Don't. Regional markets—newspapers and magazines that circulate in limited, well-defined areas—offer you neighborly help in establishing your freelance dream as a thriving business. And though their budgets may often be modest, they can give you a boost that goes far beyond their payment for your work.

Regional markets are accessible. They're bound to smile upon a writer with an out-of-the-way address, since it's one they happen to share with you. You face much lighter competition in attracting their attention and winning their support. Your relationship has a good shot at lasting the next thing to forever. Best of all, you have your chance at dusting off your pet close-to-home story proposals—fun, but hardly earth-shaking—that have special zest in your locale but have such a tight geographical focus that national publications would barely deign to reject them.

The best news of all is that regional publishing entered the Eighties in robust good health and continues to be fit, fat, and feisty in many parts of the country. For an explanation, look to the same imperatives that have brought hundreds of new titles into national circulation: Increasingly sophisticated advertisers (locals as well as the national biggies) know precisely whom they want to target with their messages. For all the advertisers who want to reach customers who are just their style, there seems to be a publication ready to help them score a direct hit—for a price, of course.

And so the regional publishing story looks far different up close than it does from a distance. For every choice metropolitan that fails or is eaten by its competition, and for every rural weekly newspaper whose presses are slowing down, you can name energetic new publications conceived to fit these changing circumstances. New weeklies—some with paid circulation, some offered free—serve city (or suburban) neighborhoods and business districts. New regional monthlies embrace the same major lifestyle topics to which daily newspapers are slowly becoming reconciled, from business and health to recreation, home and family.

Metropolitan areas that hosted one still-struggling monthly city magazine a decade ago now sometimes have several. Witness Chicago, where *Chicago Magazine* has lost none of its vitality to upscale *North Shore;* or Minneapolis, where bright *Mpls. St. Paul* continues to retain its younger readers while *Twin Cities* works to win over the older, wealthier, and more sedate.

Professional categories once served (and well) by national magazines now turn to regional, state, or even local versions as well. Agriculture is still served by *Farm Journal* and the rest. Yet in North Dakota two strong commercial entries till the same fields—*Ag Week* in the east and *Farm and Ranch Guide* in the west. The same is true in many uptown pursuits. In our nearest major metropolis, for example, *Forbes* and the beefed-up business sections of the bigger dailies overlap with readers of targeted titles like *Corporate Report-Minnesota, Minnesota Business* and *CityBusiness,* not to mention a score of even-more-specific periodicals frequently published with style and journalistic class by various professional associations.

To the freelancer intent on making a good living by the craft, this somewhat-delirious gamut of close-to-home publications represents a chance at establishing a rock-solid foundation for every kind of income-producing undertaking. Their generally modest rates (though these do vary) suggest that the category is unlikely to become the be-all and end-all of your writing career. But they pay you in more than money . . . in credits that may be cashable in acceptances from glossy markets, in reputation, and in the pleasure and insight to be gained from working cheek to jowl with real editors. They can teach you much.

Take the matter of credentials. No matter how brilliant your ideas and determined your approach, national magazines and book publishers are virtually beyond your reach until you have published credits and samples to show them. Regional bylines may not be in the same class as showing up in the table of contents in *Playboy,* but they do provide incontrovertible evidence that you can write, and have written, and that a working editor somewhere in America has already broken you to harness. (Well, maybe not quite to harness—but you've been tested and awarded a passing grade.)

Clips from regional publications fatten your portfolio with good samples and lengthen your list of professional credits. They help, too, in preparing rejection-proof manuscripts for larger national markets, since stories you develop first for regional readers may become the seed for nationally-saleable material. If they do, your regional editors will have underwritten a good bit of your preliminary research.

And the visibility you gain within your own territory will open doors. Unlike many other kinds of endorsements—casual compliments which, along with sixty-five cents, might get you a cup of coffee—regular bylines atop splendidly serviceable articles can help gain you other kinds of writing assignments. Visibility in the regional media might lead to an offer to edit a sponsored newsletter or publication, ghost speeches or articles for less verbally fluent experts, write scripts for video productions, organize public relations campaigns, or lecture to conventions or classrooms.

Take a closer look at publications in your own corner of the world. They're a bonus gift geography has given you.

Business isn't the only relationship you may develop with your regional markets. I, for one, have loved them long and well. They're the folks who welcomed me with open arms and bore with me during dry spells. They're the ones who've pointed to my submissions with pride and occasionally trumpeted my progress in their contributors' columns. Their editors have bought me lots of lunches, listened when I griped, and initiated me into some of the tougher matters that I'm sharing with you in this book.

I'm not alone in loving my regionals. Writers who work for next-door publications generally harbor a distinct fondness. Some make the bulk of their incomes from those in their own locales, functioning more like quasi-staffers than as independents. Others, like those of us in the Dakotas and other rural states, have too few to choose from; for us they represent the relish that seasons the meat and potatoes of our daily writing diet.

But I'd love my regional markets even if my shadow had never fallen on their doorsteps, for I'd be reading them just as faithfully even if my words weren't between their covers. The rest of their readers usually love them, too, for here alone they believe they'll see themselves. Many follow their state booster magazine with much the avid fandom usually associated with Trekkies at "Star Trek" revivals.

National publishing credits may get you little perks like authors' entries in the *Reader's Guide to Periodical Literature*, circulation in the hundreds of thousands (or more), and bags of enraged letters to their editors if you twist a fact or tromp on sensitive toes.

But do they prompt lovely older ladies to introduce you at church potluck suppers as "our local celebrity"?

Do they get you invitations to keynote homemakers' club conventions and lunch with the Kiwanis?

Do they put you on a first-name basis with the clerks at your favorite hometown bookstore, and get your checks cashed without showing your driver's license?

What Jimmy Breslin is to New York and Bob Greene is to Chicago, I'm a bit of to North Dakota. You, too, can be one of the "name" writers in Idaho or West Virginia. Regional markets will do that for you.

Money is the big stumbling block for many writers who have considered—and decided to pass up—the magazines and newspapers on their home turf. Newspapers, for example, are generally conceded to be low-paying, troublesome markets for full-time freelancers, since few are really equipped to function in the standard query-and-reply method so familiar in other media. While the picture seems to be brightening in some quarters, it's still a long, long way from ideal.

Regional magazines function in a more familiar way but are unpredictable in the rate department. Some do pay top writers in the range of comparable national titles, but most do not. For every *Chicago* or *Los Angeles* whose rates extend into four figures (the low ones) there is an *Arizona Highways* or a *Yankee* at twenty cents a word or a *Florida Keys* at three dollars per published inch. And some regional magazines are truly labors of love; the best you can hope for is an earnest letter of thanks and some sample copies. The regional index of *International Directory of Little Magazines and Small Presses* offers suggestions where to submit.

When it comes to writing for nothing but a byline, you know where I stand. In my opinion, no professional writer ever needs to see his name that bad! But the other markets, even those with relatively puny payments of a nickel or dime per word, may not be quite the bad influence they seem on your bottom line.

For one thing, most of these markets expect to get pretty much what they're willing to pay for. That means you'll seldom be asked to perform extensive digging or commit to large travel and telephone bills for stories for which they intend to pay fifty bucks. Because you can often draw on your own background knowledge and experience, these stories can be quick to research and write; you may be surprised to see them fitting rather well within the framework of your hourly fee.

Sometimes they don't. Then what? As a basic principle, I do not write for less than my minimum just for the sake of added reputation or exposure. I don't need it. Maybe you do. If you are just launching your writing business and feel that taking on a low-pay assignment will have other benefits—a chance to gain good-looking samples, an opportunity to learn from a respected editor—you may choose to violate Hanson's First Law of Freelance Survival. But I'd caution that if you need experience that badly, you should consider getting it in a salaried position before you begin to freelance full-time. Also, keep in mind that a market that asks you to work for little or nothing is highly unlikely to grow up to offer you highly lucrative work. You can count on a learning experience, but don't bet the farm that it'll ever develop into something better.

The vast majority of regional magazines fall somewhere within the one- to four-hundred-dollar range of payment for full-length articles (extra for photographs), and many do go higher for the right combination of writer and story. At those rates, I know you can make these markets pay their own way for your efforts on their behalf . . . and still enjoy all the side effects of writing for them.

Before you begin to bask in their benefits, however, it will serve you well to figure out just what's meant by a regional market. Then you'll want to call the roll in your own locale.

Regional markets have one thing in common, just one: They serve a readership limited by design to a particular city, state, or region. Sometimes that's all their subscribers have in common; in other cases they're further winnowed according to special interests. Either way, those readers live together on the hallowed ground known as the circulation area, or lived there once, or dream of moving there someday. So every scrap of content in the publication, no matter how far from the folds in the road map, is overtly influenced by location.

Beyond that, regional markets exhibit as much variety as the national magazine field. Brian Vachon, long-time editor of *Vermont Life* and author of a book on writing for regionals, divides them into quarters: city magazines, positive regionals, environmental magazines, and guidebooks.

(Newspapers belong on the list, too, but ought to be added with caution. Since dealing with them is quite different from magazines, we'll examine them separately.)

The regional magazines share some good points. Their editors are eminently and emphatically approachable. They want to talk to you— not just open a letter that has to be answered, but sit down, talk over ideas, and share some thoughts on your common love of your location.

They don't really expect you to be a polished professional convincingly scarred from the major market battles. A goodly share of their contributors often are nonwriters or part-part-timers fascinated with one perfect story idea or a tremendous love (sometimes even beyond words) for a single facet of the spot you all call home.

Because of their size and the good local supply of professional writers, some of the city magazines work with a more sophisticated crew. Even there you can be assured of standing in good company. Full-time serious freelance writers are rare, friend, very rare in most regional editors' offices. Says Vachon in *Writing for Regional Publications* (out of print but still found in libraries), "There aren't many full-time writers in these parts. For my money, there aren't enough part-time writers either. I'm always on the lookout for new talent."

The larger-city magazines look to me like a dedicated newspaper reporter's dream in content and bright presentation. Unlike the regionals I know best, they're usually commercial ventures dedicated to picking up where their local news media leave off—the real story, untold or unfinished in the daily news columns, or examined at length for new interpretations and new insights.

If your area is served by one, I highly recommend an expert on the subject, Art Spikol. A columnist on nonfiction for *Writer's Digest*, he's former executive editor of *Philadelphia* and author of the book *Magazine Writing: The Inside Angle* (also out of print). His book includes a lengthy chapter on city magazines that discusses in detail their needs, their attitudes, and the basic propositions that account for their being one of the fastest-growing markets in the country.

City magazines investigate all kinds of lively aspects of urban life, from where to buy the most generous ice cream cones to who controls the local porn scene. But as the metropolitan monthlies sometimes live to investigate, the regionals serving my part of the country (and most of the rest as well) belong in a quite separate category, for they exist to extol.

North Dakota Horizons and its genial, generally gorgeous brethren across this great land ring out with the sound of self-discovery and not a little pleasure at what they find. People read *Horizons* (as they do its counterparts across the country) for a fix of self-satisfaction with their place called home.

With the best available photography and exacting graphic production, *Horizons* (and *Arizona Highways, Montana Magazine, Kansas!* and dozens of others) strives to serve up the best parts of life in its territory. The closest it will ever come to an exposé is an expansion on the journal notes of Lewis and Clark on their trips through the state while exploring the Louisiana Purchase. Its approach to consumer affairs is assignments on local arts and crafts. The nearest thing to dining reviews is its one-page recipe section noted strictly for its glorious full-color food illustration of wholesome North Dakota products.

North Dakota Horizons exists to make us proud of North Dakota. And more: to provide a glimpse of home (from its most photogenic angle) for the thousands of Americans who have their roots here but who've been transplanted around the planet.

Writing for *Horizons*, and for your local magazines which parallel its sunny, optimistic approach, is almost pure fun. Stories on the characters, districts, and pastimes you hold dearest can be natural material for their pages. While they do receive a striking volume of strange ideas and maudlin poetry from those who don't understand what they're about, they are entirely open to legitimate suggestions and

submissions. The editors welcome small voyages of subtle exploration.

Those small voyages are the ones you're most eager to take—but
don't leave without a chart for navigation. Submitting prewritten material over the transom is a poor policy when dealing with regional
magazines, unless you're absolutely sure ahead of time what the editor wants.

Fortunately, regional editors are perhaps the most approachable
and helpful of their profession. Those I know are friendly, interesting
people, overworked but always eager to help you find your way if
your sense of direction is even a bit awry.

Their accessibility may come as something of a surprise; after all,
their staffs are minuscule, their duties maximal, and their time frac-
tured daily into a dozen phases of magazine production. But letting
you go off to write an assignment half-informed only adds to their
workload, for it almost always means they'll have to revise your finished product. The editors I know despise revisions.

So make an appointment and get to know a regional editor today.
Discuss several story ideas you propose to cover. Ask about needs for
coming issues; not seldom will you find the editor engaged in filling
up more than one at a time. Ask about the slant she prefers on regional
stories or profiles—or read the magazine faithfully, for the slant becomes almost instinctive after you've been exposed to it often enough.

You can find out about a magazine's prejudices if you push the right
buttons during these visits. Horizons, for example, has an unwritten
ban on photos and eulogies to abandoned barns and farmhouses.
Though some of the most striking vistas in the state are brought to life
by the bittersweet silhouette of a tumbledown family home stark
against a plowed field, the magazine officially finds no beauty in it.
Memories of the Great Depression are still too vivid to its sponsoring
organization, the Greater North Dakota Association. To them, the
empty houses cut adrift suggest family tragedies during the dust bowl
era rather than an artistically pleasing weathered landmark.

Oddly, editors' prejudices run the entire gamut of possibilities and
are as unpredictable as they are arbitrary. Some, like Mpls. St. Paul,
definitely prefer stories of those living now in their locale to the esca-
pades of expatriate Twin Citians. North Dakota Horizons editor
Sheldon Green, on the other hand, has never been averse to a story of a
North Dakotan who's made it big (and "showed 'em") anywhere in the
world, from prize-winning novelist Louise Erdrich to Gil Rud, who
spent two years leading the Blue Angels flying team. He argues they
contribute to North Dakotans' pride in the quality of people the state
has reluctantly exported since the end of the homestead boom.

The best stories I've found for our own regional magazines all distill
the essence of what North Dakotans find most distinctive—ethnic
groups and their special holidays, history pieces (rooted firmly in cur-

rent events whenever possible), and interviews with prominent or remarkable North Dakotans, from the governor's warm, farm-bred wife to a colorful horticulturist with tips on picking the right tomatoes to an elderly artist who escaped from under Hitler's thumb. (She now creates icons and coddles homeless cats in a striking old house on a hill north of town.)

There's another tie that binds the best regional stories. They're ready to be illustrated, either with a camera held in your own capable hands or by one of the proven photographers all regionals save up for golden opportunities.

The illustrations are the reason for many, many acceptances. I would go so far as to say that, given a good cerebral story with only head shots to brighten its gray columns of type, or a weaker story with striking photographs just begging to be taken, you're usually much better off pursuing the photogenic topic. Leave the other for the newspapers.

Controversy, similarly, is a factor in choosing your topics. There are two kinds of controversial topics for the regional magazine: those arguments that raise the stock of its chosen territory, and those that probably don't belong between its lovely covers.

The controversies in which *Horizons* specializes are on the order of whether ancient migrating peoples really carved the outlines in the chiseled rocks lying in farmers' pastures (for romantic and conversational purposes we have held that they did) and whether researchers who several years ago declared Fargo the windiest place in the nation knew enough not to spit into that stiff breeze.

The kinds of controversy it isn't interested in include political, social, economic, artistic, and technological dogfights. The reason is partly practical; lead time can be a full year, clearly ruling out any stories of a timely nature. The rest is purely pragmatic. Regional magazines' readers are united in only one principle, their love for a particular piece of geography. People who dote on prairies may share friendly "how do you do's," but are likely to make the oddest of bedfellows when it comes to matters of more subjective opinion like politics, religion, strip mining, and the boom in shopping malls. The rule on controversy is generally this: If it isn't upbeat, it's probably a bad bet.

The sponsorship of regional magazines can tell you more than just who will sign your paychecks. The positive regionals are often published by governmental bodies—state or local—or by quasi-public organizations, like the chamber of commerce, who have a stake in elevating the image of their promised land. When in doubt, look for advertising: While these magazines seldom take ads, privately owned publications always have it. If there's nothing but unbroken stretches of intriguing photos and prose inside, the magazine is almost surely deriving much of its budget from its publishers' direct support and the balance from subscriptions.

The magazines of for-profit publishers are more likely to take on highly charged controversies. While constrained by the same common interests among their readers, they're still in a position to experiment with their contents. How do you find out their inclinations? Just ask. That's always the best way to get an answer.

The sunny, positive regionals serve a general audience. Another type of regional publication is aimed at specialized groups: environmental magazines for readers concerned with the natural state of their region; regional farming publications, regional business magazines, regional entertainment tabloids. They're similar to the magazines that serve a national audience interested in the same specific concerns, but they're sharply limited to matters defined by a geographic area.

Many otherwise undefinable markets fit into this category of regionals. *Southern Outdoors* and *Fins and Feathers* (with its state editions) are two of them. *Minnesota Business* is another. So are the *North Dakota REC [Rural Electric Cooperatives]* Magazine, with its firm sense of place and its focus on farm families, and the bi-monthly Fargo periodical titled *Area Woman*.

Circulations can vary from a hundred thousand to a single thousand readers. Some are sold by subscription and on newsstands, while others lie in wait in motel rooms or go to association members as a benefit of paying their dues.

The most minor of these pay contributors nothing. They depend on their audience's amateur field reports or an executive director's efforts. Most, however, do rely on professional help. And there's where you can come in.

These special regionals may not shy away from controversy, provided it's of vital interest to their readerships. And the topics that interest them can be much broader than you'd predict, since even the most avid businessman likes humor and travel and entertainment, and the most go-get-'em hunter can care about conservation, hunting ethics, history and tradition, cooking and interesting personalities.

Controversial topics are of a more carefully prescribed nature. Government exposés won't find a market at a regional business magazine—unless they're of immediate interest to its businessmen subscribers. Scandal and investigative pieces can be welcomed if they have direct bearing on the publication's readers, but will be ignored if you miss the vital basic tie-in.

Granted, these publications aren't likely to assign the most sensitive pieces to those outside their organizations, at least not until their work has been proven through less touchy submissions. While well-documented articles supporting the group's positions may be considered, they have to stand up to the most rigorous standards of accuracy and interpretation, or the publication's sponsors open themselves to charges of bias and misrepresentation. Embarrassing them with inaccurate or incomplete research—particularly on topics with direct bearing on their own fields—is guaranteed death for the well-meaning freelancer who slips up (even just once).

Clearly, regional magazines can't be lumped into one or two well-defined stereotypes. They vary as much as the areas they serve, not only in subject matter, but in attitude, approach, and the appeal they offer their readers. They're a challenging group of markets which you can develop without great expense right where you live today.

Regional readers are hungry for articles about the territories they're loyal to. If you can write to satisfy that hunger, your locale has opened up a whole new range of markets for your services.

Newspapers

Newspapers as freelance markets? They provoke two kinds of reactions from freelancers, both somewhat unjustified.

Beginning writers overestimate them as a market. They don't understand that papers rely almost solely on their staffs and wire services for the copy that crams their daily editions.

More experienced freelancers tend to ignore them altogether for exactly that reason. To them, "newspaper markets" suggests the Sunday magazine supplements, or the occasional big-city paper that does buy a certain number of freelance manuscripts for its weekend lifestyle sections. Any less a newspaper than this looks like a hopeless situation.

Surprises happen to both groups.

Beginners waste untold hours querying newspaper editors or trying to peddle pedestrian stories they've already written. Usually their letters go straight to File Thirteen (the editor's wastebasket, alternately known as the round file). Newspapers, unlike magazines, are not set up to deal with would-be freelancers. Their editors work in a demanding atmosphere of imminent deadlines, and only the kindliest are likely to respond to the sight of a self-addressed stamped envelope with an explanation.

Occasionally the freelancers win, against the odds, and see their unsolicited articles make it into print. They're surprised—at both the minuscule size of their checks and the casualness with which their opus is met.

Both the beginners and the seasoned writers are half-right about selling to newspapers. The beginners have a point: Newspapers do demonstrably obtain articles, columns, and news stories from writers not formally a part of their staffs. Almost every newspaper in the nation, weekly or daily or any other, can be relied on to buy some material from freelancers if their work sounds too good to miss and they're capable of writing what they propose. It may not happen often, but it's never never out of the question.

The veterans are right, too: newspapers are not the plushest of markets. If you manage to sell to them, you may be rewarded with a check that couldn't buy hamburgers for even the smallest crowd. A figure between twenty and eighty dollars is not a bad payment at all for a story. At rates like that, full-timers can't afford to dig too deeply into the newspaper field.

But there is a way to make newspapers pay. Three, actually.

You can sell occasional stories to more than one noncompeting newspaper. This is most often done in the travel and lifestyle fields, where freelance purchase budgets are most likely to be found.

You can follow the example of other freelancers who have made newspapers their prime markets: Ann Landers. Erma Bombeck. Art Buchwald. You too can develop a column or regular feature package and syndicate it yourself to as many noncompeting papers as you can reach. The minimal payment from any one of your clients is then multiplied by the number who send you those little checks each month. Self-syndication need not be national, either; it's worked for freelancers on a regional or even a state basis.

You can, of course, develop a column and find a syndicate to market it for you. But the money will probably take longer to mount up, and the feat of impressing a syndicate is a bigger, longer job than most beginners can afford to invest their time in.

Or you can develop an ongoing relationship with one (or a couple) newspapers that take an interest in your region.

All three methods are variants of the same principle. To make freelance newspaper writing pay, you have to increase your published volume and get it in as frequently as you can. The book *How To Write and Sell a Column* by Carolyn Males and Julie Raskin can give you insight into each of these avenues.

Half a dozen writers in my own state supplement their writing or salaried income with self-syndicated newspaper columns. Another, who eventually left the area when her husband was transferred, made a name for herself as a stringer for the local daily and eventually earned herself an invitation from a national newspaper feature syndicate. Other writers—regularly plying markets outside this state—have become familiar names to readers of the several dozen far-flung Sunday newspapers which feature their work from time to time.

To sell to newspaper markets, you must find a gap in their staffed coverage and devise a way to fill it.

That's why travel writing, to name just one area, is a relatively fertile field among the nation's larger newspapers. Readers are interested in travel to every corner of the globe, and travel industry advertisers are interested in reaching those readers at a time when their receptivity is at a peak. Voilà—the travel section.

But even major papers are reluctant to treat staff writers to what they presume is a life of one paid vacation after another to gather original travel stories. (Travel writing really *is* work, no matter what editors may suspect, but the point is still valid.)

It's more economical for them to search out freelance travel articles from professionals who have already been there, or who amortize the cost of their own research travel over a series of articles and topics. Besides saving money by buying freelance stories, editors can get a wider selection of writing styles and vacation destinations than a limited travel staff could provide.

Smaller newspapers are less interested in travel freelancing because their markets don't include enough potential travel advertisers to carry an entire section. They may still group ads together with some editorial travel copy, but their wire and news services provide enough articles to make a credible, if less than dazzling, showing.

So what gaps do these newspapers suffer from? It's important to know, for gaps in their coverage are the portholes through which you can peep into these markets' workings.

Don't look for big areas of white space next Sunday. Gaps are more subtle than that. Instead, consider material that would interest the paper's readers, that's not currently being offered, and that has a logical tie-in with local advertisers which will excite the ad department. Editors and reporters are loath to admit it, but the advertising angle has more than a small impact on publishers, who in turn influence the editorial staffs they employ.

When citizens band radios were just becoming a craze ten years ago, dozens of local newspapers—our own included—suddenly discovered CB columnists. The local CBers gravitated toward these columns. Advertisers with CBs to sell were bound to notice and gravitate a bit themselves. And when the craze cooled, the features were dropped with little fanfare—a solution that the use of freelance suppliers made particularly felicitous for management.

The same reasoning lies behind the photo, gardening, home improvement, and beauty columns and stories you find scattered throughout city newspapers. Which came first, the readers or the ads? Either way, an alert writer turned up to take advantage of the situation.

An obvious gap—say, in material of interest to retired people or those on the verge of retirement—provides you with your opening. If you can spot it and prove that a local audience is waiting for it, chances are the editor will agree.

Does that mean one story on senior citizens? You might be able to sell it, though your odds depend entirely on how open the editor is to "monkeying around" with writers outside his staff. But even if you sell it, you'll be only a bit ahead; the payment is generally paltry and the impact on your career minimal.

You can overcome both problems by offering not one story, but continuing coverage of the area. That usually emerges in the form of a column, a regular piece of more or less uniform length that can be depended on to serve the same audience week after week. It simplifies the page editor's task, and also greatly improves your proposition.

Building a regular readership is, after all, both the editor's goal and your own; he can hope to attract only a handful of readers with sporadic material.

You can use the postal service to introduce yourself to the editor of your newspaper, but don't count on getting an acceptance by return mail. Or ever. A much more effective approach is to make your proposal in person, backed up with material that demonstrates your skills as a writer and the depth of material available to you.

Most columns are proposed in the same way, whether by an outside freelancer or a member of the staff: The writer develops the idea and checks to see whether it duplicates copy already in use or too easily accessible at little cost to the editor. (Public relations representatives, for example, could be all too willing to fill for free the gap you've found.)

The next step is to write not just one column, but enough for at least a month. While an editor may seriously consider your idea on the basis of three articles, she's more likely to have faith in your productive capacity as well as the strength of your theme if she can see six to a dozen samples.

The samples should be as close as possible to what you envision for the finished work. They should be presented in standard manuscript style—typed double- or triple-space with the first sentence beginning about halfway down the first page. Don't bother to have it typeset or resort to other gimmickry; the newspapers will take care of that side of production and are used to working with nonfancy typed manuscripts.

Develop a list of enough ideas to carry you through a few months as another demonstration of your idea's potential. One of the editor's first questions will be whether your premise is broad enough to sustain itself over a period of years. Yes, that is *years*. Every newspaper, from the smallest to the mammoth, will want to be reassured that you can sustain the column over a substantial span of time.

Writing a regular column is a grueling assignment, whether you're doing it as a freelancer or as a staffer. I wrote two columns for most of the eight years I spent at a newspaper, and can attest to the desperation and impending dullness you face after you've written on the same kinds of topics for years and face another ironclad deadline—and have run as dry as a glass of burgundy.

The relative shortness of newspaper columns—many run no more than 600 to 800 words—is deceptive. Behind those well-chosen words is a need for thorough background research and a deep well of variations on one basic theme. Don't take on a column project if you doubt you can sustain it. Six good months followed by one or two that falter won't help your reputation a bit, though no one will realistically expect every single column to be a classic.

Selling one editor is the first step in any kind of self-syndication. If you secure a column or an assignment to a permanent area, like reviewing films or books, you'll quickly find you put more time into that one regular project than you can hope will be rewarded by a single newspaper's payment.

With your first editor's knowledge and permission, you can approach other newspapers with the same material. Obviously your stories must have more than local appeal to be marketable outside your community. Many columns built around hobbies or activities or advice rely mostly on general information and can be broadened enough to serve readerships in several areas.

The most important caveat of multiselling is this: Never, never offer your material to another editor whose paper competes with your first. Competition doesn't stop at cutthroat intercity rivalry. Even small circulation overlaps must be considered, for what you're selling must be offered exclusively in each subscriber's territory. Weekly papers in separate counties seldom compete with one another. On the other hand, even small city dailies often do, with a larger newspaper nipping at the heels of a daily in a smaller town within its area. If you must make the choice, you're better off approaching the smaller paper than the larger; it imposes fewer limits on the other contacts you can make.

What kinds of columns and regular material might succeed in your area? Some of the more salable topics include the outdoors, hunting and fishing, personal sports and recreation, homemaking skills and human-interest profiles and anecdotes. In each case except the last, the audience is well defined both to the editor and to the advertising manager. As for human-interest stories, newspapers have an almost insatiable hunger for them. But touching people's emotions is a tricky technique that not everyone can manage.

Humor is another deceptively appealing area. A strong localized humor column would appeal to almost every editor. Oddly enough, there seem to be more would-be Erma Bombecks around than anyone would have suspected from the glum tone of much kaffeeklatsch conversation. That every newspaper doesn't already have one of its own demonstrates how many aspiring humorists fail to amuse anyone but themselves.

Wayne Lubenow defines the field of humor writing in my part of the country just as Erma Bombeck sets the tone for housewife chuckles and Mike Royko for sardonic wit applied to Chicago politics. Wayne's weekly columns, accompanied by a second feature, appear in thirty-two North Dakota weeklies. Another column and other special material show up twice a week in the tabloid *Midweek* here in Fargo.

Wayne has been a popular columnist in the state for over thirty years, first with a succession of daily newspapers and then as a full-time freelancer. He began applying his witty observations to the weekly, rather than daily, markets more than fifteen years (and one-thousand columns) ago.

"I started with just nine papers. It was a question of survival," he says. "A buddy in an ad agency suggested a self-syndicated column to me just before the annual North Dakota Newspaper Association convention. I went on up there two weeks later and talked to a few guys, and I was suddenly in business." He added more of the state's hundred weeklies as they watched his column's popularity soar, until reaching the present comfortable 33 percent two years after sending out his first column.

Each of the members of the Lubenow Co-Op—"a pretty loose name for us, since all we have to go on is a handshake"—receives a column of about 600 words each Friday along with a short North Dakota feature story suggested by one of his editors. The price for the package is twelve dollars per paper per week. "My big competition, believe it or not, is Erma Bombeck," he says. "They can get her for three dollars. But she isn't going to drive out their way during a January blizzard to write a story they want to see in print."

Lubenow's work appears in another kind of overlooked newspaper market, too—a highly successful shopper distributed to all the homes in his community of fewer than 150,000 people. That continuing relationship matches the revenue from fifteen or so of his country weeklies to bring his annual income, he says, considerably above what he could expect from any salaried job. And that's not counting assignments for *Horizons* and nearly every other regional publication with money in the budget for a contribution from a top regional name writer.

"My writing is a means of survival. My clients have a wonderful incentive system," he says. "If I don't write, I don't get paid. I've never missed a deadline for a column since I began. You have to understand that I'm completely undisciplined. Sheer economic pressure keeps me going. I just sit down at the typewriter every day, stare at it, and maybe open up a vein. . . ."

Wayne's forte is family humor; his kids have grown up and mirrored all the stages of his readers' homelife over the years. But your backyard resources don't have to be limited to your own spouse and children to prosper in the newspaper markets.

How about your whole community—its news, its controversies, its characters? You can become neighboring newspapers' eyes and ears at home as a correspondent or stringer.

Many publications have correspondents stationed throughout their service areas who feed them updates on local developments in the hinterlands. Newspapers need their stringers more desperately than most. No matter how large their staffs or how eagle-eyed the assignment editor, no paper covers every story its editors would really like within its circulation area. If you're on the spot—the right spot to fill a gap in their coverage—you can find yourself another kind of beneficial relationship between the news and you.

Where stringers are needed is outside the city where the newspaper office is located. That may mean in a city's suburbs or outlying towns served by the county seat. Papers want news of these areas, for their advertisers desire those customers' attention, and the circulation influences the rates they charge for ads.

But these peripheral subscribers commonly share one predictable gripe about that major newspaper: It never carries news of their own towns unless something really extraordinary happens, and that something is usually a natural catastrophe or horrible crime. They envy the kind of ongoing attention the paper gives its primary area, from its coverage of civic meetings and issues to personality pieces and features on local leaders and groups.

If you're living in one of these dissatisfied, overlooked communities, here's one chance that your address will elicit genuine interest and even relief (unlike the guffaws you get on a bad day in the Big Apple). Provided you can demonstrate that you're a capable reporter with time to maintain a reasonable level of coverage, you may find you've got yourself a job.

The job of a stringer isn't usually salaried. Most newspapers pay according to the total inches of copy you produce or the number of stories called or mailed in.

Your most important quality is not that you write like Hemingway, but that you're on the spot. Some newspapers regularly work with stringers and actively replace those who move or retire in a certain locale. Others are open to the idea but seldom go out of their way to seek correspondents.

In either case, your best route is the most direct one. Drop in to talk with the editor, calling first to make sure you choose a time when he's not swamped with work (and crabby). On a larger daily, talk with the state editor. Find out what kinds of news interest them and offer to submit your first samples on an entirely nonbinding basis.

Good freelance stringers find that they can generate a surprising number of local stories for their editors. Sometimes ideas are offered by the editor who's their contact at the newspaper; they may have been kept on the back burner for lack of someone with time to take them on.

With a topical column, the key to decent earnings is the number of newspapers that purchase it. Stringers stretch out their earnings rather differently. The more stories they produce, the more they earn. But they also can borrow a single page from the columnist's book and investigate the possibilities of serving more than one paper at a time.

This works best for the lucky few whose communities are within the prime interest areas of more than one daily newspaper who do not consider each other competitors. More common are situations where you can write about your community for both a neighboring weekly and a larger daily. These two kinds of papers usually don't see themselves in a neck-to-neck race for subscribers, so strong material may be marketable to both with fresh treatments and different angles.

Before you approach any additional editors, however, be sure to get the approval of your first contact. Going behind his back may cost you both markets.

You should be aware of two more peculiarities of dealing with regional newspapers. One is that few are really set up to handle the standard freelance tools of query letter and SASE. On most of the country's papers you're going to be a curiosity in the city room. Take nothing for granted; ask whether they keep score on your earnings (and check them yourself), and offer to bill them if they prefer. And present your inquiries and ideas in person or by phone. If you write and mail them, rejection is as likely to be the harried editor's wastebasket as it is the U.S. Mail.

Another problem is the fervor with which editors defend their staffers' territory against encroachments from the eager would-be freelancer. The way to get work is not to tell an editor his staff writer is rotten and you can cover his beat better. Nor is it usually worthwhile to try to sell material in an area that's close to any staffers' turf.

Try instead to find true gaps in coverage and take steps to make that ground your own. Once you've sold your services to an editor, you'll be in the enviable position of the writer who got there first. All that you've got left to worry about is turning out great copy as regularly as you've promised—and believe me, that is quite enough.

Other stringing assignments

Though newspapers are the most numerous markets that might seek stringers in your part of the country, they're by no means the only ones.

Stringers can act as on-the-spot reporters for a number of organizations. Some are strictly news oriented. Others depend upon your growing network of contacts and background knowledge of your area. All view your location as an asset, for you can help them stretch their coverage into cities they'd never reach in any other way.

I have been a North Dakota stringer at different times for several national consumer magazines, United Press International, half a dozen trade publications, a national association with an interest in legislation, and a Washington, D.C., consulting company whose clients are interested in the economy and regulatory climate in North Dakota.

My friends have managed other correspondent jobs: for *Time* and *Newsweek*, for an activist women's newsletter, for nature and ecology groups, and for consultants preparing feasibility reports on North Dakota construction projects and business development.

Some of these assignments are a real snap to identify: they are occasionally advertised in larger state newspapers. During the past six months our local paper has carried want ads seeking part-time stringers for a coal publication, a banking industry newsletter, and several anonymous advertisers who used a blind box number for replies. (I was tantalized but too busy to answer their ads.)

Other openings are passed on by word of mouth. For eighteen months I provided abbreviated daily coverage of North Dakota government and politics for United Press International, which has staff offices nearly everywhere around the world except in the state of North Dakota. The Minneapolis bureau chief responsible for the state inquired at the capitol about reliable correspondents. An acquaintance who had seen my work in regional magazines recommended me.

But many good opportunities require you to seek them out. They have this in common with most newspaper stringer slots—the opportunities don't quite exist until you create them by offering your services.

I have an informal relationship with several trade publications in industries I follow closely. I set them up in just this way, starting cold and simply asking whether they needed local information support. I knew they had a clear interest in Dakota news from watching their circulation and keeping an eye out for important developments within my territory. I studied most over a period of several months, subscribing to some (many are free on request), and reading others in the library or by borrowing copies from friends who received them. The critical point was whether they seemed to have regular correspondents already in place within the territory I could cover for them.

In most cases the answer was clearly no. In more heavily populated states, you may end up with a few yeses and maybes . . . but even then publications with real interest in developments in your area may not be at all averse to having more than one stringer stationed in your state to field local news.

Writing to offer to serve as a correspondent can be an invigorating exercise for freelancers. The reception can be a great deal warmer than the one that greets the average unsolicited magazine query. The editor of one publication for travel agents wrote me by return mail to say she was "honestly delighted to learn of a potential stringer" in my area.

Include samples of your published work and any personal background that qualifies you to report on the industry. Most editors don't expect you to be a ready-made expert, though background does help. If you have any experience at all in the industrial or business world, it will help you sound thoroughly promising. You'll find that most editors are more than willing to help you nail down the basics of their business if they're confident you'll turn out to be a productive stringer who'll be around long enough to justify their time and effort in your early months.

Consulting companies, another field for freelance stringers, are a mysterious outside force over much of the country. When a group of Bismarck business people was considering whether the community could support another new luxury motel, they contracted with one such company to explore the market. When North Dakota wanted a feasibility study on a new governmental social program, they brought in a consulting firm with a national reputation. When a problem seems to beg for further study—for instance, the need for better transportation in a rural area whose citizens are too few to guarantee it will return a profit—a consultant is often the answer.

There are dozens of national consulting firms, working in various parts of the country. Most have one factor in common when they're faced with a study in your community: As the proverbial outside experts, they lack familiarity with local ground rules and givens. By hiring your native expertise, they can save a tremendous amount of work in accumulating the background knowledge they need to give their reports credibility.

Watch your local newspapers for word of impending consulting contracts. These items turn up most often, in government news reports, but also appear in the business and finance pages and around the local chamber of commerce. You need to reach these companies very early in their planning stage if you're to be considered as a local stringer, so your own early warning system can make a great deal of difference in your prospects. (A friend at your chamber of commerce office is always a good source, as is any friendly face among the city fathers.)

To consider your help, the consulting firms need information on your reporting skills, your reliability, and your local credibility. (A local contact who's earned a reputation for exaggeration could completely undermine their own work, so they're justifiably suspicious.) Local references are a must. A recommendation from the governmental body or company that has hired them is the most persuasive reference you can have. You may find that local executives familiar with your work are most amenable to recommending you.

Fees vary, but are generally on the healthy side. Work may be assigned on either an hourly or piecework basis. Be sure that your expenses are covered, either directly or through a substantial fee. Telephone calls to distant head offices and volumes of data shipped cross-country can quickly run into a substantial expense.

If you live in or near your state capital, as I do, you have an excellent source of stringer assignments that are almost yours for the asking. During legislative sessions a broad range of clients are anxious to receive fast reports of bills introduced and enacted that affect their interests, either for news value or as their own early warning system.

Taxation policies, for example, have always been a hot political issue in North Dakota. A wide variety of special-interest groups and industry newsletters and magazines, all highly interested in regional developments, are located at such distance that they're forced to depend on local help. (Little North Dakota legislative news ever hits the national news wires.)

Some who watch your legislature with interest would like more active local help—part-time lobbying, perhaps, along with this news of relevant actions. It's up to you whether you want to take advantage of these possibilities. Lobbying pays very well, even in its more casual part-time forms. But I suspect that any business affiliation with a special-interest group damages a writer's credibility as a gatherer of news, since politicians are highly sensitive to these connections. Lobby only for groups you can truly support and defend. Otherwise, you're safer turning away tempting plums that can put you in a compromised position.

The best advice for unearthing all kinds of stringer opportunities is not to be afraid to ask whether a potential client is interested. If she's not, you'll never hear from her. But if she really is open to establishing a local contact, she'll greet your offer warmly.

Regional markets can be a solid backbone of your freelance income and a source of pleasure and reputation—a nearly perfect mixture of payoffs. Once you've explored their possibilities and considered their contributions to your overall income-producing strategy, I think you'll savor them as well, one of geography's commitments to your career prospects.

Your location is an asset in all these regional markets. If you've got the address they want, you ought to flaunt it.

7

Writing Books in the Boonies

After you've watched your finest newspaper or magazine published efforts meet their maker crumpled beneath the kindling in the camp-fire, or used to package potato peels or coffee grounds bound for the garbage, you're ripe to consider writing a book.

A book lasts. It has a life of its own, sometimes longer than its au-thor's . . . and certainly longer than it takes to wrap up what's left after cleaning fish.

Every writer views a published book as a milestone in her progress as a professional. For the self-supporting freelancer deep in the wilds of America (that is, far from Publishers Row and arch gossip at the Four Seasons or Russian Tea Room), that book can mean far more than one publisher's stamp of approval and the envy of one's literary peers.

The time spent writing and marketing your first book could be your best investment in establishing a secure, comfortable freelance in-come.

Writing books—I mean books that are published, not manuscripts languishing in a drawer—is a credential that crosses over into every other writing endeavor you're likely to undertake.

It's a source of local status, at the minimum. Such publicity can lead to all sorts of commercial work; clients will be pleased to secure some-one of your reputation.

It's an aid in marketing magazine articles, both regionally and na-tionally, especially if it helps establish you as an expert in your field.

It's a boost toward finding an agent if you decide (later, not now) that you want one. And having written a first published book bright-ens the outlook immeasurably for a second, third, or tenth.

Books offer a financial advantage that's unique among all the kinds of writing you may do as a freelancer: they continue to pay you divi-dends after you've completed and sold them. Only rarely do magazine articles, video scripts, newsletters, or lectures continue to bring in income after you've cashed the payment you agreed upon; even re-selling or syndicating them involves substantial additional effort and a dollop of good luck. But books sometimes continue to deliver semi-annual royalty checks for years after you've moved on to other projects. With a bit of negotiation and the benign smile of Dame Fortune, your advance may also pay for the time you'll spend researching and writing today in hopes of profit tomorrow.

Consider book projects early in your freelance adventure. It's good business sense to explore the possibilities (though counting on a book alone to support you from the first day you leave gainful full-time employment is simply a hallucination). Royalties, even from modest sales, can underwrite time spent in market explorations or in developing new proposals. Those checks—representing a percentage of revenue earned from your literary pride and joy—are one of the few ways to break away from using last month's income to pay this month's bills. They help build up financial security now, when you're bound to need it most.

Since the celebrity that usually accompanies authorship is also good for lining up less glamorous writing assignments, it's difficult to understand why so many writers put off this kind of project for years and years. Those writers, and possibly you, subscribe to the popular myth that writing a book is the Ultimate Goal for the would-be author, one too meaningful to be taken lightly or misapplied at a callow age. So they wait, and wait—only to increase the national census of elderly authors racing against time.

Few of us removed from Publisher's Row can boast of a New York editor friend. So we're easy prey for the rare success stories on achieving publication. We shy away from such an awesome challenge, choosing instead to take on again and again the smaller assignments digestible in more moderate-sized chunks. And we admire book authors as a special, inspired breed with a direct line to the Muse or, alternatively, an uncle or cousin in the publishing business.

Yet the evidence points to a far different conclusion. More books are being published and sold today than ever before . . . almost 50,000 separate titles in a recent year. Million-sellers are no longer rare. Today money is spent more freely on advertising, promotion, and book distribution than in any so-called golden age. For every old-line publishing house that fails or is swallowed by corporate acquisitions, dozens of successors spring up. And bookstore franchises have now become popular in shopping malls from Cape Cod to Puget Sound.

These signs point to a better outlook than you might think for your first book and an improved picture for the others you might develop.

So where do you knock on the door?

Four modes of publishing await your investigation and the sharply honed ideas you'll take to market. None is superior to the others in every way. Each is legitimate in its turn, offering its own set of advantages and drawbacks.

The four options are commercial publishers, the traditional and most obvious route to publication; small independent presses, rapidly catching up on the outside as the purveyors of quality titles; self-publishing, the former dark horse that's breaking through as a legitimate and profitable alternative; and authorship of sponsored, or premium, books. If you have a solid, well-researched idea and a grasp on its audience, one of these routes almost certainly is going to lead to your own Book Number One.

Some definitions help set the categories apart. "Commercial" encompasses the major publishing houses, whose headquarters are in New York City or one of a few other metropolises, and whose royalty structure generally offers the largest return to authors. They usually concentrate on the general adult trade (fiction and nonfiction), often handling other categories such as children's books, reference books, and textbooks in separate divisions.

Whether owned by multinational conglomerates, private investors, or stockholders, these companies have to balance their commitment to quality books with the need to show black ink on the bottom line. Established writers are far less risk than unknowns; topics that have already demonstrated sales potential are safer than those that are untried, and "more of same" is inherently easier to justify—even if it fails—than a bright but untested subject or writer diving into uncharted waters. The chances of placing your first book among their ranks are not high, especially without an agent . . . who probably won't sign you on until you've already managed to achieve first publication. Writers face ferocious competition simply getting past the lowliest manuscript reader.

Nevertheless, don't count this route out. Climbers do reach the top of Mount Everest despite the altitude, the cold, and the steepness of the climb. First-time authors do see their books published and are fully worthy of the headlines that report their achievements.

The designation "small press" is a bit harder to define. These independent companies aren't necessarily small in either scope or distribution; they may tackle the tallest subjects, and they may record sales from border to border and abroad. Their approach to money varies, too. Some are run by shrewd, knowledgeable entrepreneurs who've crafted businesses that are notably profitable, both for themselves and their authors. Others scramble from month to month with meager sales and occasional grants, plodding on to promote their highly individualistic points of view or to share their love of the language arts.

These independent publishers—mavericks or solid small firms—may build their lists on scholarship or on ideas many of us may regard as loony. What brings them into the most exciting and rapidly growing segment of the book industry is the freedom to concentrate their resources into one specialized area or a few related fields, generally promoting each of their titles more thoroughly and exploring new alleys of distribution while the large houses maintain their hold on the safer, more traditional routes to the readers.

Instead, they've pioneered often-effective new avenues of book sales through direct mail and retail operations that concentrate on merchandise other than books. Direct mail enables them to sell their wares via the mailboxes of America, permitting them to target recipients by region, interests, income, and past support of similar products. Too, they seek out merchandisers catering to their chosen readers. You will find small-press books in special small-press bookshops and occasional college bookstores in larger cities; and they're also available through sportsmen's catalogs and handicraft stores, groceries, and sports centers, and in the catalogs and bookstores serving distinct populations, from gays and feminists to survivalists and gourmet cooks.

Self-publishing is the ultimate form of verbal entrepreneurship. The author assumes all the roles of publisher as well as with its attendant possibilities and risks. Distinct from old-fashioned vanity presses that still thrive on novices' gullibility (you pay for the entire publication), these personal publishing ventures are slowly gaining respectability among book people—librarians, reviewers, booksellers and knowledgeable readers.

The risks are high; so are the potential rewards. By taking the do-it-yourself route, you come face to face with every aspect of publishing—editing (a factor far too often neglected by self-publishers, and the one that's needed most), typesetting and keyline, printing, binding, distribution, promotion, collections, and warehousing. You can proceed in two radically different ways: learning by the seat of your pants, or carefully researching each of these steps. The most difficult of all is learning to regard your manuscript baby as a creature with a life separate from your great hopes and dreams for its success.

That it can be done is evidenced not only by a long line of successfully self-published titles eventually coveted by commercial firms, but by the considerable number of self-publishers who jump to the small-press category, getting double duty from what they've learned by applying it to the publication of others' books.

Sponsored and premium books are created with the backing of an organization that helps determine their content and distribute the finished results. Cookbooks are often co-sponsored, promoting a particular brand-name product or commodity. So are books on fishing, supported in one way or another by tackle or boat manufacturers; biographies of the founders of businesses or an institution's major philanthropist; and countless others—some subtle, some obvious.

Some sponsored books are an outright endorsement of a product or service. Others are handled as ethically as commercially published titles. Whether their motives are to promote sales or support an already-popular product with more information, they can provide a means of support for us wordsmiths in the boonies . . . or our urban counterparts who recognize a frequently offbeat opportunity when they see one.

At first glance, self-publishing and subsidy or co-publishing seem the equivalent of working with a vanity press. They are not. Each does indeed rest on a certain amount of vanity or self-confidence, and the writer's presumption that strangers might benefit from reading his work. Each does require the investment of the writer's capital. But while self- and co-publishing can be forthright business ventures whose rewards go far beyond the authors' belief in themselves, vanity publishing begins and ends with ego. Unless you are fully aware and willing to assume the entire expense to see your work in print, it is a racket.

You've seen those advertisements in magazines and newspapers—"Major national publisher now looking for authors." Why, in a highly competitive business shadowed by the spectre of the voluminous slush pile, would publishers actually advertise for more? Simple. They're in the business of not selling books to readers, but of selling them to their own authors.

Vanity presses prey on the naivete of beginning writers or those who've never bothered to explore the real world of publishing (or even suspect that it exists). Their transactions begin with flattery, lead to long official-sounding contracts, are fueled by a check from the would-be author, and end with absolutely nothing. Book reviewers refuse to consider books from the well-known vanity imprints. Librarians ignore them. Bookstores won't touch them, for even if such publishers bother to send them a flyer (the "advertising campaigns" they've promised the innocent authors), they don't fit the standard discount or delivery schedules.

A similar scam begins with a letter inviting the submission of poetry or short fiction for an upcoming anthology. Such books do, of course, exist. But legitimate offers pay the writer for the privilege of including her work. The vanity press equivalent requires the writer to "invest" in publishing the collection or perhaps to pay an editorial fee or buy a vastly overpriced keepsake edition.

Perhaps both schemes have their place for amateurs desperate to see their names in print. Know them for what they are: Rackets well-known to anyone even marginally familiar with professional writing, and publishing credential paid for with a check which isn't worth the price of the paper on which it's printed.

There was a time when "publisher" was synonymous with New York. That's what made starving in its garrets seem so sensible, so appropriate . . . so right. The myth may live on among the uninitiated, but the reality is radically different.

In New York and Boston (particularly) the publishing mammoths not only live on, they are more mammoth—Simon & Schuster, Random House, Holt Rinehart Winston, and the other reconstituted houses that have emerged lately from the frenzied mergers and acquisitions. But while New York publishing has been in flux and turmoil energetic editors beyond the banks of the Hudson River and all over the U.S. are developing their own publishing enterprises.

Two great currents are roiling those distant and less polluted waters. One is specialization. Whether their nuclei lie in a regional focus or concentration on a well-defined subject (or group of subjects), more publishing companies are releasing more titles from more addresses than ever before. Most make no bones about their narrow interests: Whether they publish books for nurses or books about the Pacific Northwest, their limited scope defines them just as surely as their commitment to the actual creation of their books.

The other trend is decentralization. Convenience alone once recommended New York (and the rest of the urbanized Atlantic seaboard) as the proper site for those who aspired to literary immortality. That's no longer undeniably true. From shaping the author's manuscript (a chore frequently farmed out from the central office to freelance editors), to manufacturing (which in many cases has slipped overseas for reasons of economy), to distribution (handled via phone and computer with chains and wholesale operations all over the country), the traditional address no longer adds quite so much cachet to a publisher's image. No matter where the large firm collects its mail, the odds are high that its operation is spread all over the map.

As for the writers themselves, they can and do live anywhere. Book publishers have always given their authors latitude. Personal geography typically has far less effect on book publishing, with its stretched-out schedules and long production process, than it does on magazines dominated by tight deadlines and highly specific editorial requirements.

Here is a pleasant thought if you're accustomed to dealing with the down side of your locale: When it comes to writing books, assessing the effects of a nontraditional location is more a matter of weighing its advantages than compensating for losses.

Of course, finding a publisher for a first book is never easy. No matter where you live, you're still going to have to clear all the publishing hurdles the industry can throw in your way. Getting beyond the slush pile (where unsolicited proposals and manuscripts make their first stop) is only the beginning. You'll have to convince an editor that A) your book is commercially viable, artistically defensible and in fact likely to resemble the hot proposal she holds in her hands; and B) you're the one perfect person to write it.

These tests are not necessarily crude signs of geographic chauvinism. They're generic. You're suffering through them with the best no matter where you call home.

Commercial publishing

Rumor has it that getting a first book accepted by a national publisher is a major miracle, and that making money from the effort is well-nigh impossible.

Those assumptions, though grounded in reality, are too pessimistic. I know why.

First, they're generally based on the market for mainstream and literary fiction. Fiction always seems to come to mind first when book publishing is mentioned and its risks assessed, despite the overwhelming preponderance of nonfiction in any year's grand total of published books.

Each year perhaps two hundred or so first-time authors are published in hard-cover books. Of these, some few are hailed by critics as the current "miracle babies." Every account of their achievements includes a statement about the incredible odds against their success. That's true, given the narrow slice of the pie from which the reviewers pick the choicest plums.

But even for fiction—indisputably harder to sell than nonfiction—there's a comfortable market for titles that can earn their keep without cracking the *Publisher's Weekly* best-seller lists. Men and women in offbeat neighborhoods all across the continent are quietly crafting a living within the paperback genres of romance, mystery, intrigue, westerns, science fiction, fantasy, and horror, and recently new paperback quality fiction imprints have come on the scene. You probably devour some of their work, as I do. Every time we search out a new title it means another nickel for the author.

The second reason for the popular odds against landing a national publisher is again based on fact. Landing a contract *is* hard work. But the tales of woe are often passed on and magnified by academics, those collegiate mentors whose prospects of landing a trade book contract are about as bad as they fear they might be. Strictly scholarly tomes may be as infinitely difficult to place with a trade publisher as the self-conscious literary novels sometimes spawned during sabbaticals. While those books-in-the-making may win prestigious grants-in-aid and tenure for professors, they will likely reach only a tiny contingent of equally erudite readers.

If you're serious about earning a good living from your writing, you'll put aside your literary aspirations, at least for now, and be willing to work on the level of the vast majority of readers: Not gutter-bottom depth by any means, but rather, within the realm of entertainment and information.

And if you're serious about earning $25,000 a year from your writing, more or less, you may want to forsake the full-time crafting of fiction (at least for now) for more salable nonfiction topics.

Or perhaps not. Ten years ago I was adamant on this point. Today I'm not so sure. In the meantime, I've watched the accomplishments of two women from the most rural reaches of North Dakota, Kathleen

Eagle and Judy Baer, whose success half-convinces me to hedge that bet.

As it happens, I feel faintly like a very distant godmother. I met Judy Baer one January at a university seminar I conducted on strategies for publishing a first book. She'd traversed two hundred miles of glare ice to get there—a feat that spells serious dedication among veterans of North Dakota's lonely highways.

Though we talked exclusively of nonfiction that night, Judy, who lives in Cando, applied the same principles to writing romance. By the next time I heard her name mentioned, she was working on her third novel of love and negotiating the contract for her fourth with cool professional aplomb.

She followed the sensible analytical practices exhaustively explored by novelist Lawrence Block in *Writer's Digest* and his *Telling Lies for Fun and Profit*, and illuminated in each edition of the encyclopedic *Fiction Writer's Market*. She studied the markets for contemporary romances and chose a house specializing in inspirational Christian fiction. She reviewed its already-published novels and shaped her story and characters around its clear objectives. Only then did she write her novel. It was accepted first time out.

Kathleen Eagle, then an English teacher on the remote Standing Rock Reservation, based her own first novel on the real-life romance that landed her in North Dakota in the first place. The hero himself— now her husband—phoned me one day to ask for suggestions to help his wife find a publisher.

We talked only of the basic sales strategies common to all kinds of writing and how they might be applied to recruiting an agent, an ally (especially in the world of fiction) to help scale the desolate mountain of slush that stood between her and publication. Kathleen continued much, much farther in researching her opportunities. She succeeded in snaring the attention of an excellent agent—yes, by mail—from Solen, North Dakota. She won the top award of the Romance Writers of America with her yet-unpublished manuscript (another first for North Dakota) and is now three paperback originals into what promises to be a long, bright career.

Genre fiction has a long and honorable history as a training ground for authors who later go on to mainstream success, some without the usually required pseudonym. However, if your story-telling aspirations lie in a higher realm, your best bet lies among the small presses who do regularly publish literary and experimental fiction. Few pay authors for the privilege. Yet here, too, talented novelists have learned and broadened their craft, occasionally graduating to the mainstream and/or a larger commercial press. If this is your direction, *The International Directory of Little Magazines and Small Presses* or the small press section in *Fiction Writer's Market* should be your best friends.

Now, fiction will never be my own forte. But let's leave that case open while we consider the care and feeding of nonfiction proposals. If two serious North Dakota writers of popular fiction—both of them starting utterly cold—can bat a thousand, who am I to discourage your hopes?

Nevertheless, your prospects as a first time author seem best in nonfiction, the broad category in which competition is somewhat less direct and which lets your own expertise and geographical assets shine through.

Your locale suggests certain book topics most likely to be sold on your first time out. Each is in demand among a broad spectrum of general-interest and specialized national and regional firms, and each bears a striking resemblance to a class of those highly salable magazine stories discussed in Chapter Six.

The big six, translated into book terms, include these broad categories:

1. Travel guidebooks, celebrations of regional cultures, and history.
2. The great outdoors, from titles on how to catch more fish to compendiums of sporting adventures, exploration, conservation, and many more.
3. General instructional titles based on your own background and experience—cookbooks, hobby how-tos, home repair, gardening, computers, family management, self-improvement, and virtually anything that snags your own curiosity.
4. Religious and inspirational volumes, from reportage of current events shaded by spiritual values to Bible studies and moving accounts of God at work in daily life.
5. Lifestyle books, most often humorous but sometimes philosophical. They're hard to define but frequently delicious. Two examples are Pat McManus's *Never Sniff A Gift Fish*, essays about an outdoorsman's misadventures, and Garrison Keillor's *Lake Wobegon Days* (recognizable as far more than light fiction by anyone who shares his midwestern small-town roots).
6. Books (like this one) aimed at members of a particular profession or industry. The possibilities here are nearly endless.

Finding the right idea is only part of your challenge. The next step is to find the right publisher. Gone are the days when writers in North Dakota automatically turned toward New York when praying for their book at night. While a search of *Writer's Market* demonstrates that Gotham is still headquarters for a good share of those publishers you may approach, there are others in metropolitan areas as well.

Today national publishers—defined by their scope and general-interest booklists—can be found in Des Moines, Dallas, Cincinnati, Minneapolis, Tucson, San Francisco, and countless points in between. Not all are giants staring coldly down at writers who tug at their hems. The very largest may process ten thousand queries a year; but you'll also find hundreds of smaller firms that have penetrated deep into their chosen markets.

The giants don't stare all that coldly, for that matter. Despite its fabled inbred tendencies, the publishing world has to look beyond its ranks for new talent to churn out many of those forty-five thousand books for the next year, and the year after, and the year after that. If publishing were entirely the old boys' network (and girls', by a margin of at least two to one) that its critics sometimes charge, it couldn't show the growth that has sent sales curves up and up in the past decade.

There are still plenty of old boys and girls around, but competition for productive new authors of salable books is fierce enough that you need never be threatened by haughty attitudes. Remember, as the publishing world does, that sales of nonfiction titles seldom correlate to the size of the house that publishes them. They parallel, instead, the energy with which the publisher pursues sales. Each "marriage" of manuscript and publishing house deserves to be judged on its own merits.

How to find the proper suitor? Turn to *Writer's Handbook*, or *Writer's Market*, with two hundred-plus pages of publisher listings, and review *Literary Market Place* in the reference section of your library. Consider the true breadth of your options. You have your work cut out for you.

Look for the group of publishers that specialize in the subjects about which you're best equipped to write, or turn to *Literary Market Place*'s category index of books following the section on book publishers. You can page through these market books, or you can take a shortcut that's almost infallible: Stop at your library or bookstore and find a variety of recent releases within the same broad category as the one that you propose: other travel books, perhaps, or cookbooks, or collections of folk tales or fishing advice. Open their covers and examine their publisher's names and addresses on the title page. Couldn't be simpler.

While you're there, check the reference volume *Books in Print* to be sure that someone hasn't beaten you to the punch on your pet proposal or, for that matter, the title you've chosen. You can get some feeling here, too, for which publishers are currently interested in your subject. Watch for a cluster of recent releases which your subject might complement.

Finding their names and addresses is just the beginning of the research you'll require. Each publisher may be offering different terms to writers and a different set of advantages and disadvantages in marketing the volume you have in mind. Back again to *Writer's Market*, where you can begin to sort out those that suit your purposes best.

The largest commercial publishers have clout. Their distribution channels are nationwide. Their staffs are large and often superb. Their names open certain doors for promotion, in some cases, that result in good positioning for your book.

But the small independent presses have advantages too—perhaps even greater, depending on what you have in mind. Their expertise is far more specific than that of the industry giants. They may publish only books of a kindred nature—Colorado history, vegetarian cooking, organic gardening—but they know their fields in far more depth than the generalized giants could ever take time to develop. They often have an almost personal relationship with their regular readers. Their staffs, though far fewer in number, may also be talented and dedicated to their work. As a new author, you may receive greater, and more personalized, assistance from these spunky individualistic houses.

The giants and the feisty small-press contenders part company in the terms and conditions they offer authors. Big corporate concerns offer advances against royalties. Few small presses have the capital to anticipate a book's earnings by paying an advance; if any is offered, it's usually substantially less than what's typical of the commercial houses.

The average advance offered by a commercial publisher on a nonfiction book falls somewhere between three and six thousand dollars. It's generally considered to represent the firm's best guess at first-year royalty earnings, with actual figures computed against that sum after publication. As for the royalties themselves, they too differ. A usual rate is 10 percent of retail price on the first 8,000 copies sold, 12.5 percent on the next 10,000, and 15 percent on additional sales. Again, small presses are likely to pay less. A solid but unspectacular nonfiction book by a beginning author might sell 5,000-10,000 copies, bringing semiannual royalty payments exceeding the advance.

Smaller publishers are often hard pressed to equal these advances and terms. Again, they vary; advances are generally somewhat less, and royalties might be based on net (rather than retail) price of the volume. But they have an advantage that can add up to earnings just as great as those of larger companies. Books issued by smaller, specialized companies may be kept in print much longer than those of the publishing giants.

That longer life in print can increase total sales dramatically. Major firms, faced by the crush of new titles coming up, may remainder their stock of slower-selling titles after a year or less, while smaller companies can keep them alive based on more modest but consistent sales figures. The author benefits through royalties over a longer period and has a better chance to surpass the royalty break and earn a higher percentage on additional sales.

Subsidiary rights—book club sales, prepublication excerpts in magazines, anthologies, paperback reprints and foreign language editions, among others—is the area in which national publishers shine when compared to your other three publishing options.

The standard writer's contract assigns 50 percent or less of the income from exercising these rights to the publisher. (Veterans with some success on their records often get more favorable terms.) It's up to your publisher to take advantage of the potential for these additional sales of your material; national firms often do.

Some publishing personnel have suggested that subsidiary rights are, in fact, a major source of income to many national publishers, producing more income than books themselves. Whether or not this is true, it definitely bodes well for authors hoping to get additional income from their book.

To reap these extra rewards—and to find a publisher in the first place—you need to go back to your income-producing strategy. If you weren't concentrating on earning income as you write, you might sit down to produce your book now, then send it to market to try to find its niche. Or you can commence searching out a publisher before you've invested your time in typing out a manuscript and proceed to write it after you've found a company willing to give you a contract. That's clearly the only way for the self-supporting writer to go . . . risking time and talent only with a reasonable hope of returns.

The rest of your quest for a publisher is familiar ground. The query system you employ for selling your work to magazines is nearly identical to how you interest a publisher in your proposal. Write to an editor at the firm of your choice; you can get his or her name from *Writer's Market* or *Literary Market Place*. Describe your proposal and your own writing credentials. Sketch out your book's prospective direction and the resources it will build on, whether they're your own or dug out of some other mine of expertise. For more specific suggestions, check out *How to Write a Book Proposal*, by Michael Larsen (Writer's Digest Books, 1985).

Back it up with an outline of the book, chapter by chapter—brief but detailed enough to introduce what it's about. Slip it into the envelope you've addressed along with the ubiquitous self-addressed stamped envelope.

And wait.

Surely, there's a better way, you say? Something quicker?

Nope. There isn't. Unless you have contacts (or uncles) in the literary business, or are a celebrity, or the rare prodigy who's utterly irresistible on first sight, you aren't likely to have many other options from your vantage point in Arkansas or New Hampshire until you've proven yourself. It's the old writer's Catch-22: You can't be trusted to write a book until you've proven you can do it, but you don't get a chance to prove it until you've already written one. The query and sample chapters are the way most new writers finally break in.

But don't be crushed by the odds you think you face by querying cold and waiting. It can be done; that's how many, perhaps a majority, of books are really sold from the hinterlands. You're holding proof in your hands that cold queries without benefit of those much-desired connections can turn into warm welcomes. This author wrote a query, based on nothing but a listing in *Writer's Market*, from an address just as out of the way as yours. In a couple of months she was invited to send in a sample chapter to augment her proposed outline. Only a few days later, her mailman presented her with a contract.

The method works when you persevere, applying each lesson to make your next move smarter and more effective. You know it. That's how this book came into being and that's probably how your book will come about whenever you get ready to do it.

Unless you get an agent.

Nonmetropolitan writers I've questioned about agents disagree radically on whether they're the indispensable helpmeets they're often touted as. Some of the authors, who, collectively, have sold dozens of titles, can see no earthly way an agent could have improved their own track records. Others swear by their professional aid and encouragement. The choice is ultimately up to you. It may or may not have a major effect on your book prospects, but one thing is clear: your chances of finding an agent who will handle you are slim until you've put together a track record in major magazines or have sold your first book.

Having an agent is undoubtedly a status symbol for authors in the boonies. Their practical benefits include saving you the wear and tear of marketing your own proposals and having a third party to talk to your publisher about financial arrangements. Your cost is usually 10 or, increasingly, 15 percent of whatever income their efforts produce.

If you're not averse to talking about money yourself, and feel you know enough about the going rates to get what you've got coming, you may be better off spending your time approaching editors rather than courting agents. At any rate, put finding an agent on your list of things to do after, not before, selling your first book. By then your prospects will be considerably better.

How do you get one? By much the same method as you sell a publisher directly—a query letter, an outline, perhaps a handful of samples of your best published work. Consult *Literary Market Place*, *Writer's Market*, and *Fiction Writer's Market* for listings of agents and their areas of interests, as well as information on those who charge pre-publication or reading fees. Or, better, find yourself an agented author and ask him or her to recommend someone. (You don't know any authors? Come now. Write to one whose work you've enjoyed in care of his or her publisher. Fan letters are always appreciated, if only occasionally answered. An SASE increases the odds of a reply but by no means guarantees it.)

Think carefully about the agents who offer to review your manuscript for a fee. Many agents do in fact charge authors for the time spent in deciding whether or not to represent them. Often those charges may in fact be justified, since agents—like writers—perform a good share of their services long before the contract is signed. If you are willing to pay for a critique, it may be best to approach several individuals or firms by mail, describing your work and your credentials. A trip to New York may be justified to negotiate with those who express an interest in you and your work. You deserve a firm idea of how much you'll be expected to pay for what services before you proceed. The danger lies in teaming up with an agent who is more interested in selling quickie critiques to naive writers than selling book manuscripts to publishers.

Your most important goal is to get your proposals before publishers who might buy them. Whether agented or not, your manuscript can't be sold until it makes that potent connection with an interested buyer. You can hit it on your first query, or use up half a roll of stamps to keep it traveling among the publishing houses that seem most likely to cheer when they open your letter.

But one certainty remains. If your proposal is good, and your research and writing are sound, and your estimate of its audience is anywhere near the mark, and you persist with intelligence and chutzpah, your book *will* find a publisher. It's only a matter of when.

Small Presses

You may find a publisher where you least expect one.

Included in *The International Directory of Literary Magazines and Small Presses* are hundreds of publishing houses intent on getting their books to readers through the most efficient, direct means available. Though they're delighted to sell their books outside the areas they serve, they reserve their concentration for topics of clear and specific interest to their clientele.

Think of those publishing listings as the tip of an iceberg. For every small press that lists its requirements in Dustbooks' nationally distributed directory, you can count on another that does not, that, whether quietly well established or new and absolutely obscure, works quietly with the writers who know its markets best, and whose small staff dreads the thought of being swamped with bags of unsolicited mail a national market listing might bring.

Don't mistake the small presses as mere baby versions of the commercial firms—a sort of junior high school of book production. They're not. They're just as serious, often equally sophisticated, and frequently far more involved and interested in the fate of each and every book.

Small-press publishing, one of the fastest-growing segments of the industry, is the response to the specialized areas in which the national publishers are notoriously weak and cannot adequately do justice. These companies market books of interest to well-defined portions of the country, such as New England or the Southwest, or to clearly-identified special interest groups—ardent feminists, Lutheran clergy, professional studio photographers—no matter where they live. From the acquisition of manuscripts to the marketing of the finished results, they're famous for demonstrating a singleness of purpose that can make commercial publishers' sales representatives (and authors) weep.

Small-press books are sold through bookstores, of course. But these companies often saturate their own logical chains of distributions. Publishers of regional travel and history books, for example, might place their volumes wherever their target audience might browse—supermarkets and drugstores, tourist attractions and souvenir shops, resorts, libraries, schools, and wherever else room can be made for a stack of copies. They market their offerings through regional publications and by mail, hitting those audiences with soft spots in their hearts for the old home sod, the readers whom they aspire to know very, very well. Authors sometimes choose to approach a small press because they don't feel ready to play with the big guys. They may have stumbled across the right answer, but for the wrong reason. Standards can be every bit as rigorous; moreover, a publishing program limited to only a few titles each season can be hard indeed to infiltrate. Editors often aim at the highest quality of writing, research and interpretation. Once won over, they can become ardent advocates for your work.

Moreover, you can count on their long-term commitment to a book that proves itself. A modest first printing of several thousand may not dilate the pupils of your envious peers. What matters, though, is not how many copies are printed; it's how many times the publisher reprints your book. Some regional history, nature, and cookbooks seem to sell quietly but steadily forever. Lifetime sales of regional titles may easily eclipse those flashy but short lived nationally published books that are kept in print for just twelve to eighteen months and then remaindered.

The smaller, independent publishers, to be sure, offer some disadvantages. First among these is that most pay no advance against royalties. Royalty rates are usually less than a commercial publisher routinely offers. Some prefer to buy a manuscript outright rather than sign you to a contract that entitles you to a percentage of proceeds. Very small firms, particularly those whose work is limited to fiction and poetry, offer a range of options that might include subsidy or co-publishing, in which you share the financial risks and profits as a true partner. And still others pay you in copies of the published work.

Like little magazines and most regional publications, they are likely to mirror your own respect for writing or the subjects dearest to your own heart. For the author setting out with a homegrown idea in hand to find a publisher who will be a friend as well as a customer, they can be fertile ground indeed.

A word should be said for the small presses with a strictly regional bent: like the publication markets closest to where you live, they offer a special welcome to local talent.

Some are prosperous freestanding operations, like Falcon Press of

Helena, Montana, which distributes a catalog of regional titles that includes its own well-produced products. Others are linked to regional publications in the manner of one of Falcon's neighbors, *Montana Magazine*, whose glossy Montana Geographic Series has racked up spectacular sales in a sparsely populated region and spawned a host of cousins. These include the Dakota Graphic Society's five-volume North Dakota centennial series, in which I'm closely involved.

Small presses of the regional sort are frequently related to commercial printing companies. That is true of Adventure Publications in Staples, Minnesota, for example, whose list of history and reminiscence books includes titles co-published with their authors, and Northern Plains Press of Aberdeen, South Dakota, which publishes many of its books under more-or-less standard royalty contracts.

You may find your regional publisher on a university campus. A major share of history and nature books created for and about the less-traveled corners of America come via university presses. Some espouse ultrascholarly treatments and are open solely to those with acceptable academic credentials. Others, though, have found a source of steady support (in these days of declining public funding) in trade publishing with popular histories, books on gardening and birds and native plants, biographies of favorite sons and daughters, and sometimes-whimsical nostalgia. The University of Nebraska Press is responsible for many of the finest historical works not only on its own state, but on less well-endowed neighboring states like my own.

And regional publishers turn up in corner offices of other businesses and organizations. In Minneapolis, you'll find an active publishing program at the Minnesota Historical Society along with another regionally oriented publisher, Waldman House Press, operated by one of the partners in the book distribution company called The Bookmen.

Your best bets for uncovering small presses of every sort right in your own locale are to talk with your favorite librarian and study the regional section of the nearest chain bookstore like B. Dalton Bookseller or Waldenbooks. Too, check the state index in *The International Directory of Little Magazines and Small Presses*. The librarian is sure to have insight into the full range of locally published titles. The bookstore can help you determine which of these books are the product of publishers, commercial or small press, with whom you might work.

Note that I specifically suggest a chain bookstore. Their buyers demand a certain level of professionalism from the publishers whose books they stock. On the other hand small reputable, independent bookstores are often more receptive to small press titles, non-mainstream, innovative, the "risky" books in the marketplace.

Self-Publishing

Your third route to reaching your readers is a first cousin to regional publishing—doing it all yourself, from researching the market and writing the book to editing copy, designing pages and a cover, locating a printer, opening distribution channels, filling orders . . . and cashing the checks.

The definition of self-publishing seems straightforward at first: an author who publishes, manufactures and markets his own work. But trying to pin down these entrepreneurs—whose number may well include you—is like trying to spoon up mercury. What looks like a single smooth glob scatters into a dozen directions as soon as you scrape its surface.

A good share of small independent publishers have a self-published book in their background. Somewhere along the line it occurred to them that it's just as easy (or easier) to handle two titles or a dozen as it is to sell one. Voilà! A corporate publisher was born. That was the case with Minneapolis writer Vicki Lansky, who with her husband self-published a modest cookbook of baby foods titled *Feed Me, I'm Yours*. Bruce Lansky continues at the helm of Meadowbrook, Inc., which publishes the work of dozens of authors, many from the same neck of the woods.

A fair number of commercially published writers have self-published a book as well. Phenomenally successful computer book author Peter McWilliams and Richard Bolles, famous for *What Color Is Your Parachute?* self-published books, as did Benjamin Franklin, Mark Twain, Walt Whitman, D. H. Lawrence, and the creators of several standard reference books, from *Bartlett's Familiar Quotations*, to *Joy Of Cooking* (published by the ladies of the First Unitarian Women's Alliance of St. Louis, Missouri).

Since overtly self-published books still bear the stigma of the vanity press among reviewers and some librarians, many who set out to market their own work create a separate entity to mask their intentions. Others, like me, start out to publish others' work and eventually add their own names to their company's roster. My own little Prairie House, in cooperation with *North Dakota Horizons* Magazine, launched the North Dakota Centennial Series, written by yours truly, only after releasing a number of titles by other regional authors. My experience with their work reassured me that my own—in collaboration with my husband the photographer and colleague Sheldon Green—would stand a chance of selling at least as well.

(That hunch has proven correct, thank goodness. In B. Dalton's most recent compilation of regional bestsellers, two to a district, Book II of the series was the year's top-selling title in the area including both Dakotas and Nebraska—and that despite the fact that North Dakota has less than 30 percent of the region's population and the book was available in fewer than one-third of the three-state area's stores. Book III was the other one on the list.)

Self-publishing, along with the allied small independent presses, is said to be the fastest-growing trend in publishing today. It has spawned a national trade association, COSMEP, and a national magazine, *Small Press*.

Such publishing is not for sissies, however, whether you're taking it on as a solo or involved in a small press. Is your energy boundless? Are you so sure that your book will find an audience that you'd risk your own money to bring it before the public? Are you willing to put yourself on the line, not only as a writer but as a financier and a salesman?

Self-publishing a highly marketable, professionally produced book could double or triple your earnings over traditional royalty contract with a commercial publisher. The twin hang-ups are that it also doubles or triples your work and forces you to gamble with two precious commodities: your money and your time.

If you've had full exposure to commercial publishing, chances are that you still equate self-publishing with the vanity presses. What a successfully self-published book means is that you're not only an author but an entrepreneur, taking on a variety of new tasks that affect the outcome of your venture, an exhilarating feeling if you're looking for a challenge—or a moment of truth if you haven't yet shed your dependence on the security of a signed contract or done all your homework.

Before you even consider publishing and marketing your own book, you need to digest the hard-nosed advice in Tom and Marilyn Ross's how-to, *The Complete Guide to Self-Publishing*, as well as Aron Mathieu's *The Book Market: How to Write, Publish and Market Your Book*.

Both are encyclopedias of modern self-publishing, from idea development to the fine points of manufacturing, promotion, and order fulfillment. They'll cool the initial white-hot heat that strikes most of us when an idea is at its glorious peak of freshness with a dose of well-tempered advice, demonstrating in graphic terms that in the long run, writing is the least important factor in self-publishing success.

You need to consider that message soberly and well. Garages galore use crates of self-published books for insulation and serve as immortal reminders that quality of writing is only the last thing that sells books; what counts most of all is the quality of the effort behind them.

Yet successes are not at all rare. Here in my own state, for instance, wildlife photographer and naturalist Wilford Miller successfully published several books including *Wildlife of the Prairie* and *Animals of North Dakota* long before self-publishing even had a name. Agnes Geelan sold out two hard-cover printings of her biography of the most notorious politician in the state's history in *The Dakota Maverick*. Fisherman Mort Bank's books of lake maps are perennial sellers among North Dakota anglers. Valentina Popel published her family recipes in *Valentina's Ukrainian Kitchen*. Francie Berg created *North Dakota: Land of Changing Seasons*, still selling more than ten years after its first printing, and has gone on to publish similar books on South Dakota and Wyoming. Norwegian humorist Luther Bjerke has had a hit not only with a book reflecting his homespun humor and philosophy, but also with record albums of live renditions.

None of these books had much of a chance of finding a publishing home in a commercial or even a sizable independent firm. Yet they all succeeded because their authors believed in them and worked tirelessly, not only to put words and photographs on paper but also to sell their inventory—sometimes copy by copy.

It can be done. Profits can be made, even on books whose audiences are limited to the population of North Dakota (and even further, to the percentage of North Dakotans who love animals, fish for walleyes, or vote Democratic). The most serious hurdle, given that kind of determination, comes down to plain old cash.

If you're intent on publishing your book yourself, you need to have enough money on hand to invest in the manufacturing costs—typesetting, keyline (page layout), and printing—before sales income starts rolling in. But there are ways around that, too.

Some writers have found local printers willing to absorb some of the risk themselves and take payment for their services over the book's initial sales period. Others have turned up "angels" to finance their projects—a church diocese for a book written by its priest, a New Age agricultural group for a tome on organic farming, an alumni association for an anecdotal history of a state university. Too, there are always those nearest and dearest to you. Why deny your friends and family a good investment possibility?

Finding a backer is not so difficult if you've chosen a subject likely to pay its way once it reaches the salable stage. The more successful self-published books in my part of the country have fallen into a couple of loose categories.

One is material of demonstrated interest to a clearly defined group of readers—limited, perhaps, but hungry for information. City guidebooks, humor, and legends are the classic examples. A guide to dining in Minneapolis would be dead in the water in Cheyenne, Wyoming; given the salivating visitors and/or businesspersons from outstate Minnesota, however, its compendium of menus and reviews is a bestseller. Howard Mohr's *How to Talk Minnesotan* is hilarious to those who know the accent well, more or less incomprehensible to readers from San Antonio or Silicon Valley. A children's book on the legend of Paul Bunyan and Babe, his blue ox, sells well in Bemidji, deep in the piney woods, but wouldn't do a day's business in the bluegrass state of Kentucky.

The same is true of specialized books on Gulf sportfishing in the Florida Keys, on what to see in Washington, D.C., on mountain wildflower handbooks in the shadow of Mount Rainier, or on the saga of the rebel Louis Riel in Winnipeg, Manitoba.

Other possibilities in this group are instructional guides for outdoor pastimes, locally-popular crafts or cuisine, and histories of nearly any underchronicled city or region west of the thirteen colonies. For example, books on the traditional Norwegian decorative art of rosemaling have become best-sellers in the Nordic reaches of Wisconsin, Minnesota and Iowa. A lavishly illustrated study of the loon entitled *Loon Magic* sells well (at $39.95!) in the northwoods. And the colorful, dramatic history of Deadwood, South Dakota, has spawned countless volumes, from biographies of Wild Bill Hickock and Calamity Jane to a guidebook to the local cemetery—which happens to be the original Boot Hill.

The other sort of successful book is the one you know you can promote or sell on the basis of your reputation. Local celebrities, recognized authorities within their own fields, and those with a built-in sales advantage (like a daddy in the book distribution business), all have automatically brightened their books' prospects.

But you're not a celebrity? Find yourself one and become an astold-to.

Don't be deceived by the "self" in self-publishing, however. To produce a book you'll be proud of, you need to enlist others to perform the services publishers invest in the volumes they issue. You need a graphic designer to do illustrations, layout, and cover art. Though all printers have art departments these days, their staff artists will seldom do more than the most basic job of pasting up your copy.

You need an editor. Yes, you do. You can hire freelance copy editors and later, proofreaders; try placing a classified ad or asking someone at a nearby publishing house to make a recommendation. A meticulous English teacher can be a great deal of help if all else fails. Or talk a fellow writer into taking on editing chores for your project (for a fair price, of course) . . . if you're lucky enough to have a fellow writer where you happen to live.

The rest of the help you need is in sales and marketing. A long talk over coffee with the manager of the bookstore you frequent can give you invaluable advice on how to price your book, how to sell it to other stores, area book distribution channels, and kinds of advertising that may help sales.

When pricing your book, remember that retail stores will expect you to give them a 40 percent discount over its cover price if you sell it to them yourself. You can conserve your own time by placing it with the news and book agencies that service all the magazine racks in your area, but they'll want a cut themselves, at least 20 percent or more of the cover price, and you'll have to be willing to take back unsold books, however battered, dog eared, and damaged they may be.

Sales points outside of bookstores also may be a boon to your sales. Drugstores, gift shops, supermarkets, restaurants—all may be interested in stocking and selling a title of interest to their customers. Motels and resorts are natural candidates for selling a book of regional interest. Advertisements in magazines serving the area of the special-interest group you've written for provide other sales possibilities with a bonus: you can keep the 40 percent retail markup yourself.

Finally, keep your eyes open for opportunities to promote your books. One regional author of books on farming reaps profits through his extensive schedule of public speaking engagements. He's never without a satchel full of his latest volume for the interested well-wishers who come up after his talk. Bill Miller has sold his wildlife books through booths at teachers' conferences, ads and reviews in state wildlife publications, and workshops with students and sportsmen all over the state.

Let local newspapers know about your book; the contact will usually result in an interview. Most local television talk shows welcome visits by area authors. Newsletters of organizations to which you (or your family) belong may carry reviews, news stories, and advertisements for your book. State conferences for school and public librarians are a must; so is the annual convention of booksellers in your state. Can you get a wholesaler with annual gift or trade shows to put your book on his order form? How about setting up a booth at the state food retailers' convention to catch grocers, who are selling more and more books and periodicals these days along with the pantyhose and VCR tape? Try the local chamber of commerce's annual meeting or regular sessions; your book may be of interest to their members, and a high proportion of their members will be retailers who might stock it.

You have to believe in your book to be willing to pursue its sale with all the zeal it deserves. If you do believe—and if you relish the thought of converting nonbelievers—then self-publishing can really work for you.

Sponsored books

The fourth category of book publishing is a loose one. It includes the hundredth-anniversary history of a prominent local firm; the memoirs of a state organization entering a new period in its collective life; a cookbook promoting one of your state's major agricultural products, and a specialized history text with such a small potential readership among laypersons that no commercial publisher would touch it.

This is the broad field of sponsored books. You see its signs in photo how-to guides subtly promoting the advantages of one camera system or in some of the most fascinating profiles of industry leaders or pioneers. In some instances they masquerade as normally published volumes; in others they look like exactly what they are, books that in some way promote the goals of the company, organization, or interest group that paid to have them published.

No commercial publisher would be interested in a book on the history of telephone cooperatives in North Dakota. But the telephone cooperatives' association was. Likewise, the centennial of the Episcopal Church in the state aroused no anticipation on Publishers' Row, but was an occasion celebrated with an excellent and readable volume by

Episcopal churchpeople in North Dakota.

Sponsored books are the mirror opposites of those published through the other three routes. Instead of a book seeking an audience, you find an audience seeking a book. To get their book, they need to find their author. The author could well be you, a professional writer in their neck of the woods who can produce a readable, accurate, and creditable manuscript to satisfy their pre-established hunger.

These books pop up at the oddest times. The hundredth (or the fiftieth, or the twenty-fifth) anniversary of nearly anything can be the impetus for an official history. The need for a book may result from a promotional push for a product or a group's big membership drive. Or it may appear on the eve of the founder's retirement to chronicle his accomplishments, or memorialize them after his death.

The opportunity for the book may be part of a larger project. Our state Committee on the Humanities and Public Issues, for example, decided several years ago to publish five volumes over ten years dealing with their perspective on the state's history, lifestyle, and people; the project was born because the funds became available for grants to authors and to cover the cost of printing.

Sponsored books—some are called premium books because they're distributed as a free or discount offer—can be an inducement to buy a new product or to try a new hobby or to bank with a particular banker. Or they can be sold at full price as the foundation of someone's hopeful fund-raising scheme. (Make sure you get your payment up front if this is the case. Why depend on a volunteer and unpredictable amateur sales force?)

Do they sound dreary? Don't bet on it. There may be a certain number of tedious histories of interest only to insiders, but they needn't be the rule. One of the funniest bits of regional humor I've seen is a pocket-size "North Dakota Dictionary" sponsored and distributed by an implement manufacturer in the state. It was written by the author who coined the rallying cry "Forty below keeps the riffraff out" and included offbeat definitions of landmarks, personalities, and customs.

Sponsors of all sorts of these books have a stake in making them the best they can afford. The books are meant to reflect brilliantly on their sponsors. A poorly conceived book reflects just about as well as a puddle of spilt milk.

How do you find these opportunities to write a book with full economic security? Like most local writing jobs, it's a matter of listening for clues and keeping up contacts.

An imminent anniversary, mentioned in a newsletter or newspaper article, should be a green light for a proposal to the group (whether industry or association). Contact its president and suggest a publishing project. There are three possible outcomes: You can sell him on your new and attractive idea. You can stumble into a group already considering such a project. Or you can find you've identified one organization where no book will ever be born, for lack of money or interest or visionary zeal.

Your connections within organizations and businesses in your chosen community can lead to tips about upcoming projects. If you're interested in taking on a sponsored book, let your contacts know about your interest. You may be planting the germ of an idea that will eventually grow into a commission.

Watch the newspaper, especially its classified ads, for announced projects in search of authors. Since the job of writing a book often mystifies those who conceived it, their first instinct is sometimes to advertise for more knowledgeable help.

The income from a sponsored book varies with the sponsor's finances and your own bargaining ability. Often groups undertaking their first (and probably only) publishing project have no idea of what to pay. Base your estimates on the amount of time you will have to spend, especially in research and in clearing the finished manuscript with whatever committees are to oversee its publication.

At other times you'll be offered a flat grant or fee. Judge carefully whether it will meet your hourly rates from start to finish. A multithousand-dollar sum can sound wonderful until you figure out that it will take the best part of a year to earn.

There are no sure ways to guard against snags, but you can take certain steps to minimize them. Make sure you have a contract with the sponsor, and have your own lawyer look it over to protect your interests regarding acceptance and rewrites. Try to include a passage defining what is required for acceptance—one person's approval, a committee's approval, whatever—and mutually agreed-upon grounds for refusal. To protect yourself, never defer your entire payment until the manuscript has been accepted. Set it up to be paid in halves (half at the start, half at acceptance) or in thirds (one-third now, one-third on delivery, one-third on final approval).

If you can, work out an agreement with the sponsors on how much rewriting you will do for the set fee. Rewrites may become necessary, and not only because of your own work (as a beginning author, you may be readier to take the blame than you should be). The sponsor's goals might change, its administration might be replaced, or committee members might begin to squabble over details.

This sounds like a thorny piece of business; these problems don't come up often, so don't be put off by considering them. But do think your commission through and try to protect yourself with legal advice and open-eyed negotiations up front. The better you know the book's sponsor and the brighter its reputation, the more secure you can feel. Remember that commercial publishing houses have years of tradition and legal experts to untangle author-publisher snarls, and still some knots can be hard to work out. A non-publishing sponsor of a premium book may be taking on an author and a book for the first time ever.

Do as much as you can to make sure everyone involved subscribes to the same ground rules before you commit your valuable time.

If you receive a commission to write a sponsored book, you'll very seldom get a contract offering royalties as you do with commercial issues. If you are offered one, consider the realistic sales potential carefully and the way in which sales would be reported to you. Very few one-time publishers will have the resources to distribute, promote, and sell a book to manage respectable sales; they're even less likely to have the kind of bookkeeping system that ensures accurate royalty payments. Unless they guarantee that every member will buy a copy or contract to purchase unsold copies themselves to reach an agreed-upon minimum number of books, your royalties will be shrimp-sized.

These four publishing options offer you different means of producing your book and reaching your annual income goal. Which you choose depends somewhat on the amount of time you can invest in your first full-length project and the amount of return you must reasonably expect from it.

If you have the personality, stamina, and time to be all things to your project, self-publishing a book for an identified audience may be the most financially rewarding route. You may want to choose it if

- Your audience can be reached in an area limited by geography or profession or organized interests (like hobbies that are supplied by stores, lessons, and conventions).
- You have the outside specialists to advise you in editing, production, and distribution, and possibly have a spouse or colleague who can help you with the legwork.
- You have extra money to invest in printing and can afford to defer your returns until after the book has begun to sell—or you have lined up an "angel" to help with printing and possibly writing costs for a share of the profits.

Regional or small presses may be the route that's most effective if your project and your own schedule meet these conditions:

- It's the kind of book regionals prefer: travel, outdoors, and so on.
- You can write it while continuing to handle a full load of other writing assignments for self-support, without the assistance of a publisher's advance to help underwrite the time you spend in production.
- You desire a closer relationship with your publisher, both in creating the book and in taking an active part in planning its distribution and promotion.
- Your book has a long projected sales life and deserves to be kept in print over a number of years.

Commercial publishers might be your best choice if these factors are present:

- Your potential audience is substantial.
- You need to secure at least a moderate advance on royalties to keep you afloat during your writing stages.

■ Your topic is best suited to one of the companies that specialize in books of that kind; or it's one of the few first books of sufficient commercial power to attract strong marketing from a major publisher.

Finally, a sponsored book may be the route to take for your first volume if:

■ Grants are available to you to write it.
■ You want the security of insured hourly payment through flat fees or guaranteed sales among a sponsor's membership or clientele.
■ You come across such a project in your own locale and can handle it in your regular schedule as you would any other local commercial assignment.
■ You feel you need a boost like this to break into the book world.

Money is only part of the reward of writing your first book as an author of unlikely address. That's rather fortunate, for money is the most variable part of the bargain. It can realistically range anywhere from barely decent at first on up to providing a substantial portion of your yearly income.

When you work on your first book proposal, you'll sample new experiences that may alter your work habits for the better and make a more effective communicator out of you.

The sheer magnitude of writing a book—when compared with anything else you'll take on—demands an adjustment. Eighty or ninety thousand words is awesome. Three hundred manuscript pages is a staggering thought, especially when you've always found that most stories naturally fit into six or eight.

And yet you rise to the challenge and surprise yourself. At least, I did.

While writing my first book, I was alternately faced with elation and despair. I found that I lost all objectivity about the relative merits or faults of what I'd written while I was in the middle of it. On the days when it looked good, I was tempted to do something else to celebrate. On the bad days, I was sorely pressed not to give up.

And yet the pages kept rolling out. One hundred. Two hundred. Three hundred and forty! I'd produced more manuscript, by the time I'd completed it, than I'd put out in any other concentrated period of my writing life. And I'd done it while handling three-quarters of my normal workload at the same time.

My potential productivity wasn't the only surprising insight I gained during that project. I learned more about working with an editor than I'd ever known before.

Working with magazine editors puts you at a distance from their improvements/damage to your work. I've dealt with them mostly in the early stages of proposing and selling a story. The finished, edited copy looked different, when it finally appeared, but I'd never paid close attention to what had happened to my golden prose in the meantime.

Editing and revising a book manuscript is quite a different tug-of-war. For the first time I was working with practiced editors who questioned adjectives and prepositions, and were not amused by asides that had cracked me up at the typewriter. They made small suggestions that pared and clarified my words and large observations that helped mold form and content. I could see my work improve before my eyes, courtesy of their cool (one might say heartless!) appraisal. I'll never bridle at the thought of being edited again.

I learned to give myself a bit more distance with deadlines. Flash finishes are great when you're talking about a thousand words, but you'll be a trifle anxious if you're flapping around with six pounds of paper that needs to be turned over to a courier by four o'clock.

And I experienced both pre- and post-partum depression in delivering that book: pre- , because I had last-minute trepidations over just what sort of monster it might turn out to be; post- , because writing books is the most enjoyable assignment I've taken on as a freelancer, and I was genuinely sorry to see the little devil leave.

I've written five other books since that first experience and can tell you this: The process of incubating an idea and hatching it into a complete manuscript that emerges in full and glorious feather never becomes less daunting at its inception or less satisfying at its end. The pleasure of long-term involvement with a body of material is distinct and delightful—and there will always be moments when you believe you're drowning in molasses as you slog toward an end that's just barely in sight.

Don't put off writing your own book until you've achieved financial independence or a lofty, mature, supremely sophisticated view of life. Neither is likely to happen soon if you're sitting on the curb waiting for them to be delivered.

Take a crack at it right now while the idea excites and frightens you, while it can help form the foundations of your balanced diet of income-producing writing. The experience will help you grow as a writer, will enhance the writing prospects that you're growing into, and will teach you just how exhausting, fascinating, exhilarating, and downright fun the writing business can be.

8

Joining the Blue-Pencil Brigade

Not everyone who earns a living as an editor lives in New York City or bedevils innocent writers regularly from nine to five. You can be one of the others, fleshing out your main mission as a writer with an alter ego that teaches you more about the business, pays rather well, and offers you an outlet for your passion for grammatical and stylistic perfection. It's freelance editing, and it comes in many guises.

These editors are a little bit like oxygen. They're part of the atmosphere wherever red-blooded verbiage thrives (or surely ought to be), sharpening words and nudging them into position, clarifying the principles they're intended to express, and—if the blue-pencil pushers are very, very good—making their author's best work even better.

Like the air, part-time editors are often invisible, but they're all around us. Wherever regular publications are produced, someone must be charged with setting direction, soliciting stories, writing and rewriting copy, and overseeing production.

Wherever publishers craft magazines and books, eagle-eyed copyeditors search submissions for factual slips and scan each line for abuse of the king's English (or perhaps Strunk and White's). Wherever manuscripts are set in type, proofreaders sift for typographical errors. Independents methodically index the contents of books.

And wherever laymen set out to write for publication, a ghost—often uncredited—may haunt them, helping them shape their facts and figures (or advice and anecdotes) into what the nominal authors want them to be.

Of course, many of these duties are assumed by staffers at major full-time periodicals and publishing houses. Most of the polished publications you see are guided by full-time straw bosses. Most books and magazine copy is fine-tooth-combed by wordsmiths who are on salary. Executive assistants or public relations directors shine up their bosses' articles and speeches.

But not all editorial duties are handled by employees—not by a long shot. More and more of these jobs are being farmed out to independent contractors—freelancers like yourself. The boom in new periodicals and increased numbers of books have created a demand for more professional editors at precisely the time when publishers are looking for ways to control production costs, not inflate them further with full-time additions to the payroll. One answer to their dilemma is you.

Then there are editorial jobs too small or infrequent to justify a salaried staff editor: newsletters and magazines of associations and businesses, quarterly professional journals whose limited circulation and support preclude a staff of their own, and the editing of book manuscripts by either small publishers with a few annual issues or major houses facing occasional overloads.

All of these spell opportunity for the freelance writer looking for new horizons and regular income to underwrite his one-time assignments and market research. The secret lies in finding those that are a creative and emotional match for you. Then cultivate them well, for they spell a source of long-term security and a chance to add valuable credentials to your résumé.

The Freelance Editor

Editing local publications on a part-time basis can be ideal for the free-lancer with some background in journalism or public relations and familiarity with the graphic arts. It offers a refreshing change of pace from toiling over your own words and creative worries; instead, you wield the dreaded blue pencil over other work, often by amateurs, systematically making a poor piece better (and, incidentally, reassuring yourself of the planet's insatiable thirst for more writers of your own calibre).

Just as important, editing these publications can ease the daily pressure to build the foundation of your annual income goal one laborious brick at a time. Once arranged, an editing job pays as regularly and as often as the publication is issued. You can count on it. The time you spend now in locating and interviewing for these jobs can be written off across months or years of steady work. Once you're installed as part-time editor of a publication, you're likely to continue shepherding it as long as you care to, barring changes in its sponsor's plans or (in the case of government newsletters) reversals of the party in power. The income it produces becomes a dependable financial cushion around which you can budget your basic monthly expenses—the kind of steady support that helps take your mind off money and frees it for more adventurous pursuits, like writing and marketing articles or working on a book.

When you scouted out the community in which you plan to freelance, you probably turned up your first prospects for freelance editorships. Review your inventory of smaller publications likely to rely on outside assistance, along with those whose staffs are small and ambitions large. You may be surprised at the variety your turn up.

To begin, you may find yourself learning the trade at little or no pay. That's the bad news. The good news is that proofreaders and copyeditors are always in short supply at little magazines and other small, marginally (or not) profitable publications. The experience will tell you if this is an area you might enjoy pursuing further. At the least, you'll gain contacts and—if my own experiences in this vein serve as an indication—plenty of anecdotes to share with fellow writers.

I've mentioned before that there are only a few periodicals in North Dakota that are true markets for freelancers. That's only half-true. That gloomy census applies to those who set out to write articles, not those who edit them.

Here in Fargo-Moorhead, for example, you can find periodicals serving hospital systems, a health food chain, recreation programs, senior citizens' centers, public and private schools, a large fabric store, manufacturers of farm implements and kit cars, religious groups (both individual churches and district offices), a dozen arts groups, fraternal organizations, the chamber of commerce, the convention and visitors bureau, and perhaps one hundred more. You can munch your lunch while perusing a daily broadsheet called *The Luncheon Times*, edited by an entrepreneur and distributed to restaurants and cafes. You can find out about local events and personalities in a free monthly magazine and a quarterly aimed just at women; though they appear substantial and successful, both have been edited through most of their history by independent contractors.

On the statewide level you'll see *Bar North*, the monthly voice of the Stockmen's Association, and the Wheat Commission tabloid *Dakota Gold*. There are the Farmers Union newspaper and the magazine *Dakota Family* produced by its arch-rival, the Farm Bureau. Tabloids and a magazine are aimed at teachers by the Department of Public Instruction and the Education Association. Motor carriers have *Rolling Along*. The State Historical Society publishes a prestigious quarterly journal and a monthly newsletter. The *Dakota Bell* tolls for members of the Mental Health Association. Alumni of every college and university absorb the latest news of their old chums' exploits along with pleas for support from the dear old alma mater.

Some of these are currently edited by staffers; others are freelanced. But every one of them is of the sort that's fair game for independents like you and me. Each has something to say, and needs an editorial coach to help its sponsors state their case effectively.

I've edited several publications over the past ten years, from Fargo-Moorhead's city *Guide* to tabloids for teachers (Public Instruction's *Outlook*) and school administrators (the state Council of School Administrators' *Umbrella*). Circulation of the first occasionally reached 35,000; the second, 11,000; and the third, 3,000—nothing to rival

Newsweek, but nicely respectable in a community of 100,000 and a state with far fewer residents than the suburbs of Milwaukee.

Editing these publications had little to do with creating Art. It was more like building terrific kitchen cabinets. The work was mostly enjoyable, offering me a chance to meet contributors whom I genuinely enjoyed. Editing income guaranteed that our mortgage would be kept up to date, at least, no matter what else I did.

Since I began freelancing, I've been approached to consider editing half a dozen publications and twice as many books. In no case did I seek these out; they tracked me down after hearing of my freelance business. I've accepted some of these offers and turned down others, usually for lack of time (mine) or money (theirs). I'm convinced that an organized search and a knack for negotiation could turn up more than enough opportunities to exceed what any salaried editor in town is making on a full-time basis . . . and still leave lots of time for more creative pursuits.

Few of the periodicals which you may find yourself editing part-time are as glossy as commercial magazines. Many are hanging on by the tips of their fingers as adjuncts of other programs commanding their sponsors' priorities and attention. Some will, in fact, fold up as their fortunes change; but for every one you lose, others are sure to pop up in its place.

The rates for contract editing vary wildly from rotten to superb. Like most financial matters in the freelance realm, they're always negotiable. Factors to consider include the state in which most submissions arrive, the amount of writing assigned personally to the editor, the time it'll take you to become familiar with the insiders' jargon you may be required to speak, and your own abilities—your qualifications (old pro or novice) and the zeal with which you persuade the sponsor how badly she needs your help. Multiply all of this times the degree of desperation she feels about locating someone to take these chores off her hands, and you come up with one rule of thumb: Anything goes.

The practice of contracting for editorial service at a flat fee is most common. In my experience, the fee that's offered bears little or no relationship to any known standard or the amount of work a job requires: I know of two entirely comparable monthly publications, one paying $750, the other $150. Faced with a flat offer, rely on your hourly rate to compute whether it covers the time it will consume. When the answer is yes—celebrate. When it's no, consider whether the regularity of payment is worth accepting substandard remuneration and make your decision accordingly. Remember, many sponsors have no real idea of whether their offer is reasonable. You can always try asking for more.

Along with the checks that turn up in your mailbox, I've noticed another strong plus to freelance editing. It opens doors to meeting all kinds of interesting, involved people: your contributors and readers.

You become one of their own, even if chemical engineering or the priesthood (or whatever your publication's focus) are far beyond your intent to grasp. You receive a painless education in the field your client's publication serves as you edit its contents. Those new insights into personalities, achievements, and issues can supply you with an endless source of ideas for your own writing and an almost sure admission to the national trade publications corresponding to your local version.

For example, my freelance editing introduced me to the world of mentally retarded adults through a newsletter aimed at those who had contributed to a sheltered workshop and training center. Breakthroughs are being made every year, and are brought to my attention by their immediate applications to the local center. The elements are there for enough stories to keep me busy for months. (Unfortunately, while the stories are there, the newsletter isn't. It's one of those casualties I mentioned.)

Other newsletters and magazines have let me see into the worlds of geriatric medicine and counseling, the arts, and the tourism industry.

Locating your own editorial jobs can be a toss-up between staying alert to opportunities and the good old element of chance. I was called to interview for *Outlook* because its former editor, the overburdened staffer, had met me at a meeting to discuss developing North Dakota studies curricula for the schools. I never did follow up that most inviting hint, but that single contact paid off when he remembered my freelancing and suggested his boss call me fully a year and a half later.

Some positions—not always just the best ones—are advertised in newspaper classifieds. These ads are placed by publishers on the brink of panic, who have already beaten the nearby bushes and come up with no likely prospects. I've noticed half a dozen of these in our small local daily over six months' time.

Other ads appear where they can get a good rate: in the publications that need the editors. Make a habit of reading those that interest you. Most are filed by the local library. You can usually get on the mailing lists by calling the association or sponsor, explaining your interest as a writer, and requesting a complimentary subscription. It's a good idea to do this even if you're not currently interested, of course, for the article ideas you might encounter.

Your own writing contacts are the best source of all for these contract editorships. I've had several groups I'd written about call me back months later to ask if I were interested in helping out with their newsletters. I know of other freelancers who've secured editing jobs strictly through social contacts—neighbors, friends, friends of parents, teachers whose offices were across the hall from their husband's.

If all else turns up nothing, remember your friend the local printer. Printers are unsurpassed as a source of scuttlebutt on anything regarding the ultimate application of ink to paper, particularly on their own presses. The same printer who's helped you out with background on graphics and tips on freelance commercial opportunities can often give you leads on who or what needs editing.

He knows which publication, lacking an editor at the moment, has fallen into the lap of an unhappy association president. He knows which clients constantly complain of not having enough editorial experience to do the job they'd like. And chances are he knows when a capable editor leaves one of his choicer publication clients. He has a stake in seeing the position refilled by an ally instead of someone who might take the job to his competition.

And if he's as astute as most members of his trade, he knows down to the sixpence who has the money to afford outside help and who does not.

One other route might appeal to you. Get to know the editors of some of the more attractive local publications. Since they're usually in touch with their counterparts at other publications, or at least aware of rumblings along the fabled grapevine, they can give you leads you might acquire in no other way.

Learning to edit . . . fast

You might be stymied because, though you've written reams, you've edited little or nothing in the past. Let that stop you only if you still subscribe to the discredited theory that all editors are impeccable, cold-blooded grammarians with hearts of stone, and stiff upper lips.

The ability to write, to recognize good writing, and to improve the rest is what you need to qualify for these editorial posts. The rest you can pick up on your own through sleepless nights of trying to count out headlines and restless days of wondering how much space the average typewritten page takes up in 10-point Bodoni. (Surprise: Your real problem is that there is no average typewritten page, at least among amateur contributors. You're lucky when their copy isn't in longhand.)

The printer who publishes the magazine or newspaper you've taken on is your best source of help and inspiration. His art department will often be responsible for setting type and laying out pages. Your main duties consist of getting the copy in shape and determining what goes where . . . at least roughly. The art department takes over from there, incorporating your instructions with their own familiarity with layout, and paste-up.

Alternately, typesetting, layout, and paste-up of your pages can be handled by a graphics production company, a freelance graphic designer, or even the art department within your sponsoring organization. The last is the least likely, since a group that goes outside for a part-time editor usually lacks personnel trained for specialized type and art tasks. But there are exceptions to every rule.

Meanwhile, desktop publishing programs have turned personal

computers into sources of highly sophisticated page composition comparable to what many local printers and designers routinely produce. If you are computer friendly, this is a delightful opportunity to do it yourself. If not, consider one of the desktop publishing services that have begun to spring up across the country. (Check the Yellow Pages and tap into the local PC-user grapevine to ferret one out.)

Publications that do add these services have higher budgets and hopes than those that rely on printers. Undeniably, the presence of someone well versed in graphics and layout simplifies your own job enormously. If you work with a designer, you'll help suggest page design but not finalize it, set placement priorities for stories but not worry about the minor details, and probably end up with a more artistically pleasing magazine or newsletter than you could create by yourself with the help of the printer's art crew.

The drawback, of course, is cost. By using art professionals, you're adding a layer of expense that could otherwise be eliminated by using the printer's modestly priced services. You can often manage to compromise and get the best of both worlds by going to a freelance graphic designer (instead of a larger company that offers this service) and hiring typesetting services from those who specialize in it. Watch for outfits who, like yourself, carry little in overhead and will charge your publication's sponsor only for their time and not for your share of their rent, staff, and office expense.

After you've worked with printers and artists through one or two issues, you'll have learned enough production jargon to hold your own. If you want a more thorough understanding of the mechanical aspects of putting out a publication, try your library or technical-vocational school for reference books on printing and graphics. You might also be interested in *Folio*, the magazine about magazines, though its orientation is far beyond the average sponsored publication that has crossed my desk.

Production aside, the editorial basics for the freelance editor are similar to the rules laid down for editors of any other community publications, whether circulating among a general audience (like a newspaper) or only to your select group of readers.

When you begin working with a publication as its editor, get to know why it exists as well as how it gets into print with your assistance.

What are its objectives? Is it supposed to reflect its readers? Convince them? Inform them of technical material they need to know? Answers to these questions make a difference in the placement of stories and the slant you impart to your writers.

Who are those readers? Just "members" isn't enough of an answer. Are they members by virtue of having donated to a charity? Members in fact? Members of a profession? Who *is* the average member? There's obviously a lot of difference between the readers of the Community

Action newsletter and the state Lions Club bulletin, and quite a different approach is required to serve each of them honestly and well.

How does its sponsor feel about its past direction? Should you continue in the same vein, or was the need for big changes at the bottom of your appointment as the new editor? If you don't ask, chances are you'll never find out in any but the most explosive circumstances.

Use your news judgment when laying out the first pages, choosing what will be of greatest interest to the largest number of people.

Concentrate on involving people, not dry rhetoric, in as much of your copy as you can. When you're working with amateur writers, this can be difficult. I've seen some sponsored publications that seem to be filled with the adult equivalents of the Boy Scout's letter to parents from camp or the cheery instructions on your income tax form. But with encouragement, your contributors will mostly see the light; people stories are really easier to write, anyway.

Use as many pictures as you can get your hands on. Here's where the sponsored publication draws away from the "regular" kind. In all too many cases, it seems that they're a captive medium for fuzzy snapshots and check-presentation pictures of all-consuming triteness. Good photography, however, can raise even the lodge newsletter from the realm of gray (or, heaven help you, purple) prose to an interesting-looking bit of mail that gets read more often than not before it's tossed.

Try to do as little of the writing yourself as you can manage. If that sounds like odd advice to give a writer, consider the benefits of involving members of the group themselves as reporters for your publication. They know their audience, and that audience will pay attention to their work. They have the inside background it would take you months to acquire. Most important, members' or readers' views are the reason the publication came into being—it speaks for its constituency, not (in the best of times) to them.

No matter how nifty your style and how writerly your stories, chances are the readers will prefer to read what the lodge president has to say. If you do end up doing a good share of the writing, try to put it in others' words . . . even under their bylines, as an editorial ghostwriter.

There's an ulterior motive in this advice, of course. Most freelance editorial jobs seem to be paid at a fixed rate per issue. If you end up doing more and more of the writing—if you let the pressure on the members themselves ease up and slide onto your own shoulders—you can easily find yourself devoting an enormous amount of time to a modest job, with an equally modest return on your efforts. This is fine if you're doing it because you love your fellow Moose, but it's like sinking into quicksand for anyone seriously intent on making a good living as a freelance writer.

When you take on a freelance editorial job, try not to take too much for granted. I speak from experience. When I began doing my first newsletter I neglected to get several points of order straight.

Such as who makes the final decision on controversial or questionable stories.

Such as who has the final word on what reaches the front page.

Such as who's responsible if errors creep into the finished product—errors of policy as well as typographical slip-ups.

Do you think you need to be dealing with cabinet-level bureaucracy before "official policy" becomes an important concern? I ran into these particular hidden tree stumps while doing a newsletter for a nursing home. Every association, every client has its own set of givens. As an outsider, you're liable to discover every one of them by trial and error if you don't have dependable advice.

Editing a house organ for a client is not the time to become dogmatic about freedom of the press. It is, after all, *their* press—not your own. As a matter of policy, I always try to find one person among the sponsors who will be responsible for steering me through the thicket of musts and taboos if the need arises . . . and you may be sure I get to know that person before the need ever turns up.

As an editor, you should have certain prerogatives related to technical points. I try to make sure that I'm the one to decide which stories go on the front page, how unacceptable copy should be rewritten for simple readability, and which members, no matter what, will submit to my blue pencil before their work is reproduced in cold type.

I prefer having a member of the association or sponsor responsible for final proofreading as well. Of course I check the printer's proof myself. But I try to find a backstop—someone whose viewpoint enables her to see errors of theory as well as misspelled names or mislabeled photographs.

Even then error can sneak in. I sent an urgent story for one of my newsletters directly to the printer at the very last moment before the presses rolled. No one but I had time to read it in proof. When the finished job arrived, I found I'd called an influential elderly donor by the wrong first name, an error that would be laughed off by most people but infuriated this very generous—and very touchy—philanthropist. I came quite close indeed to eating the whole job, including the cost of a corrected reprint of all 8,000 copies. Reason prevailed, but I wouldn't want to count on it the second time around.

Finally, when any submission seems to run against my client's current thought on the subject, I like to have my contact look it over before it's used.

Some writers might object to this, on grounds that could range from freedom of the press to impingement on their professional dignity. That's something you work out for yourself. I don't object to it. I am doing a job that ultimately reflects on my client, not on myself, and I want them to be satisfied (actually, I want them to be elated) with the results. It's all too easy to be sucked into an internal squabble by defending your contributors to the hilt; personally, I don't see anything praiseworthy about finding myself unwittingly in the middle of a dog-fight.

As a freelance editor, you can earn the income that keeps your rock-bottom expenses covered while learning lessons that can improve your own magazine submissions as well.

You'll develop a much stronger grasp on the necessity of under-standing a magazine's editorial policy when submitting queries.

You'll work more closely than ever before with real live readers, and learn what moves them and what they prefer to ignore.

You'll recognize the variety of reasons that make a good piece of writing unusable under your particular set of circumstances, and ex-perience the desperation an editor feels at press time, when all that's on hand is a feeble humorous essay and three government news re-leases. You'll understand the art of compromise.

And, if you're fortunate, you'll meet all kinds of sincere people ded-icated to what they're doing, whether it's good works or the furthering of their profession. Those new friends and fresh ideas are the fringe benefits of freelancing.

Copyediting—a special knack

Editing takes two forms, each of which suits freelancers of a different personality.

One is these outer-directed editorships, where you're involved in lining up a publication's contents and seeing it through its production period. Required is someone who enjoys contact with contributors and readers, since every editor has to do a certain amount of media-tion between sponsor and audience.

The other kind of editing—copyediting—requires different sorts of tendencies. Copyeditors are responsible for the fine points of the printed product. Often unseen and even unsuspected, they bring a writer's work into smooth, literate form. Spellings are checked and standardized. Incorrect usages and misshapen metaphors are subtly corrected. Major and minor points in articles or books are checked for logic and accuracy.

The copyeditor's duties can be cosmetic or surgical. At their most basic, they require an awareness for detail, an ironbound, inbuilt sense of consistency, good spelling, and a talent for diplomacy. Some writers have these skills or have learned them through past experi-ence as copyeditors on staff with publishing houses. Others of a more freewheeling turn of mind may not.

Copyediting can lead into more advanced editing jobs that call for more writerly inclinations (though the finest copyeditors share this talent), the assignments that require serious work—rewrites, trans-plants, reshuffles, and other major creative surgery. The average writ-er's skills may qualify him more directly for this side of the work, though even here additional insight is needed: a strong sense of market and audience as applied to the copy under the knife. This sense is vital in slanting the manuscript toward its intended audience and insuring the manuscript carries the same slant from beginning to end. Also needed is a sense of logical analysis, not necessarily standard equipment for writers.

A good introduction to this possibly unfamiliar field is provided by Carol O'Neill and Avima Ruder, two experienced freelance copyeditors, in *The Complete Guide to Editorial Freelancing*. (This book is out of print but you can find a copy at your library—perhaps through interlibrary loan.) Included is a list of courses, many by correspondence, that teach editing or copyediting skills, along with a detailed explanation of how copyeditors approach a manuscript to play their part in the publishing process. Another good source of information is *Copyediting: A Practical Guide*, by Karen Judd.

Can everyone who makes a living as a writer become a copyeditor? Not necessarily. O'Neill and Ruder say, "A freelancer should love books; should chortle with glee if she finds and corrects a misplaced comma; should yearn to make every manuscript a great book."

The prospects for freelance copyediting are, frankly, mixed. They depend to some extent on where you live, though freelancers are performing these tasks all over the country. Most publishers, given a choice, prefer to work with editors reasonably near at hand.

The need for freelance copyeditors is indisputable. Of the forty-five thousand books published last year, every one of them required a copyeditor's assistance. Many were ultimately handled by freelancers because publishers' staffs were swamped and the budgets included no glimmer of more full-timers.

But competition for the best of these jobs—those farmed out by the largest publishers who, not incidentally, pay highest rates—can be fierce. The field is dominated by ex-editors, who've gotten their lessons from work within the industry and who maintain connections formed during their residencies. They tend to be thought of first when outside help is required.

If you have employment experience in publishing yourself, however, you should explore the possibilities for freelancing, first in your own part of the country, where the competition is certain to be lighter. Regional publishers and periodicals are less likely to have staffs of salaried copyeditors and may welcome well-trained freelance talent. University presses are also a possibility; a teaching background in English on the college level would obviously help you secure their assignments.

Ruder and O'Neill found in surveying freelance copyeditors that about two-thirds got their first assignments either through formerly working in the field or friendly contacts in publishing. The rest used the same method open to you: writing to publishers to offer their services. Your letter should cover any past experience related to any aspect of editing, since this is the big question in potential clients' minds. You may be asked to take a copyediting test, so be prepared to back up your claims with competence.

Publishers in need of copyeditors sometimes advertise in *Publishers Weekly.* You can buy space at modest cost to announce your own availability as well. Many magazines offer copyediting tests to freelancers; when in doubt, inquire. Contacts remain the most reliable source of these jobs, but a nicely-composed letter and relevant résumé may turn up possibilities even when you send it cold. Editors sometimes advertise their services in writers' magazines or professional academic journals, but are far more likely to get ghostwriting jobs from their ads than to reach publishers looking for freelance copyediting help.

Your first assignment is hardest to get. After you've assembled a list of editing credits the going becomes easier. Your regional clients will almost always remain the best prospects for your work.

Copyediting pays by the hour, as a rule, and it's not on par with what plumbers or even freelance writers usually charge. You can usually count on an offer well under ten dollars—five to seven is closer to average, though editors for New York houses regularly command fifteen dollars or more.

Clearly, you won't get rich copyediting. The difficulty of getting assignments seems to suggest that this is among your less profitable prospects to explore unless you already possess the meticulous eye and professional experience. If you're not already equipped to copyedit, frankly you'd be better off selecting another area of freelance writing and spending the same amount of time mastering it. The time required to break in is unlikely to pay large enough dividends to justify the effort.

But if your background is right and your list of contacts fresh, copyediting may be a way to fill in blocks of time otherwise unspoken for in your freelance schedule. The assignments may not be lucrative in themselves, but add up to another form of insurance.

Your Life as a Ghost

I guarantee it: Once you've gained a degree of reputation as a professional freelance writer, you too will start meeting men and women who want you to become their shadow, their amanuensis . . . their ghost. It's a strange, strange world, populated (in my experience) by a cast of people with often-bizarre notions about books they think you should help them write and with no insight whatever into the workings of the professional writing business.

When someone whose eyes gleam with that unusual light brings up collaboration, I'm tempted to excuse myself and stop answering my telephone until I'm sure he's gone away. But I've had just enough positive encounters to keep "no" at bay until I've heard more. After you sort the serious prospects out from the fruits and nuts, there can truly be a future in life as a ghost.

Ghostwriting is only a few degrees left of the sort of heavy-duty copyediting that verges on a rewrite. Both take another's words and refine them; both give credit to the originator of the text or tale, and not the one who readied it for publication. The difference is that rewrites are always commissioned by publishers, and thus are performed on material that's already found a home. Ghostwriting, on the other hand, is almost always speculative; you depend on the corporeal author for approval and payment.

Why do you really write? For the byline? The income? The satisfaction of crafting words that communicate well? Ghostwriting satisfies a pair of those motives, and two out of three's not bad. If you can live without the reinforcement of bylines on your work, this area can represent interesting and abundant opportunities to profit from your skill with words.

You may know ghostwriters best for the so-called autobiographies of stars and national heroes. The very best develop reputations of their own; you know them as "as told to." That association, however hallowed by tradition and Hollywood, is apt to have shrunken your notion of ghosting's scope. Those few glamour jobs obscure the great majority of opportunities for ghosts—more mundane but far, far more likely to turn up right in your own geographic corner.

Movie stars may not entrust their autobiographies to you any time soon, and you may not know a single celebrity looking for assistance in self-expression. Yet you're living within comfortable reach of a multitude of candidates for your ghosting skills: experts unable to transmogrify their knowledge into the written word; local businesspeople booked to address conventions; elected officials who want their byline (and the publicity it brings) in prestigious magazines; prominent local personalities who shimmer with wit at the microphone or even on paper, but who are blocked or too busy or just too tired to produce all their own material.

I have stepped into the netherworld of ghostdom myself and found it oddly satisfying to find someone else's expertise flowing from my own pen. I've written of financial issues that are normally over my head, historical research beyond my ken, and (my favorite) everything you need to know to catch more fish—all invisibly, all profitably, and all with the special thrill of appearing in public as somebody else and getting away with the masquerade.

You needn't be a writing legend to become a ghost. What you do need is an aptitude for working with people very, very close to the sensitive cores of their egos. Your work has to show them at their best. You have to be cooperative and flexible enough to produce a product that satisfies your own standards as well as those of the person who'll get the credit and wants to be known for only the best of efforts.

If you can uncover the essence of what clients really mean to say, and can work well with demanding but uncertain sources, you're ready to investigate the ghostwriting available in your area. I suspect you'll be surprised at the variety of people who jump at the chance to hire a professional writer to make them look good in print or at the lecturer's podium.

About one-eighth of my written output in the past few years has come from projects I classify as ghosting—that is, any written work which is publicly acknowledged as originating with someone else, and which by agreement I do not claim as my own.

Ghosting can be destined for either written or verbal presentation. I've written speeches for public officials, explaining their complicated government programs (gobbledygook!) in lay terms. I've helped a minister, gifted in the pulpit, add an informal touch to down-to-earth speaking encounters.

I've written statements and helped sketch out positions for not a few candidates for office, enlarging on their own attitudes toward the issues and helping to bring out their real personalities in tense public situations.

I've written articles for politicians and business leaders which appeared under their own bylines in trade or general-interest magazines. I've helped write a newspaper column under a representative's byline. I've even come up with the idea and market myself and taken them to the logical person to "front" them—then helped craft a manuscript that did us both proud.

I've written grant and fellowship applications for deserving educators who, though eminently qualified in their fields, have a hard time producing a professional account of themselves on paper. I've helped smooth out résumés, job application letters, nominations for professional awards, and other odds and ends that together amount to the most fascinating bunch of unexpected undertakings I could imagine. In no case have I falsified information or obscured the client's own style. I've just ironed its wrinkles or tucked back its ears or given it a bit of spit and polish. All some assignments require is to see and follow the thread in the mass of detail.

Why do clients hire writers to do what they're thought to have done themselves? People are routinely judged by their communication skills, I think. A brilliant scientist can come across dowdy and unexciting if his uneasiness with words gives him a stuffy, remote tone. A great speaker and conversationalist can fail to translate his personality to paper. A poor education or uncertain grasp of English can handicap the brightest person. The most astute of these recognize their awkwardness and want to do something about their lack of facility with the language.

Enter the ghost.

You may or may not be able to spot likely ghosting opportunities from afar. Not everyone who gives speeches that would make an English teacher shudder is open to hiring someone to improve his style. Somebody else you consider excellent may, on his own, recognize minor shortcomings or simply expect more of himself and want to add final polish to what's already a fair shine.

Unless you make yourself available, you will be overlooked. The idea of hiring a ghostwriter might not occur to many who'd consider it—not, that is, until an observant freelancer suggests the haunting thought of outside assistance.

The sales techniques that help you reach magazine editors serve you well as a foundation for ghostwriting, too. Back to the good old query. Drop a line to several likely men or women sketching out your credentials and saying you're available if a ghost may be of service.

Think over the professions that might demand well-written work of people to whom a typewriter is a foreign object. How about the local college, where research professors must heed the publish-or-perish imperative? Business people who've been asked to address training seminars or conventions? Scientists and engineers with new techniques for solving common problems? Medical professionals who have something to say about developments in their fields?

Letters aren't the only way to approach these people. In smaller communities, you have two other means of getting your message across that take even less effort—word of mouth and short personal visits.

Those who use the services of a ghostwriter aren't always too ready to proclaim it. But word of good professional help does get around. When you have handled a couple of ghostly assignments, you may find that news of your service has leaked out—perhaps by way of someone "who has a friend" you've helped.

If you want to make a concrete proposal—a journal article, for example—it's easiest to drop in and talk it over in person. Don't use hours of a near-stranger's (and your own) time, however, for ambiguous discussions that lead nowhere. If you're just feeling him out, a letter is a more courteous way to introduce the idea.

Finally, consider advertising. A quiet classified ad in professional journals has been demonstrated to get results. Find out what publications go into the offices of professionals in your area. Many national journals offer a selection of ad packages that allow you to choose which parts of the country your ad will reach. It's usually wasted space and money to advertise for ghostwriting clients outside your own area, for extensive personal contact is generally required.

And what would you think of a want ad in your local newspaper? Nothing flashy—no supermarket-size ads or tacky headlines. But a ghostwriting want ad does get results.

The angle to advertise is professional editorial assistance rather than ghostwriting, which carries a murkier connotation. Try phrasing the ad with a hint of your background ("ten years journalistic experience/former editor of trade journal"), along with a suggestion that the reader write for further information. Have a more detailed letter ready for these contacts.

Don't say too much in the advertisement itself; you're running up your cost without gaining any more in the way of benefit. A reader whose interest is piqued will respond to a short notice as readily as to a longer one. If you spend too much money on a large ad, you may even risk looking like the semilegitimate come-on experts who lure naive authors into paying inflated and ineffective fees to have material readied for publication.

Advertisements can attract clients for two ghostwriting specialties which, though radically different, present some of the fastest prospects for painlessly increasing your income.

Résumés

Some writers have provided themselves with pocket money and evened out the occasional feast-or-famine cycle by running ads aimed at getting assignments writing résumés. It's a service welcomed by anxious job-seekers and well suited to the extroverted writer's talents. The help wanted column is the ideal place to advertise—where better to reach those competing on the job market?

Writing résumés demands two main qualities—the ability to conduct a patient, probing interview (which can discover strengths and goals your client may not know he has), and an unflagging tendency to see the bright side. The actual writing is secondary to the act of "framing," with highlights on the client's best points and shadows on those not so good. Producing a good résumé is an act of salesmanship most akin to writing sunny advertising copy . . . without resorting to stretching the truth too far or outright misrepresentation of your client. (A professional résumé is not, no matter what clients may hope, a work of romantic fiction.) The writing itself requires little more than fitting your discoveries into one of the several accepted formats. (A number of books that lay out these forms are available at libraries.) Most can be prepared, from first introduction to completion, in a couple of hours or less. The minimum charge for such a service is approximately forty dollars in my area; because there is little or no competition in most communities, you may find you can charge what the market will bear. Base your starting fee on two hours' work at your regular hourly rate, then increase it in one-hour increments for more demanding jobs.

Rarely will you need to go out of your way to find résumé jobs. I never have indicated I wanted them, but have been asked to take them on anyway as a favor to clients and business acquaintances. For the limited demands they place on your time, they pay handsomely.

Speechwriting

Speechwriting is an especially needed form of ghosting in nearly every locale. At election time, candidates go through an incredible volume of prepared material in addressing all the groups whose votes they hope to win. Prominent businessmen who serve in some civic capacity may welcome a hand in preparing speeches to meet their obligations. Public officials can be steady clients for written remarks, particularly when called upon to represent the community at some larger regional or national event; I know of several writers who've been engaged to write testimony given at federal hearings on issues of major importance back home.

Writing speeches is likely to be a job that you'll enjoy, even if you can't face a crowd yourself. It demands several skills that every experienced writer possesses—the ability to interview and really listen to answers, and to closely observe the client's personality and verbal style.

You have to ask the right questions of your client to prepare a speech that she'll deliver as if she really means it. Sometimes a lengthy discussion of the topic is necessary before the client herself clarifies her position on it. Your job is to probe, to ask her to carry her own thoughts a little further until she's worked the topic through in her own mind. If your research isn't thorough enough, you may face the speech writer's nightmare: a speaker who, as she's reading her prepared text in public, begins to disagree—at first in tone of voice, finally in extemporaneous comments—with her "official" statements.

Writing to the client's personal style gives authenticity to your work. Watch civic and state officials giving canned speeches supplied by charities, for example, seeking a public announcement on their behalf—you can spot wooden, ill-fitting material just by the speaker's uncomfortable manner. A slow, thoughtful talker is mismatched with an original but high-energy statement. One whose style fairly crackles with vitality becomes impatient with ponderous academic thought.

Besides reflecting the client's opinions and his style, your speech should be one more thing: short. Gauge your speaker's normal, relaxed rate of speech and calculate to fill just a few moments less than the allotted time. (You may want to time his speech to estimate length.) Your client's audience will be grateful; and you'll find that brevity improves the reception of almost any speech.

The finished speech text looks like a manuscript with particularly generous allotments of white space. It's typed in capital orator, if you have it, or at least in a clear pica-sized typeface. It is doublespaced or, if your typewriter can manage it, triple. Top, side and bottom margins are wide to keep a nervous speaker's moist palms away from potentially smeary copy . . . and also to allow easy addition of notes, changes, and extra comments that every speaker is bound to toss in at the last moment.

The pages are clearly numbered, and at the bottom of each page but the last is a cryptic notation, "more." The end should be clearly marked too; in the heat of the moment not all speakers realize when they're done.

Charge for your speechwriting, as you do for all ghostwriting activities, on the basis of your established cost per hour. The objective is not to base the price on how long the speech takes to present, but on how long it takes you to put together. Include your time spent interviewing the client, writing, presenting it to him, and rewriting in response to his comments.

One special precaution applies to ghostwriting any kind of project for political candidates and private parties whose credit you're unsure of. Get at least half, and preferably all, of your fee before you begin the assignment. If you're prepaid half, collect the balance before you let the finished copy leave your hands.

Once given, your speech cannot be repossessed for nonpayment of the bill. Nor can you take back work you've done refining another's memoirs, résumé, journal article, or book manuscript. Individuals are more likely than businesses or other organizations to be bad credit risks, and political candidates are absolutely the worst risks of all. They have a nasty tendency to lose elections from time to time, and unsuccessful candidates quite often fail to meet the bills run up during the heat of the campaign.

Ghosted books and magazine articles offer a second option in addition to hourly fees. For books, the standard collaborator's arrangement is to receive all the advance and 50 percent royalties. However, many of the projects you turn up locally won't be taken on by royalty publishers; for a work that's self-published or printed by a vanity press, an hourly fee system is the only safe way to go.

Magazine articles give you a similar choice: split the payment (if there is one) or charge for your services on an hourly or fee basis. (Scholarly journals in particular pay minimal rates, by the way. If approached by the would-be academic author, you'd be better off quoting your regular rates than agreeing to accept some or all of the payment.)

Never, never agree to do ghostwriting on spec for your client unless it was your idea in the first place. There are absolutely no guarantees that your ghostwritten manuscript will ever be published, no matter how impeccably you've written it or how earthshaking its author sincerely believes it to be. Besides, final control of the manuscript lies with its publicly acknowledged author, not with you. The finished manuscript may be quite different than you'd expected it to be.

Because final control of the written copy rests with your client, it's doubly important in ghostwriting to have a written agreement stating your fees, the work you contract to do for that amount, and mutually understood grounds for acceptance or rejection by the client. A letter is usually adequate for small to medium-size jobs, since your potential profit and the risks entailed don't justify paying for a lawyer's services. But on any major job—say, several thousand dollars or more—a legally binding standard contract is not a bad idea. Consider your client's evident ability to pay, whether he is hiring you as an individual or on behalf of an agency or business. And the warnings of the sixth sense that usually alerts you to a project that's not quite so simple as it seems.

Cautions aside, ghostwriting can be fun. It introduces you to interesting people and reliably reimburses you for efforts performed in their behalf—a good way to enlarge your freelance income without interfering with projects that carry your name and, incidentally, a high rate of risk.

Like editing and copyediting, ghostwriting helps you master the qualities on which writing is accepted or rejected. All three forms are crash courses in clear communication. You'll use lessons learned here to good effect in every project that bears your byline.

9
Photography

Is a picture really worth a thousand words? Maybe, maybe not. It depends on the picture, and on the words. But I can attest to something better: It's usually worth extra bucks when it accompanies your own well-chosen verbiage.

Nothing can boost your nonfiction past the final hurdle quite as quickly as appropriate photographs. They can bring joy to the editor's heart and "yes" to his lips, and identify you as the kind of one-step contributor who rises quickly toward the top of the list.

Especially in less-traveled locales where stock photos are difficult to come by, that leaves you with two choices. You can find a camera-equipped collaborator to be the second member of your own writer/photographer team. Or you can learn to cover yourself with a camera.

Do the mysteries of photography seem to be beyond you? Do you use the lack of professional training and costly equipment to toss the need for illustrations back into your editor's court? Then you may be missing an excellent opportunity to increase your freelance income both through the sale of photos themselves and in the increased salability they may lend to your efforts.

Creditable photos are an asset in many kinds of freelance enterprises, from magazine articles and books that hinge on visual explanations, to commercial projects of every kind—newsletters, brochures, public relations kits and full-scale audiovisual programs.

In a perfect world of ideal publishing procedures, arranging for photographs would be the sole responsibility of the editor, abetted by a photo researcher or art director. These professionals would choose one photographer from many, as they chose you as the writer best suited to the job. They would send this paragon hither and yon in search of visuals to complement your words. Two steps, two assignments, two payments.

This pretty picture dims watt by watt as you reflect upon the realities of hard-pressed staffs who work with geographically-inconvenient contributors.

Number one: You are far, far away from those editors' offices. You are equally distant from the photographers with whom they're accustomed to working. Ergo, the expense of sending a camera whiz to stand beside you and your most appealing subjects (not only airfare and food, but idle expensive hours whiled away in airports and aboard jets) is a sizeable lump which the finance director is unlikely to swallow.

Number two: Your subjects may be as foreign to editors as the sight of sunrise glinting off the Ganges. More foreign, in fact: They could view the Ganges in the encyclopedia of your choice. What I can see from my window (sugarbeets) and explore on writing forays into the pothole country of the Dakotas is as difficult for the average editor to picture with confidence as it is for me to imagine vendors hawking pretzels on crowded urban street corners or sane women actually wearing high-fashion clothes.

Number three: Most of your best markets aren't the kinds that buy manuscripts and photographs separately unless they're absolutely forced to. The medium-sized and minor markets, including the vast majority of those in the six easy-access categories addressed in Chapter 5, are accustomed to buying words and pictures in one package. In some cases it's economic; in others it's simply the most practical approach.

When the pictorial half of the package is missing, they're reduced to searching stock photo agencies or begging civic or corporate organizations for freebies. If you've written about Fishermen's Wharf or the Tour Eiffel, that's not too much to ask; ditto if your how-to piece features a certain make and model of whatzit. It's a little tougher if you're successfully mining your local vein of writer's gold, the natural ideas provided close to (your) home by your location. Just try finding a shot of Battleship Butte, a German-Russian grandma serving *Fleishkuchele*, or a lavender sunset over Lake Tschida.

These far-flung illustrations are usually tough for an editor to obtain at long distance . . . or simply not worth the effort. If the magazine's format depends on illustrations, your story is going to be rejected for lack of Kodachrome.

Trade stories, travel stories, stories about local characters and pastimes, tales of sporting adventure and the great outdoors—all automatically gain salability when attached to a set of sharp, natural-looking black-and-white prints or a pocketed acetate sheet of color transparencies. And that's just in magazine work.

Nonfiction book proposals that require illustration become more enticing in direct proportion to the number and quality of photos which you can provide yourself. If you can't supply those that are integral to your volume, you're doubling the up-front expense and quadrupling the complexity of preparing the book for the editor who'll ultimately handle it. And you may have something to lose yourself: A full-scale photo collaborator would be assigned a share of your advance and royalties.

How-to volumes, your best bet for a first book that's frankly planned to make money, are heavy consumers of photos. Yet they require just the sort of straightforward, businesslike shots you can easily take yourself. If you can, you conserve your editor's time. The editor can visualize (or even visually double-check) the subject on which you've lavished your well-chosen words. (And you'll need to lavish fewer of them yourself, for photos add greatly to the clarity of complex instructions.)

Though your photos will cost the publisher money, you'll be the one getting it. The editor in turn saves time in searching for art or debating an unillustrated proposal's relative merits. They do allow editors to conserve a few dollars, too: Fees paid for photos purchased as part of a photo-manuscript package are considerably less than those paid for desperately needed shots selected one by one from stock photo agencies or on custom shoots by market-minded photographers.

Since the cost is less, the editor is usually amenable to buying only one-time publishing rights for your photos. As in every case, sell all rights only if that's the only way you gain a sale at all—and then negotiate for considerably more than you'd otherwise be offered for a single use.

Why? Photographs on how-to subjects, like many others including regional travel and industries, are potentially bankable time and again. You may develop a new slant and sell them again as part of another photo story. Or you may cross the line yourself toward independent photo marketing, much as the stock agencies do (though on a smaller scale).

If you develop a substantial backlog of good black-and-white prints or transparencies on topics in demand by trade and textbook publishers, you may be able to place your best work with a full-scale stock house. Your shots of the inside of a power plant, a mother bathing her baby, or a grasshopper nibbling a stalk of wheat might take on a life of their own. Proceeds from each sale would be split between you and the agency, usually 50-50. (For information on these firms, consult the current *Photographer's Market*.)

Most photo agencies, however, demand steady submissions of reliably superb quality; the competition from full-time photographers may put their services well beyond your reach unless you become a photographic hotshot yourself. You may have better results by maintaining your own files and scanning *Photographer's Market* and the market columns in photo magazines for tips on publishers' specific needs.

One advantage possessed by many studio photographers is that they often work with large-format cameras—which give larger images than the inch-wide 35mm preferred by photojournalists. Given the choice of two equally appropriate and attractive transparencies, most editors will pick the larger every time. But they can make do with 35mm very well when presented with no such dilemma.

Several newsletters offer timely information on publications' current needs. The best-known is *The PhotoLetter*, a biweekly published in Osceola, Wisconsin, by Rohn Engh. Engh's book *Sell and Re-Sell Your Photos* offers a comprehensive guide to mining this vein of freelance opportunity.

You might also take a tip from professional photographers and circulate a list of your topical inventory to likely users—logical magazines (farm, travel, and outdoors titles in particular) and book publishers, especially including textbook houses. Many will reciprocate by putting you on their own mailing lists to receive more-or-less regular letters about current needs.

And by all means, try the editors who know you as a writer first and photographer a distant second. A proven source is in all cases more reliable than an unknown; you could add a whole new facet to the jewel they already know you to be.

While you may never make your living by squashing a camera against your nose every day, the extra payment that photos will earn you does add up. Fees range from a minimum of from ten to twenty-five dollars, to three hundred or more for a color shot used large or on the cover of a smaller-circulation magazine. (Spell out who's responsible for film and developing expenses beforehand. These rather substantial amounts should be covered by the purchaser in addition to the per-photo fee.)

Your photos probably won't make you famous. They're even less likely to make you rich. But at the least, they ought to pay for the investment that basic equipment requires and the time it takes to learn to use it.

Obviously I lean toward learning to use your own camera. I love photography, as I tend to love anything that's easier than (or at least different from) writing. But you may want to consider the alternate option before you take the big step yourself—that is, working with a photographer as your collaborator.

In an ideal world, you'd be one half of a writer-photographer team. That's how top newspapers and photo magazines always prefer to assign stories (always, that is, when everything is running smoothly, about fifteen minutes per day). That, in fact, is how my photographer husband and I met, and how we now complement each other's efforts.

Marrying your collaborator is one neat way to sidestep the stickiest issue in such a partnership: convincing the camera jockey to work on speculation, rather than on a typical fee basis.

That's quite a trick. The horror with which most photographers will greet your offer should give you some measure of insight into how rare and bizarre the ground rules of freelance writing seem to the outside world. But to make your team play work, and to insure that you won't bankrupt yourself on a story that never sees the light of publication—because the photos don't quite work, because an editor is having a bad day, or because of the phase of the moon—there's just no other way.

(Of course, there are those cases in which an editor specifically asks you to hire a local photographer to take the necessary shots. That's a different case. The publisher is on the hook to pay the bill, which in my part of the country only begins at about two hundred fifty dollars a day plus travel time and expenses.)

Your ideal photo comrade is a freelancer like you, perhaps a moonlighting newspaper shooter, a studio photographer bored with bridal portraits, or one of the multitude of superb amateurs who prefer to reserve their love of the art for personal fulfillment.

If your freelancing colleague lacks background in photos for publication, be sure he's familiar with the specific needs of editorial photography before any film is exposed in vain. Most studios, for example, work with color print film. That's almost unheard-of in publishing, where Kodachrome is the medium of choice and color prints brand you an innocent. (Color prints are occasionally reproduced in black-and-white, but sharpness and tonal clarity may be lost in the process; this is strictly a last-chance tactic.)

When you're choosing your photo teammate, use your own facsimile of editorial judgment to assay his work's quality. That judgment should include these minimum standards: sharp focus, good contrast (with a range of tones from blackest black through graded shades of gray to whites that are as clear as they should be), and an ability to "see" a story in photographic terms. In other words, photos must be at least technically acceptable and interesting enough to add a striking dimension to the written word.

There's no sense in leading on a perfectly nice and eager friend whose work is clearly not up to reproducible standards. His photos won't get used if they're out of focus or mushy gray all over or simply so dull that no editor would waste space on them. If you work with someone whose skills aren't at least the equivalent of your own, you can be sure your joint efforts will be reduced to the lowest common denominator. That's usually not good enough in a market where even terrific submissions get crowded out.

Not only are you hurting your own sales, perhaps more than by providing no photos at all, you're raising false hopes and running up someone else's film and processing bills without any reasonable prospect of reward. Do that nice woman next door or your cousin's wife a favor, and don't lead her along on the callous off chance that she'll turn out something—anything—you can use.

Find someone who knows the ropes.

Or learn the ropes yourself.

I am convinced that there's hardly a writer practicing her craft who cannot master the basics of providing her own photo illustrations. I believe this partly because I've witnessed photo teachers each September initiate several dozen students in their very first serious relationship with a camera. By Christmas or Easter those same women and men, many of whom had no experience whatsoever in photography, are making slide shows and producing occasionally distinctive photo essays on their own.

Partly their example, that is, and partly my own experience. As a college freshman dazzled by good-looking photographers all around me at the newspaper, I sank a good part of my savings toward my sophomore year into a Nikkormat and the minimum number of lenses that would win me their respect (three).

The same camera has stood by me for over a dozen years. It has taken thousands of feet of black-and-white photos for publication, for reference, and for fun, along with a fair sampling of color slides.

None of those photos is going to be exhibited in the Museum of Modern Art; nor am I in line to become the next Margaret Bourke-White (or even Candice Bergen). But I've happily applied this wonderful combination of useful pursuit and avocation to dozens of other rewarding ends. Among them:

■ "Environmental" photographs of dozens of people whom I interviewed in their homes, on the open prairie, in meetings, or wherever I could catch them. Every one of them would have been happy to supply me with a black-and-white studio portrait left over from his last job application. But those shots I took capturing them active in the world around them are infinitely more interesting than the spotless self-images offered.

■ Photos to buttress investigative pieces. While these stories are not my forte, I've had occasion to use photographs to back up my own observations. However gut-wrenchingly honest the words, photos add extra credibility to your claims.

■ Copying of historical photos and illustrations of artifacts. In writing stories involving historical events and people, it's easier to get permission to reproduce those fragile, yellowing photos in all their evocative sensitivity if you can copy them on the spot where they're being protected. In some instances you can also get permission to borrow them and have them studio copied. But if you have a dear old woman's only photo of her long-dead parents, and she lives two hundred miles away in Grassy Butte, you're risking a lot in terms of good will and irreparable loss by entrusting that photo's return to the U.S. Mail. If you can snap your own copy on the spot, she'll be happier and you'll be in the clear.

Likewise, historical artifacts aren't always easily toted into the studio for perfect portraiture. Sometimes you can't even talk a leery curator into opening the locked, climate-controlled glass case keeping you from your subject. If you have a camera, you can get what you need. If not, you're in for a lengthy series of negotiations and arrangements from back home. And if the curator's only offer is to photograph the work for you, you'll have to worry about mediocre photos, hefty "service charges," or both.

If you're snapping a picture of the feisty curator himself, you can clear up another hazy area that sometimes handicaps photos' usefulness: the matter of a model release, which assigns to you the right of using your subject's likeness in print.

Many photographers go through life blissfully unaware of the model release, relying on the subject's implied agreement to appear in their work. (He didn't hit you over the head with his cane, did he?) In many cases an official release won't be necessary. But it is vital if the photo is to be used for commercial purposes (as in advertising), or if the picture is to be used to illustrate a controversial topic (sex and the senior citizen), or presents the subject in an unfavorable light.

When in the slightest doubt, get a release while you're making your photograph. At that time it's a mere formality. If you have to go back and get it later, it becomes an issue, or at least a question worthy of serious thought. When the answer turns out to be no, you're honor-bound to refrain from using what may be an excellent shot.

■ Photographic note taking. Lengthy inscriptions, immaculate records of where sites are located along a thoroughfare, and memory-jogging inventories of scenes and sources all save reams of handwritten notes on location. You can't place the museum on the wrong side of town if you've got a picture of its surroundings.

■ How-to articles. Here again, I've only dabbled in the genre. But photos have come in more than handy on stories I've written about crafts like dyeing Ukrainian Easter eggs and quilting, as well as step-by-step illustrations of pit-roasted barbecue beef and other stories-in-the-making.

Not all my photos have been published. Not by a factor of one frame in one hundred, if you must know. But they're still not a waste of my time or money.

When you work in a region that most metropolites find literally unimaginable, photos can be a valuable sales tool. Queries backed up by a few shots of the terrain, the profile, or the finished product you propose to write about are far more persuasive to editors of any stripe than the comment, "I can take great photos to go with my story." Don't tell them; show them. Photos catch everyone's attention, and I'd wager that few editors can resist paging through a packet of prints or slides filed in a plastic sheet for easy viewing.

Some of those editors may decide, after looking at your samples, that the prospects are good enough to call in one of their stable of professional photographers. You've still helped your story sell. Ditto for the times when an editor prefers an artist's rendering to photography. Photos can be the source for art that captures the spirit of a place or personality.

One of my favorite story layouts was illustrated with pencil sketches made from proof sheets of film I'd shot on location. The photos were middle-of-the-road: not bad, not good enough for the magazine's top-notch tastes. But handed to an illustrator who'd never seen the people or places I photographed, they led to portraits so uncannily accurate that one subject's daughter framed her mother's sketch. She told me it captured her like no photo ever had.

I'd warn you, however, to keep a careful eye open if your photos are to be used as the inspiration for art. Since they aren't reproduced firsthand, a wily editor may decide he doesn't need to buy any rights to use them from you. Unfair!

I don't think I need to outline how your camera can help in local commercial assignments. Newsletters or house organs, brochures, publicity campaigns—all are immeasurably improved by well-targeted photo images. You can broaden the range of services you provide your clients and increase the income that results, as well as make your assignments more effective before the public that judges them. While you do charge for your services, your client saves money, too: You can research and photograph at the same time in many cases; he need not pay an hourly rate for a photographer who needs lengthy indoctrination before he can do the job.

If you're going to become a double-duty writer-photographer, your first concern is bound to be equipment. Some photo amateurs never do get beyond this stage, spending their photographic hours endlessly discussing various camera systems' presumed advantages and the hotly debated difference between Ektachrome and Kodachrome films. They're the ones, incidentally, who may have originally turned you off on the supposedly complex and doggedly serious world of photography. Pay them no mind. Their interminable argument disguises the fact that they're too impressed with their gear to sully it by taking pictures.

No, find yourself a working photographer whose advice can guide you through the expensive maze of camera systems and accessories. A newspaper photographer may be happy to help. A working magazine photographer would be even better. But your best guide of all might be a sympathetic low-pressure salesperson at a local camera store that caters to professionals.

Don't distrust that dealer too much just because he makes his money selling cameras to folks like you. If he runs the kind of store that serious photographers frequent, he values you as a long-term customer, not just a quick commission. Once hooked, a dedicated photographer almost always becomes a customer again and again, trading up to more elaborate camera systems or buying and switching accessories or dabbling with the newest developments in darkrooms and flash attachments. That dealer has a stake in providing what you'll reasonably need to take professional-quality pictures. If he's a mutant of the breed and tries to steer you toward Hasselblads or such (the financial equivalent of a moderate Rolls-Royce in these inflationary times), keep looking for the stalwart authority you can depend on.

The most expensive camera isn't what you need. Neither, though, is the rickety bargain you pick up at a discount store or through a mail-order camera advertisement. You *can* save money by buying name brand equipment from lower-priced outlets, I'll admit. But as a beginner, you need the face-to-face service that a knowledgeable dealer can provide you. Leave the cheapies to the men (they're always men) who cheerfully polish their cameras instead of depressing their shutters, and find someone you can count on for education, for repairs, and for future advice.

Likewise, I'd suggest you avoid rock-bottom bargains and make your first camera a member of one of the major reputable photo families. Nikon, Canon, Pentax, Mamiya—photo buffs compare them constantly. But the fact is the name won't make much difference in your photos: Its effect is on your first system's resale value. If you decide to trade up to a better system someday or—heaven forbid—throw in the towel on photography completely, you'll find the name-brand equipment holds its value remarkably over the years. Brand X fares less well. The money you save by buying your discount store's weekend special will come back to haunt you at the other end of its useful life to you.

Single-lens reflex cameras are the industry standard. They're those black-and-chrome jobs slung around the neck of every modern newspaper photographer, and they enable him to impress bystanders by switching lenses, screwing on filters in odd colors and sizes, and fiddling around in an overweight gadget bag.

You needn't tote twenty pounds of goodies unless you're bent on developing your biceps, but you ought to have a few basics. Lenses in several sizes provide a selection of ways to capture your subject. As I've mentioned, I bought three when I purchased my camera, and have never seen a convincing need for more.

The 50mm lens that undoubtedly came with your camera body sees as much as the eye does, and is known in fact as a "normal" lens. A moderate wide-angle lens—I have a 28mm, though a 35mm is also useful—takes in a much broader view, allowing you to photograph the width of a room or all fifteen people seated around a conference table without backing up unreasonable lengths. (This lens gets a little fish-eyed around the edges, convenient for special effects but a pain when you have no such arty aspirations and want vertical lines to look vertical.) The third lens is a moderate telephoto like my 105mm;

with its help, you can get close-in portrait shots without smelling the garlic on your quarry's breath.

These lenses provide one of the qualities an editor hopes to see in a batch of submitted photos: variety. They're perfect for the standard illustration technique of a long shot of the subject, a medium shot, and a close-up or two. (There. You have the secret of newspaper photojournalists' photo essays.)

But editors look for more than giddy variety in your photos. Focus and exposure are the two most important qualities that make or break your photos' chances.

All that's fuzzy in beginning photographers' work is not bad focus. My own problem has always been camera movement—tiny tremors at the time the shutter is released that blur the subject just enough to cause a poor old editor to feel he must clean his glasses. Practice and conscientious effort are the only ways to correct the problem; try taking a deep breath and holding it as you snap the picture. You may also hug the arm supporting the camera close to your body, using your skeleton as a reasonably sturdy bipod.

Are all writers nearsighted? Do they all find it awkward to focus a camera wearing glasses? Just in case you're one of us, here's a tip for easier focusing. Most cameras sold today are equipped with a ground-glass viewfinder; you just twist the lens until the scene you're viewing looks sharp.

If you're nearsighted, of course, sharp to you isn't always sharp to the world. One solution is exchanging the standard equipment for a split-image screen viewfinder. Then, to focus, you merely peer at an image that's cut in half at the waist; bring top and bottom together again, and sharpness is guaranteed. Alternate models give you double vision and require you to bring the images together.

An even easier solution—though one most self-respecting professional shooters still scorn—is to choose a camera with an automatic focusing mode. Models like the Nikon FE give you the option of manual or machine-made focus, allowing you to maintain your photographic self-respect while secretly insuring that your subject will have whatever sharp edges seem appropriate.

Nikon has lately added another wrinkle to the picture with the introduction of self-focusing lenses. So far, however, their expense far outweighs their application by the non-full-time photographer.

Many cameras also offer automatic adjustment of exposures—a somewhat iffier asset. Exposure (the lightness or darkness of the finished photo) depends on the amount of light that hits your film. That's what all the monkey business with an adjustable camera is intended to control.

In automatic mode, your camera performs these feats on your behalf . . . an advantage in many situations, but one sometimes confounded by especially dark scenes or those with lots of contrast between highlights and shadows. Understand the assets and shortcomings of your particular system, which will give priority to either aperture or shutter speed; ask your dealer to carefully explain the pluses and minuses of each.

If you're using a camera without automatic exposure, you have two ways to cheat (short of truly mastering the mysteries of exposure, a goal that sometimes propels serious photographers through a lifetime of zones and bells and whistles). One is the built-in light meter which any decent-quality camera today possesses. A few field trips with careful attention to results can teach you to use it like a pro. One caution: Little things mean a lot when they happen to be the button-sized batteries that supply the juice to the meter. A weak battery results in blown readings. Change it more often than your thrifty nature suggests. Incidentally, you can keep check on your meter's accuracy by testing its readings against those of another camera of known accuracy equipped with a similar lens. When in doubt of the results, take it down to your camera shop.

The second option is a hand-held light meter, more accurate but infinitely more trouble. Carrying a simple one as a back-up is a good precaution. But do remember that it's prey to all the adversities that beset the camera itself, from poor batteries and calibration that's out of whack to the major trauma caused by dropping it on a concrete sidewalk. It also adds to the number of gadgets you'll have to juggle out in the field. Unless you're really serious about photography, get a system with a built-in meter, perhaps with the option of automatic exposure, and keep its batteries fresh.

Dim light and indoor settings pose special problems. What if your reportorial heart says "yes" but your light meter says "no"? For my money, the greatest gift that electronics have given photographers is the automatic flash unit. Gone are the guide numbers that made a mockery of elementary math as you tried to juggle them with distance (in feet or meters) to get a decent exposure. Today you can find gizmos that almost painlessly shed light on any situation you'd wish to capture. Let your budget and the territory you usually cover be your guides.

What's the final word on exposure? Kodak. His cousin Fuji and the rest all pack a lifesaver in every box of film you buy. It's that little instruction sheet which you thoughtlessly crumple with the wrapper and the box and toss into the bottom of your camera bag. It carries sound, sane advice on exposures in every sort of typical condition from bright sun to lamplight. You can rely on it to carry you through when, on location, your built-in battery has begun to ooze and you've just dropped your hand-held meter in the lake.

Correct processing can have a lot to do with your exposure, too. If you plan to use your photos commercially—and you do, for why else go through all this?—give them the professional finishing they deserve. While you may be able to recoup costs and labor of a black-and-white darkroom if you do lots of photo work, you can also for a nominal amount pay a pro to do all the mixing and fixing for you.

If a pro's nice for black-and-white, he's the only candidate for color. Color processing is a long, touchy procedure requiring precise temperatures, ultra-fresh chemicals, and a totally dust-free environment. Few of us can produce a dust-free environment, try as we might. Unless you do yards and yards of color work every week, it's unlikely that you can save money by processing it personally. Why bother?

Choose your photo lab with the care you applied to finding a dealer to trust. There is a difference between professional photo labs and the discounters whose work is sold through your local dime or drug store: several dollars per roll, true. But it's also the difference between pock-marked, off-color results and a service that won't cause editors to shudder. Ask a local professional photographer to recommend a lab, or borrow one of his trade magazines and answer a few ads yourself. Don't be concerned, incidentally, if the lab you choose lies at a distance. That's the norm for those of us in the hinterlands, since there isn't enough local volume to justify local processing houses. I regularly deal with processors in Dallas and Seattle, and my only complaint is the occasional delay in mail delivery. But if I lived my life in the organized fashion to which we all aspire, I'd avoid those tense mail watches anyway.

You may be paying slightly more for out-of-town service, but you should make it up in professional discounts on equipment and film at home. As a writer who's using a camera in your work, you are entitled to the professional discount offered by almost every camera store in America. To be offered twenty percent off list price is not unusual; cost-plus-ten-percent is often available for good professional customers. The discount will not be volunteered by the guy behind the counter. Ask!

You can't ask him *all* the questions that arise in learning to use your new toy, however. For your serious photo education, investigate the literature and the classes available in your locale.

The Time/Life Library of Photography, available in many libraries, offers two dozen volumes of useful information, from the most basic understanding of the field to specialized suggestions. The *Photojournalism* volume is especially good. Kodak offers a number of practical publications, from their *Here's How* pocket guides to more thorough examinations of any facet of photography you might imagine. Myriad books cover other photo fields. One of my own favorites is Lisl Dennis's *How to Take Better Travel Photos*. She avoids the equipment mystique and gets down to the real challenge of using a camera: creating memorable pictures.

Your camera store may sponsor seminars on using various lines they stock. The Nikon School, a traveling one-day course that covers the photographic waterfront, hits almost every state in the country annually; it's worth a trip to take part in it. Other camera systems also offer owners' seminars. Your camera dealer has the details.

Photo courses come in two flavors, good and bad. The good ones are taught by working photographers; for your purposes, the very best are offered by photographers actively marketing their work to publications. The bad ones are taught by everyone else — equipment fetishists, artists who savor every grain of sand in a photo of a beach but are oblivious to the basic art of documenting action, and well-meaning amateurs who can't teach you any better than they were taught themselves. If in doubt, ask your camera dealer about the teacher's reputation. A good one will assuredly have a measure of respect among her fellow professionals.

One special educational marketing tool may come in handy after you've mastered the basics of how to use a camera. It's seminars offered by professionals on how to take salable photos and then match them to their markets. Like writers' conferences, these workshops at their best present you with an inspiring collection of hints and hard information. Those offered around the country by Rohn Engh, publisher of the previously mentioned *PhotoLetter,* are among the best.

The best way to take better pictures, after you've learned to get film in and out of the camera and take off the lens cap, is to go out and shoot photos firsthand. Lots and lots of them. Then go over your results, resolve to improve your composition or focus or whatever's lacking, and shoot a whole bunch more.

The editor who gave me my first photo lessons always reminded me that the amount of film used is the very least of your worries when you're shooting. Consider your expenditure on equipment and accessories. Consider the time you've spent learning how to operate that camera. Consider the hours and fuel you've used getting to the location where your picture is about to happen . . . and then consider the million variables that make every shot just a little different, and just a little better or worse, than the one you've just clicked off.

Then reflect upon the fact that in being stingy with Kodak's finest, you minimize your chances of capturing that one perfect image. Do yourself (and Kodak) a favor. Shoot photos, and shoot more, and more, until you get what you want. It's the only way your labors will ever come close to the work of the pro photographers editors admire.

Don't think you'll make it? Or you don't want to distract yourself from taking notes and soaking up atmosphere to get involved with this fascinating but potentially consuming sideline?

Perhaps you should reconsider Option Number One. That is, marrying a photographer (or making over the spouse you've already come up with).

There is a thought-provoking number of husband and wife writer-photographer teams out here in the hinterlands. The teamwork's convenient. You know where your spouse is when the sun is setting or the birds ready to fly. It can be terrific fun, and it's one way to share the joys and letdowns of the freelance life with your partner.

Just picture the possibilities. There's bound to be a camera in your future if you're writing from a far-out address. Who minds if it's attached to something with even more potential?

10
Moving Targets: Writing for Voice and Visuals

Your most moving writing can give flight to more than a reader's fancy. It can actually move—exactly that, if the medium is video or its audiovisual cousins.

You can whisk an audience across space and time . . . open doors to firsthand views of lives they've never lived . . . shape a message and persuade.

Of course you can accomplish all of that—and, many would argue, even more—through the time-honored medium of the printed word. But video and its AV alternates have won a central role in our information-soaked society. While thoughtful articles and books touch their readers selectively (and while readers often prove to be at least as choosy in picking them up), the broadcast media offer the quick fix, the fast mass take. They seek out their audience actively and aggressively. And like it or not, they do deliver.

More than at any time since humans abandoned the use of sages squatting around the campfire as a major medium of communication, we are faced with a society that absorbs a substantial portion of its daily data through senses other than skill at deciphering letters and punctuation.

Where there is communication, there are (or should be) writers helping to call the shots. And calling the shots is exactly what you'll find yourself doing if you explore the market for audiovisual scripts and production.

Video in particular allows you to stretch your grasp of a story's shape and drama and color. In print, you *tell*. In video you *show*, combining motion and sound and sight through the camera's staring eye to flesh out a skeleton of your own words. Your insights provide the framework; life provides the cast of characters and the set.

These assignments give you unprecedented practice in thinking in visual and auditory terms—a skill of obvious benefit back on the printed page. You must think in action and sound and images, not adjectives and adverbs. That's true whether you're suggesting scenes or sound effects to make your point in an educational video, or slides to illustrate an audiovisual script, or an audio "illustration" to catch the listener's ear in a radio commercial.

Here's your chance to see your name in lights. Oh, little bitty ones—a credit rolled at the end of a video program, a final slide flashed across the screen, or perhaps an author's card tucked away in an AV reference file. Or you might remain an anonymous craftsperson, like even the greatest advertising copywriters outside their own domain.

Either way, you'll gain something that goes beyond strokes for your ego. There's the special sort of pride you feel for work that communicates clearly to the audience for whom it's intended.

Technology has moved amazingly fast, sweeping new writing opportunities along in its wake. Consider investigating those which have sprung up in your own locale: chances are that you'll find companies producing video product demonstrations for their salespeople, training programs for their staffs, and how-to cassettes for loan or sale to their customers. You're likely to find nonprofit organizations using videos to dramatize their fund-raising campaigns and government agencies using them to inform the public.

At the same time, take note of the mushrooming number of television stations (full- and low-power) springing up in remote parts of the nation along with new radio stations designed to appeal to specific audiences (by region, age, ethnic group, or special interest). Where there are broadcasters, there must be writers of advertising copy and continuity. (Continuity is the patter that separates programs or musical numbers, whether it's public service, station promotion, or the wit of on-air personalities.) Local cable systems often hire part-timers to manage their local-access TV channels.

And while you're surveying the field for script-writing, don't overlook a stalwart of pre-video days that's still surviving and thriving—the slide/tape program, today more sophisticated than ever. While video production and broadcast operations are more widely scattered than ever before, slide/tape programs still go them one better. They can be practical and profitable absolutely everywhere.

Video

Back in the dark ages of video—those days when public broadcasting offered just about the only glimmer of tasteful light among the titters of network sitcoms—writers of my acquaintance were evenly divided on the medium of television. Half professed deep disdain for television ("I never watch anything but 'Upstairs, Downstairs' on PBS," they insisted in those days). The rest confessed to a wistful willingness to "sell out" for what they believed were megabucks—a hopeless longing for an industry back then that seemed as distant as Hollywood's Rodeo Drive from Main Street in Zap, North Dakota.

That was five, maybe ten years ago. The first attitude, arrogant disdain, is no longer as fashionable in most writerly circles. Television and its hefty younger brother, the sort of video that's not produced for broadcast, have made giant strides toward respectability as their practitioners learn to savor the flexibility and immediacy they offer.

And as for those impossibly far-away markets, they're closer to home than ever before—no matter where you hang your hat. Video programs are emerging from spots you'd never have dreamed of a decade ago, from Beaver Dam, Wisconsin, and Brainerd, Minnesota, to your own neighborhood. Their creators range from commercial divisions of TV stations to small production houses, and from corporations to individual entrepreneurs, school systems and publishing firms.

The video revolution has come so fast that those of us in the distant trenches are only beginning to get the word. But this is no time for me to play Paul Revere. It's already upon us. Today video has become a medium of choice for an almost dizzying range of applications—public relations, education, product sales, marketing of professional services, fund-raising, training and how-to as well as documentation and reporting.

What has emancipated moving pictures from the major metropolitan areas of America is video technology itself, which has taken over many of the markets developed and dominated by the film industry. Filmmakers led the way in tailoring their craft to educate as well as entertain. But movie cameras and editing equipment are cumbersome, difficult to master, and expensive to purchase and use. Moviemaking is a costly and time-consuming proposition; its demands for specialized services and capital investment concentrate it in major urban markets.

Dramatic breakthroughs in price as well as engineering have brought video's cinema-style advantages within the reach of every kind of producer and user, no matter where they're located. The upfront expense is generally less than in movie-making. Operation is far cheaper, eliminating the need for both large crews and cartwheel-sized canisters of film. Cameras are lighter and easier to operate; editing equipment can be mastered with a modicum of effort, and special effects and titles can be generated with ease by brainy computers.

At the same time, technical refinements and dropping prices have put video itself within the reach of users inside industries and organizations of modest size and budget. Video cassette recorders (VCRs) and monitors have quickly usurped the dusty spot long reserved for 16mm movie projectors and filmstrip projectors. They have moved into the boardroom, into the classroom, into the church basement, and onto the sales floor.

Video needs writers. The better a production aspires to be, the more it needs the best ones. You may become one of them . . . one who enters this new field not only for the earning power it promises (better, I've found, than the average magazine scribbler can expect), but also for the adventure of honing your craft in a new and different discipline.

Signing up to join this revolution, alas, is not as easy as tracking its progress. Unlike publishing, video production is still in its infancy. It lacks the comprehensive marketing system that has grown up in the print business over the years. Here you'll find no etiquette of query letter and SASE, no regular listings of editorial needs, and even—outside the major production houses—no clear requirements or standards of payment.

Here on this new frontier of freelance writing, only two universal truths prevail: You're pretty much in charge of making your own opportunities; and everything's negotiable.

Finding the market presents your first challenge. National directories are of some help, including the scripts section of *Writer's Market* and annual directory issues of *Audio-Visual Communication* and other trade magazines. But the guerrilla research you've already applied to ferreting out regional magazine and book markets offers the best training for locating potential clients for your script-writing services.

To write for videos, first you must watch them. I'm not talking here of Van Halen and Cyndi Lauper on MTV (though they can teach you, too). Instead, look to the local video programs that show up at service club meetings and in the AV departments of school libraries. Scan the closing credits to begin your own Who's Who of active local producers, both in-house and independent.

Keep an eye out for locally-produced TV public service messages as well. Then phone the public service director and ask who crafted the spots. Why? PSAs (public service announcements) are frequently edited in conjunction with longer educational programs. You're more likely to see the PSAs than the full-length versions, since the latter are usually circulated by the organization which paid to have them produced.

The Yellow Pages provide some insight, too. Independent firms can be found under Video Production Services. Be aware, though, that not all who purchase listings there are created equal. Some exist to videotape the proceedings at conventions and seminars; others specialize in capturing weddings and bar mitzvahs in all their splendor. Neither have much need of your help.

But true video production companies may welcome your assistance. You have one spectacular advantage. The principals in these firms almost always come from technical backgrounds in photography, film-making, or broadcast television; they themselves are almost never writers. Yet a writer's abilities provide the backbone for the services in which they excel: You offer expertise in researching the subject, organizing the presentation, and choreographing the video "shoot"—all in addition to the script you eventually produce.

In-house video departments have similar needs and limitations. You'll frequently find them attached to the public relations or marketing divisions of corporations or, in the case of government agencies, associated with public information specialists. They're a bit trickier to track down, since their work may be known only to their own staffs and clientele. The grapevine can provide hints. Or, if you're particularly hot on their trail, tap into outside intelligence: Pry their names from the sales representatives of your area's video equipment dealers. (In most parts of the country, one or two suppliers deal with most video users. More populous areas will, of course, have more dealers.)

Forget about writing polite letters to these companies, whether they're freestanding production houses or internal departments within corporations. Phone for an appointment with the production manager for an in-person meeting.

Don't be shy if you have no solid credentials as a writer of scripts. The video field is so new that relatively few now at work in its fold have substantial prior credits. More relevant than direct experience, perhaps, is familiarity with the digging and building, fact upon fact, that's a requirement of news reporting and magazine journalism.

Video scripts require you to think in three dimensions . . . to *show* your story unfolding, rather than *tell* about it. Samples of vivid, action-packed stories which have appeared in print help sell your services. So does familiarity with still photography, either as a photographer yourself or as one who has directed others' efforts; this suggests you understand the basics of visual storytelling, which video depends on and extends.

There's a tendency among video professionals to call in a writer late in the game, after footage and interviews have already been shot according to a vague outline. They tell you, "Everything's here. Just put it together." It can be done that way, of course. Chances are good that your first script will come about precisely under these circumstances, since a producer facing a deadline with a stack of random tapes is particularly open to the sales pitch of a cool and organized writer. (At that moment he's powerfully motivated to find a savior, if he's lucky, or at least someone to share his woes.) These situations present great opportunities to prove that you can walk on water or, more to the point, dog-paddle like crazy.

Ideally, you should be involved from the beginning. You can push for that after you've piled up several solidly successful projects. In the meantime, though, dire circumstances can offer exactly the experience you need in finding the beginning of a program, matching narration (or personal testimonials) to visuals, creating transitions, and mastering the sense of timing that's as integral to good video as the simultaneous mating of what you see, what you hear, and what they bring to mind.

Video scripts are prepared in a format more stylized than the typical magazine manuscript. The left column is left for visual direction, while the right includes not only narration but other audio cues for sound effects and music. You can get an overview of how scripts are prepared from J. Michael Straczynski's *The Complete Book of Scriptwriting* or *The Writer's Digest Guide to Manuscript Formats* by Dian Buchman and Seli Groves, which presents script preparation step by step.

Your final copy is not the last word on the finished video. A scriptwriter is only one of several partners in the production process including the director, the camera operator, the editor, and (last but never least) the client. As a partner, though, you're usually a party to those changes. In my experience, you learn the trade by observing how your precious words are adapted to fit harsh production reality. No amount of coursework or research can teach video lessons as well.

What can you expect to earn? Scripts written for independent production companies are generally on the basis of a percentage of the total cost of the program, often 10 percent. The programs, in turn, are often bid on the basis of a fixed amount per finished minute. In my part of the country, that figure varies from $750 to $1,000. A writer could expect to earn from $75 to $100 per sixty seconds of script, or about $1,500 for a fifteen-minute program. Arrangements vary, however. Production responsibilities beyond the actual research and writing of the script should enter into your negotiations, using your hourly benchmark rate for purposes of comparison.

Television and Radio

The explosion of broadcasting options has not only multiplied opportunities for writers to test their gift by a new set of standards. It has also brought those opportunities within reach of nearly every corner of America. Full- and low-power community TV stations, cable channels whistling around the world via satellite, and an aching hunger for competitive programming may be delivering new markets virtually to your doorstep.

The evolution of television and radio broadcasting from a broad geographical audience to more specifically targeted markets offers possibilities.

So-called narrowcasting has led to explosive growth in the number of radio stations in many parts of the country. While some still seek the broad-based listenership that leads to Number One in the annual Arbitrons (and places a premium on advertising time), others choose to appeal to more closely defined segments of the community based on age, interests, or buying power. Increased competition means increased opportunity for writers, from creating advertising copy on a per-spot basis to providing an exclusive source of gags to air personalities in pursuit of a better market share. (Yes, someone has agonized over the vast share of their best "ad libs.")

Shifts in TV have multiplied your options, too. Today full- and low-power stations are broadcasting from communities which once received mainly snow unless Dad fiddled constantly with the rabbit ears. Not all depend solely on their staffers for advertising copy, continuity, and leadership for locally produced shows—not by a long shot. Nor do many of their clients.

Consumers have come to expect more viewing choices than the major networks and blue-chip production companies can provide. More than one hundred cable channels are bounced off satellites to cable operations that penetrate deep into even remote rural areas where electricity arrived after World War II. Not all of them can depend on re-runs of "Gilligan's Island" to keep the transmitter humming. They've developed a consuming hunger for programming consistent with the interests of the viewers they hope to attract.

That hunger has spawned a host of syndicated shows—everything from talk to teaching. Since there's no compelling need to produce them in the megabucks production capitals, many of them call odd places home; that opens doors for writers in equally odd corners of the country. You can't count on being in just the right spot, but you never know. If you can tap into an existing program at the development stage, you might find yourself on the brink of an exciting and enviable opportunity.

And for every local cable company there is a public access channel creating new possibilities for locally-produced, low-budget programming. The odds are good that you can crack it. These public-service programs offer little, if any, compensation; but they do provide a ready source of training for other broadcast jobs; that alone can be well worth your time and effort.

TV commercials aren't what they used to be—ground out cheaply and in a flash, one and all, by copywriters working under Dickensian conditions in the back rooms of the station. Faced with furious competition from well-heeled national chains, even smaller local advertisers are turning to advertising agencies and video production houses for sophisticated spots that promise high-test results.

Not all can afford the charges of full-service agencies. For them, you can help fill the gap . . . a source of bright ideas and fresh copy. With your help, they can depend on video crews from the stations on which they advertise to execute an exciting finished product.

The same is true in radio . . . and then some. More stations, more competition, and more at stake in winning and holding an audience mean greater effort poured into what goes between Top 40 hits and "time and temp."

When the need to communicate expands, so does the need for writers. All of these markets demand a river of copy—some of it written by staffers, but another portion certainly destined for the desks of free-lancers geared for motion.

A great deal of written material goes into local programming for ra-dio and TV, from advertising and spots promoting their own programs to public service messages, editorials, short specialty clips, and spe-cials. Radio uses most of these, and more—including many of the spontaneous ad-libs of those quick-witted on-air personalities, a good share of which are read verbatim from comedy services and joke books.

News programs, the most obvious use of writing, only occasionally offer freelance opportunities. They're usually handled as a full-time job or as no job at all, since many radio station announcers just rip copy off the news service wire and read it over the air. Nevertheless, an enterprising independent may find a niche either as an occasional expert on a specialized area or as a part-timer, especially on the week-end shift. If you're launching your freelance business light on creden-tials, you might want to investigate this further.

Station promotions and public service announcement copy are probably written or rewritten by employees. Here, too, you may still play a part-time role with the station. Comedy quippery can be also lucrative, but only if you have the peculiar turn of mind that can produce hilarity on demand and in great volume.

But there are more dependable opportunities:

■ Regular programs of five or ten minutes (or more) once or several times a week on topics of special interest to you and listeners—the outdoors, hunting and fishing, cooking, consumerism, travel.

■ News programs aimed at special-interest groups to which you have a pipeline—minorities, senior citizens, residents of outlying com-munities, farmers.

■ Editorials promoting the station's viewpoint. (These are very often ghostwritten.)

■ Series of public information segments around which advertising can be sold in special campaigns—back-to-school tips, Christmas safety, local history anecdotes, outstanding area personalities, or whatever appeals to you and the ad manager of the station.

■ Interview or talk shows that require more background or prepara-tion than station announcers are interested in investing.

Freelancers have one big paradox in their favor when proposing these kinds of projects. It's the media's age-old quandary: Local pro-gramming draws local listeners and local interest, not to mention lo-cal advertisers—but costs far more to produce and air than canned programs created elsewhere. Small stations have neither the staff nor the time to do as much original community broadcasting as they'd like. As with a gap in newspaper staff coverage, these weak spots in ra-dio or television programs present an entrée to creative freelancers.

Like the other media, radio and television exist—at the very bottom line—to make a profit for their owners. The profits come from the sale of advertising. Any idea you propose, therefore, stands a good chance of being accepted if it will appeal to listeners or viewers whose attention, in turn, will cause advertisers to brighten.

The classics in my part of the country are hunting and fishing programs. One well-known full-time outdoors writer, though he had no previous experience in radio, produces five-minute broadcasts run during drive time on local stations; their sponsorship by outdoors firms is almost guaranteed.

You may be able to adapt your own writing specialty to the same practical considerations, especially on radio. Consider topics that interest not only you, but their potential audiences and sponsors. If you write regularly about cooking, for example, how about a program on gourmet masterpieces? Grocers or retailers of kitchen equipment might be interested in supporting you. If you're well informed on travel, how about travel agencies, airlines, and hotels?

Another approach is also possible for news in the public interest, even that which has no automatic moneygrubbing associations. Radio and television stations are licensed by the government and need to demonstrate, at renewal time, that they are serving the public interest. Civic-minded programming can help them satisfy this requirement and also lend that local touch to the program schedule that means so much to faithful listeners.

Senior citizens' news falls into this category around here. So does a talk show concentrating on Indian issues and guests. Programs related to local charities and worthy causes can also provide good material for your freelance program—and help build up a public service record for the station that sponsors you.

Use your hourly rate as a benchmark for remuneration for your broadcast efforts. You may have to start off at a lower total income if your goal is to have your program aired by more than one station (as outdoor programs often are); if station management is doubtful about your program's drawing power among its listeners, you may also want to start at an amount less than your ideal hourly income. But if this is the case, be sure that your fee goes up as the program's success (in terms of attracting listeners and advertisers) is demonstrated. Like everyone else, broadcasters seldom give raises in payment based solely on merit or gratitude. If you don't ask, you'll probably make beginner's wages for as long as you pursue the project.

Everyone benefits from local freelance programming: you, of course, but also the station, the advertisers, and the listeners. The station can sell your sponsorship at a premium because you reach a selective, interested audience. The advertiser not only reaches customers with his message; he also gains a bit of philosophical fallout for taking an interest in supporting sportsmanship or gastronomic excellence or whatever you've cooked up.

Producing your own radio programming may smack of stardom to you. (Actually, it's something less than that, but you *can* count on at least a tinge of notoriety in your community.) There are other freelance assignments associated with radio, however, which might be equally or more lucrative in the long run.

Writing commercials can be financially rewarding and often downright fun. Packing a substantial message into a tiny bit of time with thirty well-chosen words is a challenge that reminds me of crossword puzzles or party word games. Humor is welcome in advertising, and you can be as creative as possible to help distinguish your message from the audio clutter around it.

You have two avenues to freelance copywriting of commercial messages. One is to approach the advertising managers of local radio. Their own copywriters are traditionally overworked, and they may welcome an opportunity to shift some of their work load onto capable freelancers.

The drawback in freelancing for stations is the payment. Station copywriters are not only worked to a frazzle, they're also underpaid, as a rule. While a freelancer should always expect more than the going hourly salary for similar services (remember all the money you save clients?), the top limit is apt to be fairly inflexible with station management.

But you can go straight to the source of ad messages, the advertiser himself. A business that books time on radio or television is a good possibility for freelance commercial copywriting. Unless it's a major national franchise with a big ad budget or uses canned co-op commercials provided by the lines it sells, it's likely to rely on copywriters at the stations to come up with motivating nuggets of ad persuasion. Retailers in the small-to-medium range probably can't afford ad agency services for their commercials; yet they're bound to be dissatisfied with the sameness that even a dedicated station copywriter gives to the messages he writes for the advertiser's account . . . and his competitors'.

The advertiser, moreover, is less likely to blink and stammer when you mention your hourly rate. Advertising, even on smaller radio and TV stations, is extremely expensive—a major entry in their annual budgets. To spend that sum without presenting a fresh, clear message that brings in customers is folly. So clients are inclined to substantially reward someone who can make their investment in airtime pay off.

Commercials proven to bring in customers allow you to virtually write your own ticket with local advertisers. So does a flair for the inevitable occasions that elicit advertising with little content but lots of good will—Thanksgiving, Christmas, Easter, the Fourth of July. At all these holidays ad salespersons urge their customers to wish the public well with the verbal equivalents of gooey greeting cards. Yet all the yammering about joy, warmth, patriotism, and motherhood becomes deadly dull over a day's time, sort of like audible wallpaper. Put a flick of originality into those messages—to make the client stand out just a little from the competition—and your holiday shopping or vacation money is assured.

Not only businesses may be interested in your talent for writing radio messages. Nonprofit organizations (those that raise funds for disease research and charitable work, for example), government agencies, service clubs promoting public projects—all need the same kind of skill you provide for commercial clients.

Public service announcements are run at no charge by radio and TV stations for the same benevolent but pragmatic reasons that interest them in your program suggestions: as evidence of their commitment to the public good to offer at license time, as well as to actually serve their listeners.

As with your commercial copywriting, you'll probably submit PSAs double-spaced with extra-wide margins for production notes. You'll seldom, as a freelancer, go ahead and record or film the announcements that are to be issued to stations. That chore is generally carried out by the station's staff (for small organizations, at no charge) or by ad agencies (for the biggies who can afford full campaigns over large geographic areas).

At smaller stations in areas like mine, typed public service announcements are entirely acceptable; they're read over the air by the staff announcers. Direct them to each station's public service director, usually an individual with myriad additional chores who simply opens the mail, screens PSA requests, and inserts them into a logbook for announcers' use. The screening in my area is relatively perfunctory; the critical test is whether the request is for charitable purposes or has a visible profit motive, which is a universal no-no. (Those who want to profit from ads are supposed to pay for them.)

Finally, there is the unique subject of disc jockey quippery. Not many people have the knack of knocking out topical one- or two-liners that can be marketed to radio personalities. If you have this rare gift, you can apply it for moderately good rewards to writing on-air material, either for the nationally distributed humor services like Robert Orben, or by marketing your own material to disc jockeys in your part of the world.

Drop in at a station and talk your proposal over with an announcer whose work you admire. That person will probably be able to show you samples of the publications the station subscribes to. If your own samples sound good, the announcer may agree to pay you a set fee for a set number of jokes and comments on a regular basis.

You won't get rich by providing sharp-edged comments to one announcer; but there's no reason that good material be limited to one. You're free to market the same work to others—provided they're in noncompetitive markets, usually at least 250 miles apart. Work through individuals, not stations, when selling on-the-air material. Disc jockeys are a notoriously nomadic lot; the good ones work hard on their ratings, and fresh humorous material is one weapon they can use in building up their followings and bettering their prospects for the next move.

Television offers many of the same kinds of opportunities you find in radio. But the differences in the two mean that the possibilities for a freelance writer are both better and worse.

Better, that is, if you can convince station mangement to engage you to work on the larger, more expensive, and more committed scale required by TV's programming procedure, advertising rates, and special demands as both a visual and audible medium.

Worse . . . if your local stations are closed to all but full-timers, or if you're not ready to put in the time necessary to do good TV work, or if your personality and inclinations clearly rule you out as television material.

The rule holds true again: The smaller the station, the better the opportunities. Large urban operations may welcome occasional freelance copywriting assistance but little more. Smaller TV stations, however, respond to the same needs that propel radio management— more local programming, better ratings, demonstrable interest among high-ticket viewers who inspire advertisers when gathered around one time slot.

Writing commercials or "continuity" is no one's idea of the glamorous television business. . . . not, at least, at a smaller operation where the job is one step above receptionist. In the very smallest settings, the job may not be even a full-time assignment. In others, those who currently hold the copywriter's title are anxious to tackle other station assignments to broaden their experience, head into more inspiring positions, or simply avoid the inevitable ruts that face those who think in terms of minutes and fractions thereof.

For all these reasons and because good copywriters are scarce in smaller markets, the field presents a freelance or part-time writing opportunity. As with radio copywriting, television work comes in two categories: employment by the station, where you come free with the advertising contracts, and freelance employment among advertisers. The latter pays better and, oddly enough, is often easier to come by.

The TV copywriter has a double challenge. He or she has to create not only a memorable message in capsule form, but a visual accompaniment that catches the eye while the ear is being seduced. Experience in working with audiovisual projects is invaluable background for this work. (The reverse is true too: experienced copywriters are in a good position to go into audiovisual production.)

If copywriting is the bottom of the TV creative heap, producing or even hosting a regular program is near the top. You may have a shot at it if you've compiled an impressive background and reputation as a writer in a consumer-oriented field, or if you find an opportunity to research and write for an on-air personality or locally originated project.

My first experience in television grew out of my background in the news media and availability as a freelancer. Like many public television stations around the country, my area's Prairie Public Broadcasting originates a relatively ambitious amount of local public affairs programming. I was recruited to produce a low-budget "Washington Week in Review," with North Dakota journalists from Bismarck and Grand Forks and Devils Lake and Crosby sharing their insights about the statewide news stories of the past seven days.

Did I have experience in TV control rooms or with video cameras? No, but that barred neither me nor you from broadcast production. Like so many hidden freelance opportunities, it requires not a high-technology expert but someone with the skills of a generalist (not infrequently coupled with the patience of a saint).

As producer of "North Dakota This Week," I was responsible for the "soft" work that led up to the taping and editing of the program. I monitored the state's newspapers and kept in touch with the coterie of journalists who graced our panel at more or less regular intervals. I lined up each week's participants and arranged their travel to the studio in Fargo, a substantial task in a state whose airline service varies from poor to none. I picked each program's topics and prepared a script for the moderator, whose casual style belied the careful work that went into his conversations.

Lack of background in television production didn't handicap me at all. My role was in working with participants, something that comes natural to a writer. The technical side was well covered by the station's regular production crew, who could just as well have been shooting and editing a how-to program on Ukrainian cooking or a college hockey game.

Television production won't bring you fame but it can bring you professional respect. The better you do your job, the more spontaneous, natural, and *nonproduced* the finished program will seem to its viewers. It also offers you an introduction to broadcasting, the satisfaction of mastering a medium most writers regard only with curiosity, and the steady financial return that a freelancer requires. It presents you with a potent new credential as well, one that can easily lead to other forms of video writing and production.

To find your own production jobs, talk with station managers or program directors about their plans, needs, and programming daydreams. Your experience as a writer recommends you (especially if you are a veteran of any related audiovisual field, from educational video to slide/tape), as well as your knowledge of your subject matter and your willingness to consider the station's priorities.

You need not only react to their plans. You can propose your own as well. In both public and commercial television, a sound proposal that serves their viewers and fills their needs will get a serious listen—especially if you've assembled the research and practical expertise to make your idea work. In commercial television, you can even go one step farther: Pre-selling your idea to several potential advertisers is the most convincing endorsement you can bring along.

Rates of pay vary as wildly in radio and television as they do in the no-holds-barred magazine business. You might earn $15 to $25 per spot writing continuity for a small television station or a fraction of that for each page of gags you put into the mouth of a hometown radio personality. Freelance copywriters are paid by the hour or by the spot—seldom well, but on a nicely regular basis.

The production of regular programs or specials demands a different approach. Your hourly rate comes into play in negotiations; while you're unlikely to get the full amount on a long-term project, it offers you a guideline to what you can afford to settle for. So might the program's budget; a percentage may be allotted to its writer much as in non-broadcast video production. Rates in my area vary from several hundred dollars for the script treatment for a television documentary to just under $1,000 for production of a weekly public affairs broadcast.

Slide/Tape Programs

Once the darling of audiovisual departments, slide/tape programs have lately taken a back seat to the more glamorous medium of video. Yet they deserve serious attention, not only for their particular strengths but also for the substantial financial rewards they offer free-lancers. Nor are they limited in any way to larger and more progressive communities; even more than the burgeoning field of video, they're within the grasp of every kind of sponsor and writers in every locale.

Slide/tape programs have two major points in their favor. They offer the ultimate in flexibility. Slides can be switched with ease to keep a show up-to-date, especially when the script is crafted with an eye to adaptability. (Audio tracks, of course, are somewhat more difficult to alter; nevertheless, they can be re-recorded with far less effort than it takes to edit changes into a completed video program.) Even the presentation can be adapted to suit the circumstances under which it is shown. A smooth multi-projector show can be edited down to a single projector and programmer, if need be, with the loss of some degree of style but little problem with content.

Too, they're relatively inexpensive and straightforward to produce . . . and well within your reach, if you decide to take responsibility for the entire creation. Your earnings reflect the degree to which you make each show your own baby. If you're writing a script for a third-party producer, expect a fee derived much as video rates are, based on perhaps 10 percent of the budget.

If you become the contractor for the entire project, you get to keep what's left after the photographer, "talent" (the narrator), recording studio, music license fees, and duplication costs are paid; if you've bid the job correctly, you ought to be able to count on at least 50 percent of the final figure, including your own earnings as writer and director. Even better, you get to add "producer" to your own list of bona fide professional credits, just like those two renowned Stevens, Mr. Spielberg and Mr. Cannell.

My first slide/tape assignments were for scripts alone, presented in manuscript form and sent into the maw of an advertising agency. The agency secured 35mm slides to illustrate the copy, contracted for a narrator and music, and pulled together the many pieces into a polished and impressive whole.

I got my initiation into full-scale production by a fluke—a client who had thought of a writer first when considering a slide/tape program, rather than looking for someone who could take pictures. While I heartily agreed with his judgment, it did cause me some doubts (as it might you), for I'd had no hands-on experience with planning photography or recording the narrative for a project.

Three methods that got me started are just as available to you: common sense, a trip to the library, and enough humility to ask questions of those more experienced in the field than I was at the time.

Common sense is the most useful of the lot. Chances are that you already know how to illustrate an article; if you daydream when you write, as I do, you've probably produced many a mental movie. You also have a lifetime of experience as a consumer of visual images in movies, on television, and through all the slide shows and filmstrips you have absorbed as a student and captive audience.

All this background is ready to tap when you plan your own project. You know more about the rhythms and techniques of the photo side of AV than you may now think you do. You surely know enough to hold your own with the specialists you'll engage to handle parts of your project: the professional photographer and your choice of experienced narrators.

A trip to the library or a bookstore can put more technical information at your fingertips. Kodak has an excellent booklet on producing slide shows. Photo magazines (especially the trade journals aimed at professionals, like *Studio Light* and *Technical Photography*) carry articles on slide show production from a visual point of view. A more thorough overview is presented in *How to Create Super Slide Shows* by E. Burt Close.

These publications may at first baffle you with their talk of multi-image slide shows, dual projectors, dissolve units, and as many ultra-sophisticated techniques as AV wizards can dream up to make themselves difficult to replace. But for your purposes, worry only about learning the basic slide/tape setup: a slide projector (usually a Kodak Carousel), a cassette tape recorder, and a programmer to advance slides automatically by encoded inaudible impulses. You can even skip the programmer and introduce new slides with an inconspicuous tone recorded along with your narration.

Books and articles can give you a chance to learn AV language. But for practical translations of the jargon, your best prospect is detailed, candid conversation with the team of freelance specialists who'll help you create the professional slide/tape production you have in mind.

As I've said, a professional photographer is an invaluable member of the team. Try to find someone locally who does commercial, not studio, work. Though they use their cameras like artists, studio photographers seldom get into capturing live action outside of weddings and other formal occasions. Studio photographers are also accustomed to working with color negative film in larger camera formats. (This refers to the size of the film or negative.) The photographer who's right for you uses 35mm cameras, the only practical size for slide shows, and has thoroughly mastered the ins and outs of working with color transparencies. Don't worry if this doesn't mean a lot to you. It will to your photographer, and you can refer to Chapter 9.

If your community is minuscule, you'll have to work with whatever photographers are available in the area. Just make sure they're used to slide film and candid documentation. A moonlighting newspaper photographer might be your ally, or a college teacher of photography. Or you can solve the problem as handily as I have, and marry a professional photographer to make sure he's nearby when you need him.

The other member of your slide/tape team is a professional narrator experienced with recording on tape, dubbing music and sound effects, and rendering a polished performance of your scripted copy.

Your local favorite radio or television broadcaster is probably the person you need. He has the training and the voice to bring out the best in your script. I've worked with professionals as well as with eager amateurs who had no experience but glorious vocal cords and a willingness to work cheap. In every case, I now would choose the pro over a dulcet-toned volunteer, even if the pro talked like a duck.

My favorite narrator doesn't sound like a waterfowl, however . . . more like the voice of Zeus as a young man. An FM radio broadcaster and TV weatherman, his mellow, fluid voice makes even forecasts of midwinter blizzards sound inviting. Besides his ability to make anything seem reasonable (an asset to a weatherman), he has incredible breath control. That proved to be a real asset while I was still getting the hang of writing for AV, which requires shorter sentences.

Your broadcasting buddy brings another plus to your team besides his performances, however. Most likely he can use his station's studio facilities for recording after hours. He also has access to their extensive library of music already cleared for commercial use. (Never, never just use a popular tune to open and close your production. Songwriters and performers get royalties just as writers do, and you could be in for extra cost and controversy.)

These team members work with you as freelancers themselves. You can choose to pay them personally, passing on their charges in the bill to your client, or you may decide to have them bill clients directly. In either case, your professional interests mesh nicely. They, too, may be approached to produce other AV projects. After you've worked together once, you're likely to be included in other projects drummed up by your two colleagues.

You needn't worry about a big investment if you begin producing slide/tape programs. Your narrator should have access to recording equipment, his station's, or his own. Your photographer always comes equipped. The only piece of equipment you might want yourself is a slide programmer which puts silent impulses on your taped narration. These impulses make a slide projector advance slides automatically during the course of the program without any manual effort or distracting audible beeps or buzzes to signal when a new slide should be shown. The unit can be purchased for about three hundred dollars and hooked into the slide projector I assume you already have; or you can rent it from an audiovisual supply or electronics rental firm.

So you've got the technical side of production down pat. What you need now are clients. Your regular local writing customers may be looking for audiovisual programs to buttress the printed information pieces you've already produced. Or try government and nonprofit agencies with a need to reach the public, or the public relations or personnel managers of local companies. These jobs are found wherever you turn up other commercial writing clients, as we'll discuss in the next chapter. Make your interest in AV known and go out looking for your first project. After it's completed, others will find their way to you through references and hearsay.

Scriptwriting is similar to gathering information for any article. Talk with your client to establish what message you're working to communicate. Who will its audience be? Will it be shown within a preordained period of time, or must it be timeless to allow for future updating? Will it be used in one easily controlled location, or sent out to borrowers all over the area? (They could be equipped with anything from Model T projectors to sophisticated AV labs with cushioned chairs for the audience, which increase average attention spans by at least five minutes.)

The answers to these questions make a great deal of difference in the same way that a magazine's special readership profile influences its approach to topics. One of my first slide/tape programs, for example, was for the state emergency radio network. Much of the information was technical in nature and would be fascinating to other radio specialists—but incomprehensible to the general public. Our audience was to include legislators, who fund the network; law enforcement officers who use it but sometimes don't understand how to get the best from it; and finally, the general public, homemakers' clubs, high school classes, and visiting dignitaries.

The director wanted the program to explain the duties of his chief officers. But the program's life-span was to be forever, more or less, and the people holding these positions could change.

It would not be sent out on loan, so one concern, varied equipment, was eliminated. But it would be carried into the field by agency personnel armed with only the machinery they had on hand: one Kodak Carousel projector, a battered tape recorder-programmer they borrowed from the office next door, and the office extension cord. This ruled out some of the more spectacular techniques we could have used—dual projectors and a dissolve unit to eliminate black space between slides, stereo sound and the like.

We resolved the question of the audience's comprehension of radio technology by taking the safest route, making it understandable by virtually anyone who had no background whatsoever. While this benefited the visiting homemakers, it helped no less the lawmen and legislators who might be loath to admit their lack of expertise. We decided that those better versed in radio technology would be able to question the director after the program, since he would be on hand to show it in person.

The problem of musical chairs with staff positions was also easily solved through one of slide/tape shows' most adaptive features. We mentioned the positions, but not names of the individuals, in the narration. We used photographs of the current personnel to illustrate these portions. If titles are shifted and new managers hired, new slides can replace the old; the narration, which is much harder to alter, can stay exactly as it was recorded.

Slide/tape scripts are usually typed in a special format that allows room for notes about illustrations and sound effects. Double- or triple-space the copy, leaving an extra-generous margin on the left side of the page; about three or four inches is usual.

The script is augmented by a photo-shooting "script" called a storyboard. Block out the approximate number of slides in the program; then sketch out (in words, if you're no artist) the general content needed. You can scribble these views back into the margin of the written script for your own reference; present the storyboard to your photographer with a heart-to-heart talk about objectives.

I have never worried too much about music and sound effects, as the narrator I work with is a master at matching them to my scripts. If you're not blessed in the same way, suggestions for sound additions to the narration should be added at the appropriate spots in your script.

Be sure to mark them off with parentheses so they don't slip into your flowing prose when it's being read for posterity.

A few hints may help you plan your first program. Length is limited not by the engrossing material you uncover, but by the attention span of an audience usually parked on hard folding chairs or sweaty plastic seating. Fifteen minutes is a good outer limit.

Plan to use lots of slides. For some reason writers become niggardly when allocating slides, perhaps hoping to avoid distraction from their precious scripts. In practice, slides work in just the opposite way. Good illustrations highlight your script, while bad shots or too few shots create boredom over the best of sound tracks. One slide per fifteen seconds is none too many; five or ten seconds each is a better ratio. Of course, if you get into elaborate shows involving two projectors (or more) you'll need more slides than for a straightforward project. Series of slides flashed quickly on the screen create a feeling of motion that is an improvement on the choppy slide-advancing rhythm.

A "good" image for slide show purposes isn't necessarily one you'd choose for your living room wall. It's one that augments the script—tells a little more, or makes an idea clearer, or merely occupies the audience visually while the narrator delivers a phrase that demands more of their attention.

Your first indication that a slide is up to your standards is that it's in absolute focus. While most people edit slides on a light box or by holding them in front of a window (daylight's closer to what they'll really look like), you must go through your slides at least once in a projector to check for sharpness. Slides are tiny; what looks focused when you eyeball it can look like flannel when projected the size of wallpaper across a screen. Out-of-focus slides give viewers headaches, not to mention the trouble they cause the poor woman trying in vain to focus her projector.

Artistic merits, in slide shows, are secondary to clarity. Simple, uncluttered images are best. Backgrounds should be quiet or harmonious, allowing the subject to dominate the screen. Good color is vital; you've probably seen, as I have, embarrassing sequences of slides that are greenish, half off horizontal, and which decapitate or cripple the subject by awkward positioning of her figure. Throw out every slide that fits this description, even if it's your only picture of a Tasmanian wombat. When you're really in a pinch, you're better off with an artist's rendering, a graph, or some other diversion than a photo that causes gastric distress. (Incidentally, those Martian-green indoor slides that turn up so often are caused by using film color-balanced for daylight in a room lit by fluorescents, which have an entirely different color temperature. Blame them on your photographer; she certainly should have known better.)

I look for one other nicety when editing slides: I want all horizontal views. While some perfectly acceptable slide shows use both horizontal and vertical pictures, they're an unnecessary distraction for viewers. Choosing all horizontals also makes your task easier if the slide show is to be converted to a filmstrip, since filmstrips rely without exception on that format.

Watch out for clients who just want you to write a script to accompany slides already in hand. The slides in hand almost always are of the wrong subjects, have that greenish look, or were recently recovered from a crushed file folder, a drawer into which mimeograph fluid was spilled, or a shoebox unearthed in the storeroom. You find that you're writing around an impossible collection of images. When the script ends up choppy and awkward, you—the writer—will probably be blamed.

You want to produce good programs. One good program leads to another, for nowhere in the country are slide/tape shows not received with interest. As a freelancer, your charges are much more reasonable than the client's other alternative for production, an advertising agency. You may also find that your community has never had anyone making really professional AV productions. One good effort then raises the standards of all who see it, creating more business for you in the future.

11

Bread and Butter Writing

Your career as a freelance writer has all the elements of good drama: an unusual setting, a struggling hero, unexpected joys and sorrows, and the potential for a happy ending.

Now it's time for a word from your sponsor.

All the highs and lows of a writing life can be underwritten by commercial writing in your own neck of the woods.

Scoff. You're entitled. You don't read about such things as annual reports, brochures, publicity campaigns, grant applications in books about Making It as a writer. But those are the financial support beneath some of the brightest writing careers in the country.

Sure, you've never read about them in author's bio-notes on book jackets or in the little italicized comments at the end of a magazine article.

Yet it remains an uncontestable truth that you can smooth your creditors' furrowed brows while launching your freelance livelihood by finding and fulfilling a whole spectrum of unsuspected local assignments. They go under myriad respectable names—public information, public relations, research and information, consumer education. They're all commercial jobs; you're engaged and paid, not by an editor, but by a client who wants what your words can accomplish for his company, his public agency or, as often as not, himself.

Commercial writing. Does it sound like a step down from the lofty books, articles, and media work we've been examining? It's actually a step up in dependable financial support. Commercial jobs, in my experience, are more likely to return your necessary hourly income without argument or compromise. It's a step sideways in technique. The same skill you use to gather and concoct other writing assignments serves you well in working for a commercial master.

A master—is that it? That aspect of commercial work is, I think, the reason it can be a step down in just one category: status. If you've worked in the news business, you know that reporters regard flacks as hack writers (and, privately, as people who make more money than reporters, which is immoral).

That attitude dies hard. And yet many of the newspapers I'm familiar with would be sorely pressed to cover their territories with the thoroughness they value if their flow of public statements from politicians and authorities were cut off; if no more business news releases filtered down to the business editor; if no food distributors or clothing manufacturers or home decorating companies sent recipes, fashion hints, and interior design tips to their women's or lifestyle editors; if information centers sponsored by industry weren't there to fill in the sketchy background on stories of even the slightest technical nature; and if all the sports departments of the world no longer got a steady flow of photos, bios, and news releases from college and high school athletic promoters.

The dignity of any assignment is in the eye of the acceptor. You may never know what commercial reasons led to a magazine sale, but they're there nonetheless. Books are published in the hope they'll make a profit. Outright commercial assignments come with no less practical purposes. The difference is that your clients are up front about what they hope to gain from your work. Layers of editorial and publishers' swathing protect you from that knowledge in many other markets.

If you dig back far enough in the origins of this insidious attitude, I think you'll find the traditional antipathy between artists and businesspersons. You may be an artist, but you're in business, too. (A respectable common ground for you and your business clients.)

The wealth of commercial writing opportunities in good old Bismarck surprised me, as I've told you, when I was taking my first excited steps toward freelancing. Wherever I found an organization that needed to get its message to the public, I had a potential freelance writing client. Their reasons vary—some want to persuade, others aim at pure information, and still others forge a combination of those two motives to promote their projects, their ideals, or their products.

Sometimes, I've found, their reasons are more ambiguous than anything else. While some commercial clients do know exactly what they want written, many more have only a general idea that something needs to be done. Not precisely what it is, or who it's for, you understand—filling in those blanks is going to be up to the writer.

As a freelancer, you're a temporary partner of the client who contracts for your services. You have to work together to find out what her needs really are in the way of written work. Together, you arrive at the best way to fulfill them.

Freelancers from outside your client organizations really are in a better position than staffers to identify and analyze many of these needs. Staff members have been steeped in the traditional dos and don'ts of the company. Their familiarity with how things have always been done can hamper the ability to see problems in a new light. They're bound, by their salaries, to hallow sacred cows that an outsider (benefiting from ignorance) can ignore.

Commercial work varies most from writing for other kinds of publication in who ultimately gets credit for your work. In magazine and book writing it usually reflects on you. In commercial work, your clients bask in the glow of your job successfully done, or carry the burden of factual errors or mistaken approaches that affect their ability to reach their chosen segments of the public. Most commercial publications carry no bylines. In fact, their creator's identity is only rarely considered; the few readers with a real interest are other potential clients who observe and remember a job that served its purpose well.

But don't let the anonymity of commercial work convince you that it doesn't deserve your better efforts.

Commercial writing does have a mercenary nature, to be sure; your writing is not to satisfy a Muse or a cause, but a straightforward exchange of product for payment. But so is all the work you take on in the course of your freelancing.

The real reason so much commercial writing is mediocre, I think, is that the writers sometimes felt they didn't have to respect it. Much of it is put together carelessly by nonwriters, to be sure. Yet I've seen enough dull, pedestrian commercial prose composed by ostensible professionals to wonder.

The assumption that commercial jobs are something less than magazine or newspaper writing has led some highly competent people to write down to their clients—to turn out work that'd make a beginner blush—work they'd never consider foisting off on an editor but which they think is par for the commercial course. It's all too easy to act out your worst expectations: If commercial writing is a routine mechanical exercise to pay the rent, then it gets written routinely, mechanically, and confirms these low opinions.

If you believe you can toss off a less-than-professional product for a client just because it is, after all, public relations work, you may be quite sure that what you've written won't be something you'll point to with pride. Of course you'll make excuses for it. You should.

Just because commercial work pays better, is readily available, and even appears almost unbidden at the far-flung freelancer's door is no reason to underestimate the quality of challenges you'll meet in pursuing it.

Commercial work is not free money. You'll work for it just as hard as you do for the most gratifying and ego-satisfying publication. If you're prepared to respect the part you play in bringing information to the public on behalf of your clients, you won't regret trying out this application of your craft.

There are two main assignments for which commercial clients may seek you out. One is to write and produce publications of any kind, from brochures, annual reports, and catalog copy to the newsletters and house organs we looked at in Chapter 8. The other is to plan and carry out information campaigns through the news media, direct-mail contacts, and other routes you chart to reach the interested public. Related to this area are audiovisual projects, discussed in Chapter 10.

Of course, not all clients for commercial writing and production come looking for you. While you're getting started, you'll approach them—in most cases—a time-consuming practice, but one that can't be sidestepped if you're going to use these opportunities to reach your income goal.

Advertising agencies often use presentations to impress and secure new clients. They bring samples of work they've done for customers with whom their quarry will identify, an explanation of the services that they provide, and more than a few fast words about how effective their past efforts have been in reaching donors, increasing sales, or convincing voters.

As a freelancer, you're in a similar position. You have to convince your future client that he needs your services as a writer, that you can provide a full range of help in getting the message into finished form, and that you've already succeeded in achieving these goals for others whom the prospective client respects.

Your presentation needn't be elaborate. A folio of samples is a necessity, along with an edited résumé mentioning past clients or projects. (Be sure that past clients have no objection to being listed. Those who hired you to ghostwrite often do.) Beyond these props, you are your own best evidence that you know how to communicate and can relate well with the person you're calling on. Be pleasant. Be bursting with ideas. And—unless you're encouraged to stay—be brief.

Cold calls are the hardest. You can avoid many of them by choosing prospective clients with an eye to your own personal resources. In which fields or businesses do you already have contacts? Where does your background lie? (My own years with state government provided a natural access to other state agencies I'd already worked with.) What connections can you dredge up—shared memberships in service clubs, in-laws in common, playing racquetball together at the Y? When all else fails, turn to the best recommendation of all: Choose those people whose work you genuinely admire, and offer to become part of their team. Honest respect will get you fifteen minutes of the busiest man's or woman's time.

I've never felt that I was competing with anyone for the jobs I've been hired to do. Many of them didn't exist until I made the right contacts, which suggested to some clients that a project should be begun. A freelancer's availability has often been the reason that a new plan was put into action.

Beyond that, freelancers are positioned differently than advertising agencies, for example, which do compete—ferociously—for accounts. Few agencies deign to take on work that adds up to less than four or preferably five digits: their overhead makes small jobs unprofitable. But the same projects can be extremely lucrative for you.

Once you've convinced a client to try you with an assignment, she's unlikely to look up half a dozen more freelancers and listen to their claims before making a decision. The kind of commercial work in which freelancers specialize usually amounts to small change in the corporate budget. While hiring an ad agency represents a commitment of a chunk of money large enough to demand justification and careful comparison, the projects you'll take on are more of a convenience which an executive can easily work into "fees and services."

What kinds of figures are we looking at? I base my own costs, as I've said, on my basic hourly rate. When figuring a bill, I try to include every minute legitimately spent on a project, including discussions with the client, writing and research, travel time, hours spent working with designers or printers or the news media, the whole works. Yet it's a rare brochure for which I charge more than two or three hundred dollars.

The budget of any brochure includes far heftier sums than my own fees. Printing always equals, and usually doubles or triples, the sum I've billed. Graphic designers who charge by the hour or the job can earn at least as much as I do, especially if given free rein with the artistic side of the project; none seems to do much for less than a hundred dollars.

The client would encounter these costs even if she had her file clerk or sister-in-law patch together some information for a brochure she was planning. By contracting your professional services, she's actually protecting a far larger investment. The best-designed, most finely printed brochure will miss its goal if it is poorly planned and written.

Printed communications

Organizations have any number of reasons for producing publications, from the logical functionality of the annual report to ambiguous institutional brochures cranked out because the competition seems to have one.

Done right, each shares the need for a well-chosen slant, fine-honed selectivity in presenting material, and appropriately flavorful writing to attract and hold readers long enough for the message to sink in.

The answer to those communication challenges has to be concise and punchy. Researchers have shown that a brochure has three seconds flat to catch the casual reader's interest. If his interest is piqued, you gain another thirty seconds to lure him into reading it more fully. Only the best material clears these two hurdles to get the reader's full attention—and unless he's really fascinated, you have three minutes from that point to get your entire message across.

Are you nervous yet? The same quick hook and sticky lead make good magazine articles successful; but as one writer in a big fat magazine, your role in catching readers can be a little blurry. In a publication you've produced yourself, your central role is unmistakable. If you don't succeed, the brochure gets tossed aside without a second thought.

As a freelancer, you face a fascinating challenge when you take on a one-shot publication project. In an all too finite space you have one chance to convey that all-important message to the reader, who's usually no more than casually interested in paying attention to your performance.

And before you ever get to that prospective reader, you've got weeks of work to do. You need to identify your message and your audience, organize your content, and do the actual writing.

But you also have to come up with an orderly design, with or without the help of the fascinating breed called graphic designers. You have to proceed from idea to concrete type and illustrations . . . find a printer who'll do your work at a reasonable cost . . . resist (in most cases) all temptations of gold foil on parchment and four-color art and still create a classy product. Finally, you usually have to badger every party involved to meet your deadline, which is always too close for comfort.

When you're done, if you've done well, you'll get your rewards. A brochure or similar publication that you create from start to finish is among the most satisfying pieces of work you can drop into your sample file.

Don't be overwhelmed by the task of working through the production process—working with graphic design, type, and printing. Those are areas where you can call in your own outside experts to carry the ball. Nor are those areas as difficult to understand as you might think; their mystique lies mostly in your unfamiliarity. Look at the brochures and reports you pick up around town every day. If your pickings are like most I've seen, you're probably sure you can do a better job yourself.

I've handled hundreds of brochures and reports for clients ranging from the Mental Health Association to our local junior college, and can attest to how quickly you become acquainted with the basics of laying out designs and badgering printers. As a nonartist, I've occasionally been baffled about how to communicate my ideas for art or express my reactions to that which I've seen. As a nonprinter, I've been befuddled more than once by talk of printing two-up, saddlestitching, die cuts, color keys and separations. I've learned—and you will, too—not to be intimidated by the technical side of production.

Though parts of the process have little to do with your skills as a writer, you've still got the best credentials to oversee it. You've come equipped with the ability to recognize a theme, present it in a manner most likely to reach the readers, and, with any luck, concentrate on it with enough stubbornness to prevent your goals' being lost from sight.

The production of any printed brochure requires a certain amount of experimentation if you haven't been through the process before. Taken a step at a time, there's absolutely nothing mysterious about it—nothing that requires a degree in graphic design, or public relations.

What you must be is observant. Watch what others are doing in your part of the world. Note which pieces capture your own interest and which leave you cold. When you encounter a real loser, think about how you'd have made it better. (You already do the same when reading magazine articles; just transfer your professional rivalry to these new targets.)

I had a great store of others' printed work on hand when I began—not by design, but because I'd already squirreled it away as a source of potential story ideas and background data. If you haven't already started your own bottom-drawer file of brochures and other printed matter, I'd advise you to start today.

Call it a "swipe file"—but don't be horrified by that hint of larceny. These samples of other work illustrate techniques you can use yourself, in your own way, to improve work you do for clients. Don't waste a second thought on the ethics of so-called copying. There are very few ideas under the sun that haven't appeared in some form before. Every advertising agency I ever visited had its own swipe file of idea-starters stuck away somewhere, collected not only from its own city but from wherever its personnel happened to stray.

Ask yourself three questions when you're considering a piece you really admire: Why was this produced? Who is supposed to read it? Does its style match or contrast with its message?

Any brochure worth the trees that died for it provides answers at a glance through its slant, its choice of material and the graphics and style that flavor it. Slant, selectivity, and presentation. They're what make good printed projects work and poor ones mystify their readers.

The most successful projects, without exception, are those where the writer has a well-organized idea of what his work is to say and who's going to read it. No matter how dazzling the graphics and impressive the printing, fuzzy focus or lack of direction will undercut its effectiveness.

A set of department brochures I revised for our community college, for example, had suffered from an undefined target audience. They were handed out to service clubs and community leaders when the president was called on for a program at the college. They were given to prospective employers of graduates by the placement staff to sum up the educational programs students had completed. And they were also apparently supposed to speak to students' questions about enrollment—which had little or nothing in common with what the local Lions Club wanted to know or the concerns of prospective bosses.

We decided, after a surprisingly lengthy debate, that the material was primarily intended for prospective students. They needed to know what they should have as aptitudes and background, what they could expect to learn in each department's curriculum, and what kinds of jobs they'd be qualified for at graduation. Once this had been determined, the remaining steps—gathering hard information from the teachers, working with a graphic artist on designing covers and layout, and supervising printers and production—were just means to an end.

Another of my favorite projects was an institutional brochure for Pride Industries, a workshop preparing mentally retarded adults for outside employment. Pride needed a piece that would be everything to everyone: information to be used in drumming up community support, in reaching parents of prospective trainees, in finding jobs for graduates, and in approaching potential donors the financially pinched facility desperately needed.

We chose to address the community (instead of the smaller, more specific groups). The folder's simple, inviting graphics carried a clear description of how trainees reach the level of employability on the open job market. Large, uncluttered photos of men and women in training backed up the copy's claims. Only one small panel carried a message referring to the need for financial support. A separate flier with more information on fund-raising was inserted only in those copies that went to possible givers. By resisting the temptation to tell too much, we greatly increased the folder's impact and its chances of being read by those who picked it up.

Ever wonder why you see so many architect's sketches of new buildings on brochures that fund-raisers give you? I think it's because the client was seeing her project from her own point of view inside the institution, and not from the waiting-to-be-courted position of the mildly interested outsider who reads it. That new building may be Nirvana to those housed in the old cramped, musty quarters. Outsiders, though, care only that the program is doing well, that the community needs what it provides, and that their support can help it fill that need even better.

Brochure copy and illustrations call for all your writerly judgment and precision. The standard brochure, an 8½″ × 11″ sheet folded to fit into a No. 10 envelope, allows space for only a few hundred words unless you cram them into microscopic type.

There's just room for the essential, appealing facts. Don't bemoan all the good stuff you have to leave out. Any piece you write is only one link in the communication between your client and his public; you'll live to write more on another occasion.

I usually have a rough layout in mind when I approach a graphic artist to help design a project. That's not because I'm an expert at graphics, but because I love color and felt-tip markers and have a childlike passion for messing around on paper. Giving your artist some idea of the direction you want to take is a good idea, to be sure; but if I weren't so fond of my Marvy Markers, I might concede that providing too much can limit his own approach to the project.

Finding your graphic artist is as important and elemental a pursuit as picking the narrator and photographer you work with on audiovisual projects. I suggest you try to find a seasoned artist working as a freelancer. Some might be set up already as you are; others may have retired to raise families or progressed up someone's corporate ladder past the point of doing artwork themselves.

If your community college has an applied art department, as ours does, you will find a coterie of trained professionals on its faculty willing to do freelance work. Creative art departments may also harbor some excellent designers; but be sure your new team member has a background in preparing artwork for printing. Many artists and art instructors do not, since graphic design shares the same kind of suspicious status in the art world that commercial writing does in your own.

Don't be sidetracked, as I was at first, into using art students to do your design. I've learned the hard way that even the best students lack the experience required to produce a really top-notch layout and design. You're better off, too, working with someone already experienced in carrying out freelance assignments. Your hands are full enough with writing copy and supervising production without also teaching a newcomer the ins and outs of conducting a freelance business.

Alternately, you might want to learn the basics of layout and graphic design yourself. That local college art department may have an evening course designed for those whose vocational fields are other than art. Just be sure it's not a basic art course; though those classes can be fun, tips on oil paints and landscapes are ill-adapted to graphic design.

There are several very good books explaining the basics of graphic art production and printing stocked at the local library. After you've become fluent in the jargon of the trade, you'll find you're capable of communicating with printers and coming up with rough layouts that can be transformed into finished art at reasonable cost.

After you have the copy typeset you and your artist can produce the finished master version of your brochure ready to be printed, called a paste-up, yourselves. You may also choose to have this mechanical work done by the printer's own art department, which usually performs it at a most reasonable charge.

Both you and your art partner should have a say, along with the client, about the paper on which it's to be printed, the colors of ink, and the special effects selected to dress it up. You'll want to decide beforehand and then call several printers for price quotations. (You may be surprised how dramatically those quotes can differ for the same job.)

Once the project is in the printer's hands, you sit back and wait for the next development. Such as delivery two weeks later than promised. Such as having the inside printed upside down (or worse!). But in most cases your real surprise will be what a polished, good-looking piece of information you've succeeded in producing.

Of course, not all commercial publications allow you as much latitude as brochures. Annual reports, for instance, closely follow a prescribed format. You can translate business jargon into English or brighten it with striking illustrations. But an annual report is still what you have to end up with; vary it too much, and you've created something else altogether.

Other commercial jobs offer much warmer receptions to creative copy and design. A catalog aimed at consumers can be a pure joy to conceive. With the enormous expansion of direct-mail and retail or wholesale catalog selling across the country, your chances of becoming involved in such a project are far better today than ever before.

You find catalog work by following leads to businesses who need printed inventories of their stock—gift shops or department stores, of course, but also wholesale distributors of plumber's pipe, suppliers to do-it-yourself mechanics, and manufacturers (smaller book publishers, perhaps?) looking for a conduit to businesses. Those who've issued catalogs in the past are the best initial prospects. Printers may also have leads on businesses considering new publications, since the first step in producing one is often looking for bids on printing cost.

Catalog work is the best exercise you can give your store of adjectives. Writing descriptions is a circumscribed process, limited by length, similarity of products, and legal rules on false advertising. If you say it's warm and cuddly, it had better be just that; if it's plumber's pipe you're pitching, your claims and measurements had better be exactly on the mark.

Catalog work pays either by the hour or by the printed page. If you find you have a facility for striking, succinct descriptions of hubcaps or fine china, you'll find the per-page payment more rewarding, as hourly rates are rarely on par with the figure you use for a benchmark.

Producing any kind of commercial publication freshens your thinking, and fresh thinking is a necessity for the freelance writer. Too, my commercial endeavors have filled me in on a dozen subjects that I'd been curious about or never dreamed of; all this is fodder for more traditional kinds of writing.

The danger is that commercial work may be too seductive—that it'll capture more and more of your time, cutting down on the writerly work you began freelancing to accomplish. But finding yourself struggling to apportion your time between too many fascinating projects is good trouble. You'll never be bored again.

12

PR Prospects

As a commercial writer on the loose, sooner or later you'll be approached to take on a media campaign. It's a tribute to the news media's impact that every special-interest group in town—government, business, charity, religion—is eager to harness them to carry their message to the reading or listening public.

There's no special trick to producing the mundane, monotonous news release—a page or two of double-spaced copy liberally larded with mentions of your client's product or project. It works . . . not well, but well enough to satisfy most media groupies and allow you to collect your fee.

But working with the news media can be much more rewarding, both for you as a writer and for your client. No matter who the media are in your part of the world—a rip-and-read radio station and a county seat news weekly, or several competing TV stations, a daily newspaper and a host of eager radio AMs and FMs—you can serve them as well as your client with a good, professional media program.

You can use your skills and savvy to bring people out for a nursing home's ice cream social and to air a politician's rebuttal. You can help the public learn more about screening clinics for diabetes or free immunizations against the flu; you can aid a business in presenting its story to the public or help consumers use their products more wisely.

Performing these public-spirited functions can be an excellent source of income for the freelancer with one eye on his income goal. These jobs are readily obtainable, they work into your weekly writing schedule without major adjustments, and they pay well for the generally enjoyable duties they entail.

Freelance writers can be the very best choice for handling media campaigns . . . and the right prefreelancing background is a great help. Years spent in journalism (newspaper, television, radio, or wire service) or corporate or governmental public relations are optimum. That experience gives you automatic familiarity with the means by which news is made.

If you lack that familiarity, you need a crash course from those who have it. The *Public Relations Handbook,* a weighty anthology, can provide some insight; another good book is *Professional Guide to Publicity* by Richard Weiner. (Libraries may have both of these out-of-print titles.) The Public Relations Society of America has an excellent series of booklets on every aspect of publicity campaigns.

Talk to successful staff publicity people. Meet with news directors and a city editor or two to learn exactly what they'd like to see. The purpose of your reading and questioning should be to demythologize the news media. If you share too much of the public's awe of headlines, you won't be able to effectively feed your client's information into them.

Learning how to work with the news media is a fascinating educational pursuit, and if you've got reporting experience under your belt, you already know how many other news releases yours will have to compete with for a limited amount of space. Standing between you and that public are the reporters and editors who decide what, finally, is news in your community on any given day. To get your message to the public you'll have to convince these astute observers that it's interesting and worthy of being used to fill their precious space or time as a legitimate story.

You also, incidentally, empathize with the skepticism with which news releases are greeted by news editors. Since releases are sponsored and produced by a client, they're immediately put to the test of public interest versus the client's private agenda.

Yet news releases and those who write them perform a valuable service at all kinds of papers and stations, from the very smallest to the largest. The smallest may use their offerings to fill space that otherwise would have to be taken up by the product of expensive staff time. The largest—those with sizable reporting staffs—can afford the luxury of checking out or, at least, rewriting your releases.

What do they have in common? In every case, they depend on you and your counterparts to keep them in touch with what's going on in the community. Without news releases of employee promotions, new branches opening, and new lines added, most business editors (a traditionally overworked breed) would have only the thinnest columns in their Saturday business pages. Without nonprofit charitable groups' releases on recognizing or treating diseases and handicaps, many women's or lifestyle editors would find their sections sparse on Sunday.

And without the kind of continuing, pointed communication with the public provided by a steady stream of news releases, the editors of every department would be more isolated than they care to be from coming events, community concerns and, yes, even ambitious politicians' thinking.

Once you've established yourself as someone who can deal with the media, you have three ways to charge clients for your services. One is by straight time billing for all your assistance, based on your established hourly fee. Another is to agree on a flat rate for the job, based again on your fee and the hours involved, but computed as one sum. (This is especially helpful when dealing with clients who, unaccustomed to dealing with freelancers, gape at the mention of an hourly rate as substantial as yours.)

The third method is to receive a retainer and remain available to handle the client's media work as the need arises. Because it guarantees the receipt of a check of a certain size each month, some writers and most public relations agencies prefer it.

I don't. It seems to me the retainer system is an unnecessary security blanket that encourages a lot of wasted time on my own part and money on the client's. While payment is supposed to average out with services performed over a period of months, I've found that the issue of that check creates a desire in the client to get her money's worth—right now, whether media contacts are appropriate or not. At the other extreme, you might go for months with few demands placed on you and then be called to take on an unexpected and time-consuming project. The client, who's been helping support you during quiet times, justifiably expects you to drop whatever else you're working on and come to her aid. With freelance deadlines and work loads as unpredictable as they are, you cannot count on being at her beck and call.

I prefer to take on each job as a discrete unit, wrap it up nicely, and present an equitable bill. I believe this is fairest to my clients. It also allows me to keep my independence. Last-minute callers are forced to be realistic about my other commitments. In the long run, I seem to come out at least as well financially as those who cling to the security of retainers.

So you certainly needn't feel like a mendicant wheedling favors from the news media when you're involved with news releases and press conferences. The function the writer fills is an important and persuasive one; the better you fill it, the more you learn about communication yourself.

News releases come with as many motives as there are clients waiting for your services, or trying to get along without a writer's help. Usually you can count on their belonging to three distinct, but overlapping, groups.

The promotional: These are the workhorses of the news release world. They're probably the kind you think of first—announcing to the public that a car wash, rummage sale, open house, or arts-and-crafts show is coming up on a certain date at a certain place and time. These stories cause the widespread public confusion between news and advertising, since in a sense they really are "free advertising." (Editors wince at those ill-fated words.) But they're also legitimate information for media who pride themselves on informing the public. Investigative reporters are often chagrined at how members of the public value these promotional stories more highly, in many cases, than their thorough, insightful articles, which give a well-rounded picture of an issue . . . but don't do a thing to get folks out for the benefit auction.

The informational: This second type of release embraces the gamut of information offered the public, from straight stories of employees' promotions or attendance at banking school to elaborate human-interest features on advances in the treatment of cystic fibrosis.

These stories can be difficult to recognize when they reach the news columns. They may be helpful pieces on how to use a particular mustard in preparing wonderful picnic foods, or travel stories that mention the pluses of vacationing in RVs . . . a certain model, by the way.

They're the staple of business and women's sections on many smaller newspapers, though routinely laundered of their obvious brand-name connections. But never mind; a certain number will mention that company's mustard, and anything that gets the customer thinking "mustard" will be of ultimate benefit to the firm which commissioned the release.

United Funds across the country use this principle in creating "hard" news—that they've reached a certain percentage of goal, week after week, until the moment they hit the top (and prompt an editor-assigned photograph on the front page of the newspaper's local section). So do ethnic associations, helping build a public sensitivity to the pain caused by the more subtle forms of prejudice.

The argumentative: Public figures' statements to the press generally start out as news releases. When an up-and-coming local politician gets his name in the paper again and again, commenting on his opponents' doings or sayings, you can be sure he has initiated it.

During the legislative season, many apparently spontaneous controversies begin as press releases issued by someone ready to fight. The replies, too, come in by mail. Reporters are sensitive to these challenges and rebuttals that use them as a medium; but since such exchanges are often of public interest (if only because crowds always gather for a good fight), they generally continue to accommodate the ever-more-public figures.

Candidacies begin with news releases and carefully planned news conferences. So do "waves of public support," often originating at a typewriter of the association that endorses the candidate's position.

These pieces, of all the types of news releases, are most apt to be mistaken for "real" news . . . and reporters' acceptance is heightened by the urgency they convey. When the media pick up on these released statements and pursue them on their own, they're demonstrating the thin line between public relations and straightforward news.

All of these releases provide both direct and indirect access to newspapers for you and your client. First, your story may be used as you prepared it. But it can also produce the best kind of repercussions: By creating media interest in your client, it might initiate thorough and ongoing coverage of his programs or industry.

One little news release cast adrift on the sea of information can have only a limited impact, unless its message is momentous, like the adoption of a new homestead act or a decrease in local taxes. In most cases, it will carry only the most superficial kind of information to the public.

The secret of a good media campaign is repetition and goal setting. By planning not one, but a year's worth of news releases and other contacts with the news media, you can help create a much deeper understanding of the message you're trying to communicate to the public.

That's the reasoning behind the old adage "I don't care what they say about me, as long as they spell my name right." But since most of your clients will be looking for genuine understanding of their goals, rather than voter recognition in the polling booth, you'll be aiming for more than mere reiteration of a name.

You may also want to consider how exposure you get through the mass media can be built upon through other avenues. Look to newsletters, upcoming programs, and face-to-face contacts with the client's own constituency (whether members of a nonprofit group or a store's customers), where this information can be discussed in greater depth and detail.

But before you can build on anything, you have to master the techniques of reaching the right people in the newspaper, television, and radio news worlds.

In war, you're counseled to know your enemy. In the competitive arena of public relations, you'd do well to know your friends. Knowing the reporters and editors who will receive your client's releases can save you a lot of time and unsatisfied curiosity about whether or not a story you've written will suit their needs and, thus, be used.

The three most valuable contacts on your daily newspaper staff are the city editor, the business editor, and the women's editor (or "lifestyle," or "family," or whatever term is used locally).

The city editor is your gateway to local and state news of general interest, the great bulk of the newspaper. This person is both influential and extremely busy. She oversees the staff of general-assignment reporters who may be assigned to your subject area, and makes the decisions about whether to cover specific events and controversies.

Since the city editor always has a tight schedule, you may want to ask her if you should talk to one of her reporters. You can spend much more time with the reporter, as a rule. You should be able to develop an ongoing interest in your subject area by helping her master the basics, providing background information and story leads. But the editor is the one who ultimately decides whether a story makes it or not; so meet her first.

The business editor, on all but a few major newspapers, is a harried individual who relies heavily on businesses themselves for news tips. This may change in the future, as editors recognize the wealth of vital information and juicy story ideas awaiting them in the business community. But in the meantime, the business sections of all too many papers (and business segments on TV) depend on news releases issued by those the stories mention.

After talking with your business editor, you may find this is a fertile field for stories about trends, personalities, and other topics in your client's area. Chances are the editor will be glad to receive something unusual to enliven her section. On many smaller dailies, including our local paper, business news is too often confined to announcing which real estate salespeople have changed firms, which door-to-door salesmen have won sales awards this month, and who's been hired or retired at local banks.

The women's editors of this country are the unsung heroines of hundreds of good causes. Their section seems to have a deeper commitment to public service topics than any other department of the average newspaper (just as the woman who hosts the afternoon talk show on your local TV station is more interested in charitable works than anyone else on the staff).

Women's departments or their renamed counterparts tend to be the best targets for coverage of health-related stories, consumer articles, benefit events, and education topics. Since they usually have a specific number of pages to fill in every edition—and often are understaffed—the editors are generally receptive to longer, detailed stories that can readily be edited to fit a given news hole. They can also be counted on to do the original follow-up stories that mean so much to public awareness of your client's goals.

How do you find out who these people are, much less what they want of you? You read (or watch) their work closely. And then you stop in to introduce yourself and ask their advice.

Personally meeting your news media contacts is the most worthwhile way you can begin any project. It lets you explain why your message is important and of interest to their audience. It lets them see a face to attach to your name, and inspires a little extra interest when they get your articles in the mail. And it allows them to easily ascertain whom to call for further information on any of the stories you send them. It's the beginning of an easy alliance that can help you get your information across more clearly and prevent editorial misunderstandings from creeping in.

When I was arts editor of the newspaper where I got my start, I depended heavily on organizations to send in news of what they were up to. With a good share of two states within my working territory, I could no sooner know all that was going on than could a sports editor get by without all those proud coaches who call in scores after they've won the game.

One woman, who cared deeply about the local symphony orchestra, set an example of the ideal public relations chairperson. She made an appointment for coffee or lunch once—only once—per symphony season. At that time she'd give me all the background information she had on the upcoming concerts and guest artists, and we'd talk over features that might be developed around them. We'd talk about symphony concerns—how the fund-raising was going, whether the women's auxiliary was planning an active year, the rapidly increasing cost of sheet music. And after we'd said goodbye, we wouldn't see each other for another year, though we'd talk by phone and she'd send updated information by mail.

What Evelyn did was offer me a tiny initiation into her world and its concerns. Our discussions paid off for me in dozens of ways, from ideas for stories to a much better understanding of the symphony. Best of all, our contacts created trust. When I had a question about the symphony, I knew I could count on Evelyn for an honest, informed answer.

I've tried to create the same kind of trust myself in some cases, and—because I've got my fingers in too many pies from time to time—counsel my clients to pay the personal visits themselves. Those chats contribute more to your success in placing stories than could any amount of advice about how many words, how big a margin to leave, or other mechanical tricks of the trade.

Nevertheless, there are a few rules about form that can make your releases look more professional.

The basics include double-spacing on white nonerasable paper with a deep top margin and generous room left on the other three sides of each sheet. In an upper corner, offer a name and telephone number to be called for further information. If the moment of release is crucial, note the right day and time. But be forewarned that news desks tend to be too busy to worry about filing and saving releases; involved instructions on timing any but the most earthshaking announcements cause editorial pain. To be safe, don't mail your release too early (if timing is a problem), and note "for immediate release" at the top.

The guideline on length is the shorter, the better. But don't adhere to this logic so closely that meaning is lost to brevity. It's more important to convey your point than to be short at all costs. If you run longer than one page, make sure the critical information (the who, what, where, when, and how) is in your first one or two paragraphs—insurance against chop-chop editing.

As long as you're going to the trouble of writing a news release, try to make it do the best possible job for you. If an event is going to be held by the Boy Scouts to benefit some charity, tell what that charity is and why the Boy Scouts are behind it. Ice cream socials in the abstract are less than compelling; an ice cream social to buy lifesaving equipment for a rest home might garner a good many more readers' attention and support.

On the other hand, if your release is a less timely, more substantial one—aimed at explaining how to recognize a disease, use a product, or choose a vacation destination, for example—you can allow yourself a bit more luxury in length. Two or three double-spaced pages is usable for most publications. Go longer than a thousand words, however, and they'll run into space problems. The ideal length is probably around 500 to 600 words.

Sometimes this just isn't enough to do justice to the scope of information you feel the public needs. Consider dividing the topic into several subtopics, trimming each installment to a versatile, compact size. You'll want to advise editors that the stories in the series are closely related, and may be most effective if used in consecutive editions. Sometimes they'll accommodate you and sometimes they won't, depending on their own pressures. But if your information really is of public interest, you'll usually be pleased with how they choose to use it.

What about photographs? They can sometimes be a convenience to the publication you've approached. But most naive publicity photos are a total waste of time and money. It's up to you to know your medium's policies and needs.

What kind of action? Study the photos taken by the newspaper's own staff. Guest speakers who visit local institutions, committees arguing over proposals, well-dressed visitors getting down on the floor to play with kiddies in a nursery ward—all sound less than compelling, but stand a far greater chance of being run than the traditional shot of two people shaking hands and staring at the camera.

Your subjects will be stiff in front of the camera during your first shots. Remedy that, and get natural-looking photos, by taking a whole roll of film or even more. After the first few foreboding clicks, they'll become used to the camera and stop making self-conscious jokes about breaking it.

Before you spend a great deal of money on shooting, however, take the precaution of calling the city editor and asking if he might be interested in seeing some photos. Given the track record of publicity shots, the best you can expect him to offer is weak encouragement. If he says anything but "Absolutely not!" you're in business.

If you have reason to believe a newspaper will use your publicity photos, deliver them as quickly after the event as is humanly possible. Photos from a convention that ended three days ago, though weekly papers or trade magazines may still want them, are as welcome as dead fish on a daily's doorstep.

Straightforward head shots of a person who's a principal in your article are appreciated and frequently used, especially if the individual is a prominent member of your community or a visiting personality.

With consumer- and product-related stories, photos are definitely useful to the editors. But check with them before you take any shots or hire a photographer. Many newspapers have firm policies about publicity stills. As a rule, smaller papers tend to be more receptive; the more care the paper invests in its staff photography, the less likely it is to accept yours.

Certain photo ideas which sound brilliant to your client elicit nothing but laughs from the news media. Be wary of the prototypical check-passing picture. You know the kind—the head of a charity accepting a check from the head of a donor group, both flashing gleaming smiles at the camera. There is scarcely a newspaper left in the world that will use those pictures. Speakers shaking hands with the president of the ladies' group who sponsored them are equally deadly.

Appetizing, original photos, on the other hand, are almost always welcomed by editors. Though not every one will be used, because of space considerations and all the little decisions that go into making up newspaper pages lickety-split, the occasions on which they do appear make them worth the effort. Stories with good illustrations invariably get better play—and are noticed more often by the average reader—than those that compete without them.

A photo that may get favorable consideration is simple, and looks as if the subjects didn't know the photographer was present. It involves people acting and reacting with each other, and should be self-explanatory enough that a long typed caption (called a cutline) isn't needed to make sense of it.

Making the television or radio news is a bit different than getting into a newspaper. Often the same news release is sent to all local media. While it may get used all around—especially if it's very timely or newsworthy—its chances are often better in the electronic media if retailored to suit the needs of those who'll read it aloud.

News stories for TV and radio should be shorter than those meant for newspapers. And they should avoid locutions that, though perfectly reasonable when used in print, sound awkward aloud. Run people's titles before their names—"noted author Norman Mailer"—rather than as clauses set off by commas—"Norman Mailer, noted author." Include phonetic pronunciation of difficult names. If you want to make your package look especially professional, consider typing it in the Orator typeface, which uses all capitals for easy readability.

Know a little about your local radio and TV stations before you send them your releases. Most of all, learn whether they have their own news departments or if their news broadcasts are of the rip-and-read variety. If the latter is the case, they're unlikely to use anything you send them. Save a stamp and forgo the temptation.

If you're sending photos to the newspaper, you might also want to consider providing them to TV stations for use with your release. Save your black-and-white prints, however. Though they're the standard for newspaper reproduction, there's not one thing a color TV program can do with them. Provide color 35mm transparencies (slides)—not color prints.

And, be careful whom you send your photos to. Your local radio news director will be happy to joke confidingly about the number of lovely, expensive photographs the station receives with news releases every week. No matter how terrific they are, photos just don't work on radio.

Two other aspects of dealing with radio and television may enter into your media planning. They are the news conference and the public service announcement.

In some parts of the country, scheduling a news conference is the standard way of getting TV and radio coverage and, to a smaller extent, attracting newspapers. This naturally applies only to the most important stories you wish to get before the public and those that are very timely—visiting authorities, fund drive kickoffs, discussions of an important local issue.

Elsewhere, the news conference is used only for items of cataclysmic proportions. Talk to some of your TV friends to find out the traditions in your area.

If you learn that news conferences are commonplace, you'll be able to use them as a shortcut to good coverage. Best of all, they reach the electronic media, who are much harder to attract than newspaper reporters in other circumstances.

Choose your time and place carefully. Because of TV deadlines (and those of afternoon newspapers), morning is often best. Remember that many smaller TV news staffs don't come to work until 9 a.m. or later, as is also the case with smaller morning papers whose push comes in late afternoon. Ten in the morning is generally an ideal time. Days earlier in the week are also more effective choices. Mondays are usually slow days in the news business, while Fridays tend to be very busy. Only skeleton crews work weekends.

Select a location that's easy to find and offers these important features: a simple, plain background for your speaker, and lots of electrical outlets for video and radio equipment.

Prepare a written statement and, if necessary, written background information to give to reporters as they come in. Though your speaker may repeat this material verbally, a written reference can be a real help.

Allow about five minutes for an initial statement and then open your conference to questions. If it's slow going, you might want a staff person on hand to ask a few starters.

Above all, convey your central message as clearly as you possibly can. Try to keep press conferences uncomplicated. The setting lends itself to striking single statements rather than involved technical data.

The other special electronic-media technique you can use is the public service announcement. If you're promoting an event of some kind that's open to the public, a PSA can be a source of free publicity that can equal or surpass a small paid ad campaign.

Unlike newspapers, radio and TV stations are licensed by the federal government; and with this licensing comes the obligation to serve the public's interest. For smaller stations that can't afford a great deal of original public service programming, this often takes the form of frequent PSAs, which are in essence unpaid mini-ads.

A good public service announcement should be short—no more than fifteen or twenty seconds when read aloud. It should be as clear and direct as you can make it, because it's rarely supported by any kind of visuals (especially on radio!). Double-space it on plain white paper, using Orator type if you have it handy.

When a radio or television station has used your public service announcements, it's simple courtesy for a member of your organization to write them a letter of thanks. It not only shows your appreciation; it also gives them concrete proof that they're meeting the community's needs when relicensing time rolls around.

Saying thanks, in fact, is a good policy to follow in all your dealings with news staffs.

Too often people engaged in pursuing what they consider good causes forget that the news media have no real obligation to cover their stories. The media's obligation is to the public who reads or watches their news, not to those who want to reach that public through their good graces.

Of course they should be serving the community, and of course you've done them a favor in bringing a worthwhile subject to their attention.

But remember to say thank you.

The news media get all kinds of responses when people disapprove of what they've done, but rarely earn more than a resounding silence when they've done a good job that benefits their audience as well as special-interest groups.

Say thank you. Call it or write it. You'll find it does more for a continued pleasant working relationship than all the free lunches your client's budget can hold.

Grants

Another kind of public relations effort stands distinct from all the others. It's writing grant applications and reports. Though the general public never notices them, they're a fact of life (indeed, lifeblood itself) for many agencies of government, nonprofit charitable and educational institutions, and even individuals looking to better themselves under someone else's philanthropic support. While the changing tax climate and federal cutbacks have had a serious effect on organizations that count on this support, grants continue to offer at least a degree of opportunity for those tenacious enough to ferret out surviving programs.

Grants have an intimidating reputation.

Do they make you think of Rockefeller's foundation, and Ford's? Of endless piles of bureaucratic forms and certifications? Do you imagine foundations paying writers to spend months ensconced in comfortable isolation "for art's sake"? Do you fancy piles of money there for the asking? Or, conversely, such fierce national-level competition that they might well be labeled "elite only"?

Make friends with the grant-writing process, as well as those wonderful people who hand out the money. It might be one of the best things you do for the sake of your geographically underprivileged writing career. No matter where you live, there are foundations and other potential grant-makers whose purposes and contacts with groups they fund hold promise for your salable skills.

A handful of grants is distributed each year to fund artistic works in progress. Among these, grants to writers are few and far between. If your work borders on Bellow or is well received in national poetry circles, you might investigate further, most notably into the National Endowment for the Arts.

On the other hand, if your aspirations (like mine) are more on the order of craft than Art, your chances of getting a grant yourself are not at all strong. But your chances of working on grant applications (as a writer who can prepare a readable, persuasive proposal for the funding agency's consideration) are very good indeed.

I have seen dozens of grant proposals that were drafted in Bismarck then sent winging their ways all over the country. Most of them had two things in common: They were shots in the dark whose prospects were as poor as the results they achieved. And they were the dullest piles of pages ever. Deadly dull. If I were the foundation director who had to plow through those wordy, stilted, self-consciously erudite packets of pontification, even I—who greet the postman's arrival as I do Santa Claus's—would get an unlisted mailbox.

Do you see a mission here? A writer who can bring to grant proposals good will and clarity of communication is like a breath of mountain air. If you choose to hire out your skills in the grants field, you'll find you can accumulate any number of grateful customers—grateful, because they hate writing dull, ineffective proposals as much as you'd hate reading them, and "customers" because the financial stakes are high enough that they can well afford to pay a writer to increase the odds of success.

Who prepares grant proposals? They might be nonprofit charitable groups or professional associations looking for outside financial support. Or government agencies designing pilot projects in cooperation with local groups. Or community-based committees organized to find a way to fill some special local need.

The grant-seekers could be requesting support for a shelter for battered women . . . planning a series of informational meetings on public policy . . . trying to convince someone to buy the local YMCA a few dozen volleyballs to keep troubled youngsters off the streets . . . or asking for equipment to better treat hospital patients. Imagine the most exotic scheme to solve a social ill, and the most mundane, fundamental local need possible: Chances are that grant-seeking groups in your own area have equalled the wildest and most basic and every conceivable degree in between.

Over twenty-six thousand incorporated foundations exist around the nation, funded by families or corporations or a mixed bag of special interests. Though the majority are headquartered in New York and along the eastern seaboard (with offices, no doubt, right next to the editors to whom you've been writing), almost every state has anywhere from a few dozen to a few hundred located within its borders. North Dakota, of course, is the exception. At last count there were approximately five . . . but every one of them was active in supporting projects that fit its definitions of good causes.

As a writer, you may be contacted to help a grant-seeking organization put its case in order. Your role is to clarify the reasons they believe their project is necessary; sort out specifics of how they plan to go about filling this need; develop a plan to evaluate whether the potential project has done its job for the sake of the grantor, and then—after all this groundwork—write a succinct, persuasive grant proposal for your client to present to the foundation it believes will be interested.

Grant writing has a lot in common with the garden-variety editorial query. You'll feel right at home. You'll do initial research to determine where the most salable story lies, then dig a little more to learn how to go about getting it. Finally you wrap it up into a sales letter that falls onto a desk crowded with other queries, before an editor or foundation administrator whose needs and prejudices often can (but sometimes cannot) be foretold by studying past history and stated market requirements.

The best grant proposals are no more than ten pages long, typed double-spaced in what you already know as manuscript form. Granting groups usually require this information:

■ An introduction of about one page which sums up the proposal in an attractive way and gives an accurate boiled-down version of all the material that will follow. Often this is the only part of the proposal automatically read; it has to be good, or the idea truly revolutionary, for the screening committee to want to read further.

■ A summary of who your organization represents and what its purposes are. The group's track record is important; any past successes in comparable projects should be highlighted.

■ A rationale for why the project is needed. If it proposes a shelter for battered wives, is this a widespread problem? Do you have figures? Are there figures now available on battered spouses seeking help? Why was your project's approach selected as the right way to go?

■ A précis of how the project will work. The granting agency doesn't need or want a thoroughly detailed rundown of every move you've planned; all that's really wanted is an overview of how you'll go about using their money and how you'll take the story to the public.

■ A plan to evaluate how the project is working. If you're looking for sponsorship for public meetings, will you pass out evaluation sheets? (Though limited in usefulness, these are the classic cliché of evaluation and rank approximately better than nothing.) Will you follow up existing data? What's really wanted is some indication that the organization applying for the grant plans to assess whether their approach has been effective, rather than taking the money and running.

■ The budget. While you won't be responsible for developing it, urge your group to include not only what they want the foundation's money for, but also what they plan to get from other sources. Government agencies gave birth to the terminology of "hard matching" and "soft matching;" the former means money or tangibles purchased, while the latter includes the blue sky of grant administration—volunteers' time, the use of a corner of somebody's office, a telephone, some photocopies of the grant proposal. Harder is always better when it comes to matching grant money.

You can put this material together in two ways. The traditional method is to break out separate categories under roman numerals in familiar outline form. The more readable style is to put it all together in narrative. If you choose the outline format, try to keep your total package under a dozen pages. More length is not an improvement from the viewpoint of the granting agency, the reader that counts most in these cases.

If you lean toward the narrative—the typical writer's slant, I suspect—try to get your message across in the same space as a long magazine query. Two pages of single-spaced, readable data will gladden the hearts of some screening committee. Five pages is the outer limit.

The tone you want is the same friendly, straightforward, confidence-inspiring one you use in writing unknown editors. Don't be a supersalesperson; but don't go too far in the opposite direction and employ the verbal weapons of academia to sound serious and unassailable. You'll end up sounding serious, all right; total boredom is not to be taken lightly.

Your organization may know which are its most likely funding sources. But if their ideas are still ambiguous, you can add to your proposal's chances by reminding them of a truism in the grant-writing field: The closer to home, the better.

Not only foundations should be considered for the funding proposals you'll help develop. Well-heeled area corporations and state organizations are equally likely to be interested in helping you out, as are some government agencies.

The best question to ask in identifying a funding source is not "Who has the most money?" but "Who can get the most out of this project?"—in public approval as well as actual progress toward goals it supports. Those nearby clearly have more to gain from positive local impact.

I've written grant proposals aimed at national medical foundations, as well as community foundations, university departments that give cooperative education grants, and state organizations, including the Bankers Association and the Farmers Union. I can assure you that local sources, no matter what their structure, are much easier to sell on a grant project. They believe in the betterment of the local (or state) community and benefit from being identified with public-interest issues.

Their self-interest is similar to that of the editors who screen your queries. While you've set out to fascinate the editor, he has to keep his own constituency in mind, whether it's potential readers and advertisers or the public with whom an organization's future good will lies.

Your own self-interest lies, of course, in the commercial side of grant writing. While you might get satisfaction from helping good causes, you need to safeguard your own source of support—and that has a lot of bearing on how you set up your payment.

Some grant writers build their own fee into the budget requested in the grant, so that the applying organization can better afford them. This appeals to your client. It means you have minimal impact on their regular budget, which is already tight or they wouldn't be looking elsewhere for money. The grant writer sometimes feels this gambling approach gives him or her the justification for a larger fee.

The danger is obvious. If your grant proposal is rejected, you may not get a cent for your labor. And the proposal can go down the drain for reasons that have absolutely nothing to do with your role, from an ill-conceived project to simple lack of money to pass around among too many deserving applicants.

Unless you can afford to gamble, require your own payment be a transaction apart from the grant itself. The organization should have enough faith in its own proposal to invest in your services. The cost of professional writing help is insignificant next to what they hope to gain.

There are ways, however, that your services can be built into a grant to help its sponsor make sure the project succeeds.

Most grant projects have a publicity budget, both to reach the public whose needs the grant is intended to serve and to make sure the sponsor gets the credit he expects. Good publicity depends on written communication, from press information plans to published materials for the people the project hopes to reach.

Some grants also rely on outside administration, assuming that the sponsoring group's staff can't take on the extra work. A freelance writer is in an unusually good position to help them make contacts, plan meetings, and take care of details. Unlike most people in the work force, you're free to take on short-term obligations that have a definite termination date.

Finally, you can be on hand to write the second most important document of the whole grant-seeking, grant-administration cycle—the final report.

The foundation or company that gives the money does attach a few strings to it. Of primary importance is that the grantor be informed of what happened to their cash. A financial statement is mandatory, of course. But that final report can be much more (and much more stimulating to write)—a candid, informative tale of the project in action. Such a report is a courtesy to the granting agency, like a long thank-you letter; in addition, it's superb future grant insurance for your client. Chances are they'll want support again some day for another project. A strong, honest final report leaves an impression of confidence, competence, and good will. It's commensurate with the good investment your project really did prove to be. (Calling a dud a dud, by the way—in better-chosen terms—doesn't hurt your standing as much as you might think. Everyone knows some grant projects don't work out in history-making splendor. Admitting it, but explaining the reasons behind the weak points, inspires future trust in all but producers of real fiascos.)

Each kind of commercial writing has its own rewards. Working with brochures and their printed brethren sharpens your precision with words and sensitizes you to graphics and printing quality. Reaching the public through the news media prompts you to appreciate how news is made, how messages are made memorable, and how the public actually fishes its information out of the flood of words around us every day. Grant writing puts worthy petitioners together with worthy donors—a service that enables you to do good works and generate more assignments for your well-honed writer's craft.

The variety of commercial assignments available to you is ultimately limited only by your own ambition and spirit of adventure.

You can take on enough of these handy, handsome jobs to underwrite your basic expenses while you invest the rest of your hours in projects like books or magazine sales that have a deferred payoff. You can have fun and reap the rewards of commercial work and still find—and face—new challenges.

13

Speak Up!

Authors are nearly as famous for talking about their work as they are for writing it.

Fortunately, such talk need not be cheap. Call it what you will: public speaking, consulting, teaching, workshop production, or convention planning. Talking about your work can be unexpectedly profitable, both in cash and writerly benefits.

If you're shy about microphones, think of these opportunities as simply "writing out loud." They can be good ways to pry your fingers loose from your keyboard and rub shoulders with other creatures in the world outside your office. They offer welcome respite from the rigors of writing while setting up new challenges to stretch your abilities. They can propel your career forward, sometimes far more rapidly than other marketing strategies. And they pay, to boot.

At first, public speaking can seem a daunting challenge . . . especially to those more accustomed to the sheltered notoriety of the byline rather than the right-now rigors of five hundred eager faces waiting to be impressed. After all, many of us chose writing in the first place for the way it camouflages our native timidity.

We may speak out bravely, but in other people's voices—and in print. We may participate in the great events and directions of our times, but as observers cloaked from nose-to-nose accountability by the nature of our craft.

Coming out as a speaker or teacher violates that personal anonymity. It opens up exciting new possibilities to communicate, but at the price of new and daunting risks.

Nevertheless, the rewards can be tremendous. If you're a certain kind of writer, you may discover that these direct opportunities to persuade, amuse, inform, and touch the lives of a living, breathing audience offer a rather thrilling new avenue for plying your trade.

Think of it: You may hear yourself formulating well-founded opinions that you never knew you held, right in front of several dozen intelligent adults . . . who are actually taking notes!

You may uncover layers of self-confidence that have lain, unnoticed, deep beneath the normal strum of day-to-day satisfactions and anxieties that are all writers' lot.

And, yes, you may learn how fear affects altogether unpredictable parts of your body, from knuckles that throb and feet that fall asleep to a tongue that without warning turns to rubber.

Don't worry. The adrenaline willies offer good aerobic conditioning, and they go away the instant you hear applause or cash your honorarium.

In a field where excellence is seldom paralleled by wealth, seminars and speeches are the gravy. They pay, sometimes out of all proportion to the magazine rates or royalties the same information would garner in print.

At the same time, they add bulk and respectability to your credentials as a communicator—an extra dimension that can ultimately increase the salability of your articles, books, and services.

They're rich in the sort of direct give-and-take for which response-hungry writers pine away.

Best of all, they're a bonus . . . a dividend. Here you can be repaid in a fresh and unexpected way for the last-minute assignments and late-night rewrites, the hours of unpaid research, and the inevitable rejected queries that have seasoned you as a genuine professional.

Yes, you receive a check. Better yet, you collect face-to-face affirmation of your hard-won status as an expert in your field, a person to whom others will drive miles to listen. Often they even ask questions, note pithy quotes, and say "thanks" at the end of your session . . . three miracle drugs of amazing benefit to writers accustomed to demanding editors and occasionally unruly clients.

The lecture circuit is a fine old tradition among authors. Its current practitioners range from better-known mainstream personalities like Ellen Goodman, Tom Peters, and Jane Brody to others whose highly specific reputations are buried deep within their own disciplines.

Here you find historians with regional or esoteric specialties, tax and finance experts, writers on the arts, and how-to gurus in areas as diverse as home sewing, freshwater fishing and, yes, freelance writing.

The podium has supported a host of writers through the lean times as they stretch to find their own professional niche or weather dry spells in their markets. For others, speeches and workshops have been a way to build a reasonable living from excellent reviews and reputations that, sadly, are not always reflected by hot sales figures or fat royalty checks. Others still have learned that even minor success with the written word can become a key ingredient in success as a seminar leader or public speaker . . . a point which serious but over-shy writers ought to ponder.

Pull out the promotional material from the last workshop or lecture you attended. The symbiosis between writing and talking about writing is almost certainly reflected in the biographical sketch of the speaker or instructor. Figuring large among the credits is a book or two or other publishing credentials mentioned to create the almost-automatic aura of well-tested expertise.

Which came first, the book or the speaking contract? That line may seem blurred if the expert at hand handles the microphone like a pro. But delivery smooth as butter seldom earns an invitation to join the agenda. At the heart of the matter you'll usually find the book—and not necessarily a block-buster, at that, or even a title directly related to the speech at hand.

Bylines are second only to advanced degrees as harbingers of credibility; off the college campus they probably rank Number One. The implication that authors are by definition experts may be a personal comfort or a hilarious contradiction, depending on the present state of your own publishing fortunes. Nevertheless, it gets you past the starting gate.

You need be neither an actor nor an egotist to enjoy and profit from out-loud opportunities. A guest spot on "Today" or a major lyceum series may be well beyond your comfort zone (but not impossible, given the power of a timely topic and the devouring hunger of the human-interest media). A convention workshop or community education class may be just the forum, though, for stepping out from behind your desk and dealing direct.

Out-loud opportunities are your ticket to taking advantage of all you've learned as a writer, both about your own profession and your topical specialties. For you have a pair of directions from which to choose as you approach the podium or the blackboard.

Your writer's calling is the more obvious choice. Pick your own focus—anything from the love of language (or its dark side, tales of hideous word abuse) to savvy insights about how to shape and communicate a message.

Essentially it's a license to talk about yourself. For most of us, what could be more delicious?

Or you can address the body of knowledge you've distilled into writing assignments, drawing upon the painstaking credibility you've earned in your areas of specialty. The same elements that have tickled your keyboard may click with a live audience as well, from the stock market to the livestock sales ring, from homeowners' how-tos and history to light humor.

I'm convinced that deep within just about every mild-mannered, modest writer lurks a secret exhibitionist—a ham.

This alien being draws force from everyday writer's tasks. Its confident fingerprints show up on magazine queries, beneath the polite pitch. Its grinning shape can be glimpsed during interviews in the warm glow of a perfectly shaped question. Its voice can be heard in the silent way we shape a piece of routine copy, larded with deft verbal twists that perhaps 999 of a thousand readers are guaranteed to miss.

But toss a microphone into the hand of this Clark Kent of communication, and out comes a beast of a different nature.

The finest speakers I've ever heard are writers first and last. Their persuasive power comes from the polish they've rubbed to a high gloss during desperate grapples with manuscripts and deadlines. Their sparkle comes from finally being allowed to turn loose some of the good stuff that never fit anywhere but between the lines.

I met my own podium-crazed alien only after years of world-class shyness. For a decade I cleverly cloaked it in my 9-to-5 identity as a reporter, using the newspaper or magazine for which I was working as my on-the-job armor. Only after scores of interviews did I begin to notice that I genuinely enjoyed asking people nosy questions under circumstances that almost guaranteed they'd have to answer. Nor did I think the less of them for having opinions—lots and lots of opinions, reasonable and otherwise.

They gave me permission to admit in public to having my own, along with the courage to express them out loud and in person. No matter how odd I might sound, by then I'd quoted scores of people odder.

The rest was easy.

In a world where everyone seems to be talking at once, it's reassuring to discover how many are eager to listen.

Testing and mastering your skill as a speaker is a far simpler matter than it might seem to one still used to keeping her own counsel. Opportunities to talk to groups abound in towns of every size, granting you free tuition as you assemble your own list of credits.

Of course they don't pay; schools, churches, service clubs, and civic groups seldom have budgets for regular programs and don't invest them in unproven speakers even when they do. But a reputation worth charging for begins with a series of smaller successes on occasions like these, and one thing leads to another.

My own testing ground was in high school and college classrooms, not as a student but as a guest lecturer. There comes a time each quarter when students grow restive and tidy lesson plans turn to mush. That's when teachers send out the call for guest speakers or, alternately, schedule field trips on which their classes can witness actual human beings applying the principles which have been inspiring essay questions since September.

I first carried the proud banner of the Real World into classrooms as a teenage newspaper reporter, working English and journalism classes up and down the Red River Valley. I was selected by virtue of my junior tenure on the staff and motivated by a simple creed: When your editor says, "Do this," never say no.

I doubt those first talks were spellbinding. Especially on muggy May afternoons in solar-heated auditoriums, my audiences might better have been described as semi-comatose.

Nevertheless, I learned the two most helpful lessons a speaker can muster: No one has ever applauded less because your talk was too short. Also, never leave the floor wide open for questions unless you're prepared to enter the Twilight Zone. (Most of mine fell somewhere between "Why does your sports department hate our school?" and "Why doesn't The Forum publish 'Doonesbury'?")

Years later, those lessons began to come in handy. The mere novelty of surviving as a freelance writer resulted in my first invitations to speak at writers' conferences, teachers' conventions, and career days.

Those who had attended earlier talks or workshops sometimes called to invite me to talk to other groups with which they were involved. As those referrals began to run farther afield from the topic of professional writing itself, I branched out into more specific areas in which I have experience.

When you're first asked, you'll probably respond much as I did at first: "Oh, I don't know anything to talk about." Wrong! If writing is your home plate, then applications of that ability to communicate form the bases—working with the news media, writing and editing internal publications, crafting an advertising message to reach a target audience.

If your background lies in these fields, similar opportunities await you, paid in cash or just experience. What audiences might want to hear you? Students with an interest in writing. Groups that harbor would-be writers—retired teachers' associations, writers' and fine arts clubs, historical societies. Businesspeople who can benefit from a better way with words. Political action and public interest groups.

It sometimes baffles me why the average person becomes so curious about our craft. But nonwriting friends remind me that what we do for a living is something of an arcane art to those unfamiliar with what we take for granted. You may find, as I have, that you have a ready market for your talks on convention programs, annual meeting agendas, professional improvement workshops of all kinds, and your local school system's adult outreach program.

I stumbled across these potential markets when a state health department staff asked me to fill one slot on a day-long regional workshop—"how to work with the news media." I arrived half an hour early to size up my audience and was treated to an eye-opening program on spermatozoa, chromosomes, and surging hormones: I'd been booked as the only nontechnical speaker on an agenda for family-planning workers.

It was an inspiring experience, one which was reproduced in four other states in as many subsequent months as a member of the workshop's traveling team. In every city I was intrigued to learn that my topic, basic media relations, seemed as technical and jargon-ridden to my audience as their field was to the general public.

I learned that the simple act of calling an editor to suggest a story on their interesting, timely, and controversial programs was completely foreign to most of them, who nevertheless could not imagine why they weren't getting the coverage their work with teenagers certainly deserved.

Get to know a reporter or editor! (They scribbled in their notebooks.) Deliver a couple of news releases every year without fail, and hand them over in person. (They looked skeptical.) Hire a professional writer to handle your news-making needs. (Light bulbs flashed above their heads.) Don't stand in awe of the news media—they need you as much as you need them. (Applause! For a moment I felt like a star.)

Since then I've talked to chambers of commerce, political action groups, United Way volunteers, senior citizens, nonprofit associations, social workers, retired teachers, women's business conferences, public employees, and Rotarians and their ilk. The roster is a mixed bag, but the message has been much the same: not "somebody ought to do something," but "you should do this . . . and here's how." The basic message has undoubtedly fueled a million talks on a hundred topics, and it still works every time.

My fees have run the gamut from twenty-five dollars for a brief talk that took half an hour away from my writing schedule to two hundred for an evening seminar sponsored by a university continuing education department. Longer sessions naturally bring more—from several hundred for teaching an adult education class on four consecutive Mondays to nearly a thousand for a keynote address and several break-out sessions at a regional conference that required both extra preparation and travel time.

But I've done nearly the same talks before many other audiences for little or nothing beyond the contacts and the pleasure of their company. Some of those groups undoubtedly possessed budgets at least as large as those of the fine folks who paid me. The difference between the two was small but disproportionately significant. I quoted a standard fee to the first group. I neglected to mention it to the second.

Which has led me to formulate a principle you may quote as Hanson's Law of Reimbursement: Unless you ask for an honorarium, you probably won't get one. Unless you try to increase what you're offered, you'll be paid the minimum. If you do ask, the likelihood of their coming up with a reasonable sum is in direct proportion to how much they value your visit. If a group you know has paid others but declines to pay you, cross them off your calendar. After all, you can always use the time to write.

How do you get started? If your background doesn't now include some speaking experience, you probably start by talking for free. Your first public-speaking encounters can help you quickly determine whether you enjoy contact with an audience or lose several days' good work time dreading it. (If the latter turns out to be true, drop the idea after a few experimental attempts. The rewards for local public speaking are not so enormous that they should threaten your writing schedule and peace of mind.)

Everyone who's stood on the business side of the podium has his or her own method for organizing a talk and conquering stage fright (which never goes away entirely, but has a way of returning at the oddest times).

Since I've spoken on the same topics several times, I have notes on file from which I work for each new engagement. I retype them, inserting a few comments directed specifically toward the current audience and sometimes rearranging them to include fresh thoughts added by a previous audience's questions. I also try to find a couple of current examples (when my subject is the news media) to give more immediacy to my basically timeless themes.

My notes (typed on five-by-seven-inch file cards, three or four for an hour's talk) would mean nothing to anyone but me. You'd see single words, names underlined with wavy lines, exclamation points, question marks, handwritten additions between the lines. I go through these hieroglyphics several times before getting up to put them to use—not to plan every word I'll say, but to have a firm idea of how each topic leads into the next. Otherwise it's easy for me to get lost on a tangent with no graceful way to find my way back to my conclusion.

A sense of direction helps, too, when you interrupt your planned talk to field questions from the audience. They're an invitation to losing your place. The outline helps me keep to the point at hand; offbeat questions get postponed until a more appropriate spot in the talk.

I always ask for questions and answers . . . and seldom get them when I want them. That could be a peculiarity of Great Plains audiences, who are super-polite; it could also be because nothing blanks out your mind like the necessity of asking something intelligent without warning. At any rate, questions are a valuable way to make real contact with the audience, and deserve special attention. When I can, I plant a starter query or comment with someone in the audience—one of the sponsors, perhaps, or someone who's come up to talk with me beforehand. One question can prime the pump and produce a virtual torrent. If not, thank the audience and sit down.

One of the great advantages of living in rural areas is that word of your availability as a speaker gets around very quickly. If you've educated or charmed one audience, that message will spread to others looking for a new face for their programs.

Alternately, you can advertise your service with a letter or simple brochure. Get quotes from those to whom you've already spoken, with their names; their comments count for more than all your own claims.

Check your local chamber of commerce to see if a speaker's bureau has been set up. It provides a list of men and women willing to talk about a wide variety of professional and personal topics, some for a fee; it's circulated to service and professional groups and provided to convention planners. If no formal speaker's bureau exists in your community, talk with the chamber staffer who works with convention groups. His personal suggestions influence many others looking for help in putting their programs together.

I never expect to make the professional lecture circuit. Maybe you will, when your best-seller gives you a national audience for your expertise. The rewards there can be excellent.

But the regional speaking engagements I've booked have more than satisfied me. For an hour out of my day, I can often earn the equivalent of a good sale to a minor magazine or half a local brochure, whichever's greater. When you add in the publicity I've received for my writing business and the fun I've had in meeting these new groups, speeches are one of the finest little extras I've encountered as a writer.

Consulting

Being asked for your advice is a heady experience. Basically, that's what consulting work consists of: giving advice, and being paid for it.

For a writer, consulting usually means ghostwriting. It can also, however, be the purchase of a few hours of your time by a client who can't afford (or won't pay for) your primary services: critiquing a public information program, for example, and giving reasons why it has failed to get the expected reaction from the news media; or finding ways to retailor government information programs so that listeners can actually understand them.

I've included consulting in this chapter because most of my pure consulting jobs have grown out of speeches I've made before professional groups. Grown out of them? Sometimes they've almost duplicated what I told the group for a far more modest fee. Nevertheless, I've apparently touched a chord here and there, and I'm more than happy to offer the analysis (and often, reassurance) they desire.

Not all freelancers, however, will find the way to consulting opens for them so easily. My background in the news media and government has provided me with something of specific usefulness to share with clients, as well as a way to measure the effectiveness of what they've done in the past. If your own work experience is short on these tangible skills, consulting may not be the best possibility for you to pursue until you've built up background expertise. An attempt to bluff your way through is all too apparent to the client who's agreed to pay for your assistance, and may sour him on other projects you might propose in the future.

Putting your experience to work as an information consultant requires three distinct steps: talking to your client to find out his real message and the audience he hopes to reach; studying what he's doing now, as well as his past efforts, and matching them with evidence of success or failure; and developing a report to the client on your findings and suggestions for future directions. While the report is usually given in person, a written version helps satisfy him and reinforces your conclusions.

The difference between consulting and actually accomplishing commercial writing tasks is the contrast between teaching and doing. In most cases your role as a consultant is to offer an ideal course of action, tempered by the limitations of which you're aware.

Your role, as a locally based freelancer, can lead in either of two directions: Applying a program that's worked elsewhere to the area which you know firsthand, or translating a client's knowledge of the local market into effective ways to communicate with his special segment of the public.

For this reason, you have two target groups of clients. One is the organization or company from outside your area that's well staffed on its own, but unfamiliar with your own community. These are the people to whom your knowledge of local interests, prejudices, and history is most valuable.

The other is quite different. It includes smaller local groups or businesses with "homemade" publications and relations with the news media. While they may not want an outsider to take over these functions (for prideful or fiduciary reasons), they welcome the professional expertise you can bring to their planning.

Personal contacts are the easiest way to turn up consulting jobs, but the first move is usually up to your client. The same people whom you approach as potential commercial clients may instead turn out to be sources of your first consulting contracts. Your reputation and credentials as a proven freelance writer are your best references . . . presented to top advantage when you're invited to expound on them from the speaker's podium.

Normally you will charge more than your basic hourly rate for consulting services, since you're offering highly distilled information rather than personally putting it to work. Try to find other consultants locally (perhaps in management) to get an idea of the going rate. Talk about fees with the client before you begin; you may find the client has a figure in mind that is higher than you expected, for consultants command substantial sums in every field. I accept these jobs for nothing less than a hundred dollars, increasing the figure based on the amount of time spent in researching and preparing a report.

Teaching

The third kind of face-to-face opportunity is teaching. Perhaps education is the world you're trying to leave behind by turning to freelancing. Or maybe you've never considered yourself equipped to help others learn an intangible art like writing. In either case, the economics of freelancing can be reason to reconsider and look into what opportunities might be awaiting you.

Teaching noncredit or evening classes makes use of your experience in the most generous way—sharing it with others to help them avoid some of your own costly mistakes and to help them polish latent talent into salable writing. It's also a change from days alone at the typewriter, and it helps pay the rent.

In the back of your mind, do you admit to a low-grade resistance to teaching others to become your local writing competition? I know I do; writers are insecure creatures, especially when we're not used to others typing away on our turf.

Yet I wouldn't let such doubts keep you away from such an interesting adventure. You suffer from overconfidence if you believe one night class under your leadership will equip enrollees with ammunition to take your own hard-won assignments. And more writers (even some conscientiously trained by yours truly) don't really seem to hurt the market for freelancers. Oddly enough, I've watched new writers make it better for all of us here in Bismarck, familiarizing more contacts with freelancers and (in the case of inept ones) making the professionals look all the better in comparison. Writing compatriots stimulate your own thinking, keep you on your toes . . . and give you someone to commiserate with when all's not well on the writing front.

The give-and-take between you and your students can help you see your vocation from a fresh, excited viewpoint. Enthusiasm that's slowly seeped out of your daily grind suddenly returns with a rush. You appreciate your life as a freelancer when you share it with eager disciples.

Part-time teaching opportunities vary dramatically in the amount of preparation time required, in the kinds of students whom you will meet, and in remuneration. An evening adult education class may be based on what you know by heart, spruced up with a sturdy course outline and attended by those with little insight into the who, what, why, where, when, and how of writing. On the other hand, a college course for which credit is granted demands not only academic preparation but a substantial amount of time spent planning lectures, working with students, and critiquing their work.

Other forms of education fall in between. Writers of poetry and literary fiction can apply for "Writer in the School" programs sponsored by their state affiliates of the National Endowment for the Arts. These involve concentrated visits to elementary and junior high school classrooms, directing young people's discovery of the power and pleasure of words . . . an often-delightful experience that can renew the visitor's own vision.

At the opposite end of the spectrum are commercially produced seminars and workshops, promoted by a corporate or organizational sponsor or by the speaker. The odds are good that you've attended some of these yourself, as I have: Everything from how to catch more fish (according to a noted outdoors writer) or how to sew fashionable clothes (by a noted author and home economist) to how to profitably publish books (as suggested by the publisher of a newsletter on that arcane topic).

Most consumer seminars are offered in conjunction with a local sponsor—fishing classes by Muskies Unlimited, for example, and sewing workshops by fabric stores. These can net the speaker a tidy sum in addition to a chance to plug books. But the greatest potential may lie in seminars produced by their speaker (perhaps under the bland title of an institute or consulting company that's in fact a sole proprietorship).

As usual, the promise is proportionate to the risk. The speaker books the room, arranges the publicity, buys advertising, orders coffee for the students, and collects what's left after expenses. That can be a nice amount for successful sessions that draw dozens of participants who each pay tuition of from $25 to $100 (or much more).

The best guide to entering the workshop market is Jeffrey Lant's book *Money Talks*. Along with his *Unabashed Self-Promoter's Guide*, it's an eminently practical handbook of step-by-step instruction in breaking the barrier to sharing your expertise with others for a fee. He's utterly frank in an area which more genteel advisors pussyfoot around—the immodest and undeniable necessity of tooting your own horn. (Even the price for his self-published handbook—thirty dollars, or three to four times the typical book of its kind—serves as an endorsement of his brashly effective beatitudes.)

Convention Planning

Making your living as a freelancer is a matter of flexibility. If you're really good at staying flexible, if you like people (but perhaps need a push now and then to get reinvolved with the world outside your office), and if you're in the market for a boost to your income that interferes very little with your writing routine, how about considering occasional bouts of convention planning and promotion?

Unlike other options I've explored as a freelancer in the boonies, convention planning is only partly dependent on time at the typewriter. Research, diplomacy, and a flair for communicating with the public are the main requirements—writing is only a fraction of the assignment.

Why, then, include it in a book for freelance writers?

I've found that putting together a public hearing or workshop from time to time is an ideal way to reinvolve myself with the human race. I can see the signs that I need to work with people again: I begin to enjoy hearing the telephone ring in the middle of a chapter, or I encourage the UPS deliveryman to share complaints about his route, or I'm tempted to discuss metaphysics with the door-to-door religion peddlers who are usually the bane of the at-home worker's existence.

Jobs planning meetings and seminars are real plums among your freelance pickings, paying well and making relatively modest demands on your work week. And you, a freelance writer, are exactly what the planners are looking for. You can easily accommodate a temporary assignment and, unlike others who may also be available at the moment, possess continuing connections with the working world.

Jobs as meeting planners are among those bonuses I promised you for working as a writer where you're least expected. In metropolitan areas, staging conventions and meetings may be handled by staff members who concentrate in those areas, or turned over to firms that specialize in putting gatherings together. In smaller, more remote communities like mine, the opposite is the case. Staffs are spread thinner, and there are few or no full-timers plying this highly specialized field. Conventions and meetings come up infrequently enough to gain a lot of attention among their sponsors—and to inspire a mild but real sense of panic in the overworked, overextended men and women responsible for seeing them carried out.

Your skills and freelance work schedule make you an ideal candidate for these undertakings when they do come up. The meeting's sponsors are looking for someone with professional credits who's plugged into local promotional and professional circles. Yet most with these qualifications are already employed full-time, and a juicy six-month job still isn't sweet enough to entice an employee into leaving a permanent position. You'll probably find when you apply for these positions that your own credentials are easily the best of the field of unemployed or underqualified applicants, while your freelance style of doing business is exactly what the doctors (or the plumbers, or the social workers, or the ad hoc planning committees) ordered.

I wouldn't have become such an avid supporter of meeting planner jobs, I think, if I hadn't agreed during a weak moment to try one myself more than a decade ago.

The time was early 1977, remembered by feminists and their opposites as International Women's Year. A national conference on women's issues was to be held later in Houston; to prepare for it, all fifty states were charged with holding their own conferences to discuss major concerns and elect delegates to the big convention.

Those were the first days of my freelancing, and friends still tended to worry that I was really unemployed. One who was a member of the planning committee asked if I'd like to take on the part-time executive director's position to publicize, organize, and generally nail down the meeting.

Did I jump at the chance? Of course not. I was a writer, not a trail boss. But those weeks of waiting for editorial acceptances had already begun to stretch a little longer than anticipated, so the salary was distinctly appealing. Most of the duties, besides, tallied neatly with work I knew I could handle: writing brochures and press kits, news releases, federal reports, and the like. Of course I could book a few rooms and order coffee and work with a committee of twenty-six fine, outstanding women, most of whom lived some hundreds of miles away and were unlikely to be around often.

Famous last words. But through the ensuing brouhaha—inevitable with any sizable, strong-willed steering committee—I learned enough about pulling a program together to savor future opportunities in the field. The meeting did get off the ground in four months' time and was quite a success, one of the larger voluntary nonpolitical meetings held here in recent years. It has led to other statewide meeting assignments on topics as far afield as revisions in our state commitment code for the mentally ill and how to handle the daily stresses of farm life.

I've taken on several series of meetings in the years since then. They've enabled me to meet all kinds of people from stress-ridden farmers to the head of the state hospital for the mentally ill to perfectly amazing women activists who've gone on to national prominence. Those projects have helped me set up some ground rules that apply to any meeting:

■ Identify the committee members or leaders of the sponsoring group who are likeliest to do what they say they will. Do not, under any circumstances, ask the rest to help with matters that will affect the smooth flow of the meeting you're planning. Let the procrastinators be in charge of subgroups that are clearly identified as their personal area of action; then develop contingency plans in case they do fail to remember to come.

■ Have the chain of command spelled out for you before you accept the assignment. Then stick to it, ignoring all enticements to take shortcuts and alternate solutions after the decisions have been discussed and made.

■ Watch for signs of serious internal dissension among the sponsors. If they're arguing or show signs of getting a good row going, the benefits of the assignment won't be enough to prevent you from wondering why you were born.

■ Have fun with the job. Taking it too seriously is foolish, for it's only a moment in time (and without a byline, at that). The potential for real enjoyment is very high in planning meetings, making new friends, solving day-to-day problems with common sense, and being paid to have your mind opened to new concerns and issues.

Successfully planned meetings lead to other kinds of assignments

as well, especially those more closely related to your writing expertise: public information campaigns, newsletters and publications,
even speechwriting or ghosting for the nonverbal experts who "star"
in your show. I guarantee you'll come away from the experience with
at least a fat handful of new story ideas, even the introduction into a
new field. And don't forget your salary as the meeting's planner.

Tracking down these assignments is not just a matter of knocking on
doors and showing your samples. There's a less tangible element involved: You have to be ready to stand up when they call out for volunteers. The wider your network of friends and acquaintances and the
more who know of your freelancing, the better your chances of pounc-
ing upon opportunities when they first come into sight.

Some opportunities simply turn up in the want ads. These are sponsored by the unfortunate souls who don't know anybody dependable
who is free to take their part-time, short-term project. Don't be afraid
of applying for these, even if they are blind ads. If you find you're not
interested after learning more, you can always say no. And if the
sponsors' original plans aren't to your liking, you may be able to
negotiate changes that suit you better. More than any other position the
sponsors will ever advertise, these jobs are flexible and open to negotiations on services to be provided and salary to be extracted in return.

Another spot to make your predilection for planning known is at
your chamber of commerce. Even in smaller communities like mine
they are busy establishing convention and visitors' bureaus to attract
and serve those planning major gatherings of all kinds. Their motives
are clear—conventioneers spend (according to the national average)
about a hundred dollars apiece for every day they're in town. The
more convention-planning services available locally, including your
own ready assistance, the more appealing your chamber's delegation
can make their city sound.

The managers of several of my state's convention bureaus have been
stalwart allies for turning up leads on meeting-related assignments.
Each of them regularly fields questions about who's available here to
handle a whole bundle of meeting-planning tasks, and often has re-
ferred coming conventioneers to me.

Your commercial writing clients are also sources of information on
meeting-planning jobs. They may be interested in your service themselves if you let them know of your interest, for public relations personnel of business and government are often the contact points for
sales meetings, professional seminars, and conventions.

Ask a few critical questions of anyone who proposes to hire you before you accept any of these planning positions.

Can you work in your own office? The right answer is yes. Otherwise, the job can easily eat up much more of your writing time than it
should require. If it doesn't fit in with your writing schedule, it's probably not worth whatever it pays.

Will you be reimbursed for basic expenses like telephone, supplies, and mail costs? In almost any legitimate case the answer will be yes, but be sure to get these points cleared up before you spend any money out of your own budget.

Is there a clerical support staff? Don't agree to become a glorified secretary. A lot of paper must pass through the mail to bring the average meeting or workshop to life.

What is the chain of command? Get it laid out clearly, then go over it again. Try to have it in writing, just in case.

What functions will volunteer planning committee members play? Who gets the final say on conflicting plans? Again, get answers down clearly—then circulate a copy among the committee to insure that everyone understands.

Some of these questions may seem unnecessarily mechanical. But they're going to come up in one form or another in the course of planning any gathering. Since your position is a novel one for most groups, there is no fund of tradition to fall back on. Safeguarding yourself with a job description and a very clear body of instructions will prevent the kind of nervous eruptions of temper or dissatisfaction that undermine even the best-laid plans.

Planning meetings of many kinds can be a refreshing break in your writing program. It enlarges your professional contacts enormously, both among local sponsors and the visiting city managers who attend the gathering you've pulled together. One job leads to another; one or two meetings well planned and well received may elicit more offers than you can easily manage, and you'll have the luxury of picking and choosing the most interesting.

Face-to-face assignments present you with variety, satisfaction, and a chance to recharge your creative batteries. Whether you speak to a convention or help plan it, teach a class or advise clients one by one as a consultant, you get to share your professional insights and gain new perspective on your own field through the eyes of others.

You get paid for it.

It can be fun.

And it's the ideal antidote to writer's cramp.

14

The Adventure That Never Ends

In theory, writers ought to write. But that's no simple matter.

There is something in the universe that plays April Fool with those of us determined to make our way with words. This trickster invests deft words in creative hands scattered from coast to coast, then plunks the bulk of the publishing industry down on a single polluted island between the East River and the Hudson.

It spins tabloid yarns about million-dollar authors, yet declines to smite magazines that still pay five cents a word.

It plays Cupid with the love of language, then dowses that flame with full-time jobs larded with meetings and policy statements and guidelines and gobbledygook, only occasionally seasoned with an actual chance to write.

The alternative is freelancing—a goal, a process, an adventure in which ideas are the fuel and fulfilling them is the profit. But of all the world's business ventures, it's among the most widely doubted, ranking right down there with worm ranching and professional macrame.

Maybe because writing looks like so much fun, it seems too frivolous an option for the serious-minded. "Experts" are happy to support that discouraging thought, often pointing to that miserable 1979 Columbia University-Authors Guild study of 2,200 published authors whose median income was $4,775.

A host of surveys and articles suggest that all professional writerdom settles into three layers like an old-fashioned gelatin salad: On top, the big-name authors, floating happily amidst cherries and whipped cream; then workaday salaried writers populating the vast murky middle; and finally, struggling freelancers at the bottom of the bowl among the sunken nuts and weary shredded vegetables.

Don't you believe it.

Ask any cross-section of these otherwise-employed experts, from big-time magazine editors at writers' conferences to strangers in a shopping mall, and they'll be happy to echo the same set of options: Starve or hang on to your job.

Nonsense.

There is something abroad in the land that wants to believe in suffering for art—a special pain more poignant than ever borne by those who suffer for insurance sales, say, or asphalt paving.

And there is something in the universe that conspires, with a giggle, against writers in their prime.

Writers, if they are very good, are all but inevitably rewarded with promotions that set aside the skill that distinguishes them.

Newspaper reporters grow up to be editors. Poets become professors. Authors evolve into critics, and even advertising copywriters are reborn as agency vice presidents.

Writers, in short, are recast as men and women who talk about writing. And talking about writing not only possesses a luster easily equal to that of actually producing polished prose. It pays better to boot.

This is the law of the pen-and-ink jungle. This is the real writer's curse . . . not the threat of rejection, a drafty garret and popular disdain, but the threat of success—yielding to practical working necessities that hogtie the very talent that once made a youngster dream of writing as a career.

The public sheds few tears over this gentle irony, preferring higher drama for its myths about the creative life. Its taste leans more toward sensitive souls ravished first by carping critics and then by self-destructive drink. It adores tales of genius novelists left to languish until their dotage.

These stories add up to not only poignant legendry, but a nice selection of subplots for soap operas.

We who earn our livings with words know how far-fetched such notions can be. Ours is a real profession with real supply and real demand. The reality is seldom melodramatic, though it occasionally shares some common points with situation comedy.

If we are adept and we are ambitious, if we follow the all-too-normal path, there's a desk without a typewriter waiting somewhere in our futures . . . or, alternatively, we'll be passed over for promotions and left toiling at the same old dull assignments for the rest of our working lives.

The would-be writer waits, patient, in the closet. We seldom acknowledge it, even among ourselves, except on those agonizing days when the act of writing seems more penance than benediction.

Yet in twenty years in the profession I've seen the same story played out time and again. Throughout the communications industry, writing is an entry-level job (or nearly so). Few writers outside of the focal point of national publishing can manage to carve an entire career from their profession if they expect the same perks that other fields provide. Their fate is to hit the ceiling widely shared by all the creative fields: Singled out for their own creative excellence, they move on to overseeing others who do the fun stuff.

The best and most aggressive writers (outside of a few metropolitan areas where career ladders reach up toward the stratosphere) are frequently rewarded with exactly the opposite of what seems logical. They're promoted to nonwriting management jobs.

Sooner or later an employed writer's progress amounts to official permission to stop writing. This step up is supported with fatter paychecks and heftier status. Next thing you know, he starts quoting Lee Iacocca and parking his big Chrysler in a reserved executive slot. He makes life more stressful for those still wrestling with keyboards in the city room, the public relations department, or the magazine's freelance stable. And he daydreams aloud (over Tanqueray, vermouth and double olives, perhaps, at the local country club) about how he'll get back to writing someday: Then, by all that's verbal, he's going to finally show the world!

There is another way . . . one that plunges you into the thick of your craft while allowing you to explore new avenues, polish your skills, and continue to grow as both a creative individual and a solid citizen whose mortgage payments are mailed on time.

There is another way to maintain both your enthusiasm and your family's lifestyle . . . to test unknown waters or to dive more deeply into those you know best . . . to choose risks equal to your comfort level while building credentials and expertise to allow yourself to pass smoothly in and out of the corporate world.

Welcome to the great adventure of the professional writing world. Welcome to the business of freelancing.

I can't teach you how to write. That's the first vital step. It's up to you to learn your lessons well.

But I can tell you, with absolute assurance, why the struggle and doubts are worth your while.

Of all the world's professions, writing is the closest to a perfect choice . . . and the freelance format makes it nearly ideal. You can spend a career mastering a subject or a medium that commands your interest, molecule by molecule; or you can plow fresh ground whenever you feel the need to pioneer. You can perfect highly specialized skills and build deep, wide bodies of expertise; or you can flourish as a generalist, whetting your appetite for new experiences. No matter what you choose, the door stands ajar and the welcome mat is out. You can always count on fresh air.

Freelance writing is a great adventure, an adventure that need never end.

When I wrote the precursor to this book at the age of twenty-nine, I was still thinking of beginnings. A dozen years as a newspaper reporter, minor bureaucrat, and profitably self-employed writer had prepared me well to preach the gospel of following a dream—of daring to launch a freelance business no matter where you lived.

Then I was thinking of guiding newcomers' initiation into the nearly invisible society of far-flung freelancers who've carved out successful careers in locales as unlikely as my own. Now I know there is great adventure, too, in full membership in the club.

I learned this lesson not only by getting older but from responses to that earlier book. Many of these letters I had half-expected, given its premise. They came from men and women on the verge of considering full-time freelancing—some of them well prepared for building a business on already-demonstrated skills, and others just beginning to develop the experience and facility with words that might someday make writing a practical career option.

But other letters opened my eyes to the broader potential that lies beyond those first giddy years of living by your words alone. Creative freelancing works for beginners, yes. That I knew. But, as they taught me, the ritual of religiously scanning the horizon for new opportunities never grows old. It can continue to direct writers down new avenues throughout their careers, no matter how fond they are of the dear old familiar streets they know by heart.

For instance, I heard from a magazine freelancer in California whose name I recognized immediately. Despite his stellar track record with the best-known computer-user publications, he'd begun to feel the effects (he said) of editorial shake-ups, mergers, and announcements of suspended publication in that volatile specialty. He waxed enthusiastic over the suggestion to broaden his focus. He'd moved into script-writing for how-to videos and scored with proposals for several sponsored books. For him, creative freelancing works.

I heard from an expert copywriter transplanted from New York to the Carolinas, where he'd always longed to live—and then marooned by internecine politics within the small-town ad agency he had helped create. He had begun to despair, he said, of staying in the community where he'd always dreamed of retiring. But he took another look. In addition to the modest businesses whom he advised as a consultant, he broadened his income base by developing seminars. He also tried his hand at writing for several regional markets which he'd originally dismissed as inconsequential; they proved him wrong. He wrote that he was confident now of surviving in his chosen locale. Creative freelancing was paying off for him.

I heard from not one but two former high school teachers situated on opposite sides of the Rockies. One chose freelancing and resigned her job in an orderly manner. The other seized on writing after massive education cutbacks cost her her job. Both testified to making progress toward their goals in towns far smaller and less prominent than my own in North Dakota. I grade both of them "A." As freelancers, they created their own choices where others swore that none could exist.

And I was amazed that readers sent flurries of missives that essentially said, "Me, too." Through their notes and calls, I became acquainted with writers in Texas and Ohio and Wyoming, Michigan and Nevada and the Florida panhandle. One writes about horses for media of every sort. One works strictly with newspapers, flourishing as a versatile stringer capable of handling everything from lifestyle profiles to police investigations. One got rolling in the recreational vehicle field and stayed there. He has parlayed the RV equipment reviews and travel pieces that launched his career into a full docket of manufacturers' public relations, annual travel guides, how-to manuals for owners, and contractual editing jobs.

Others stayed with freelancing for a time, and then were swept along by the currents it created into full-time jobs tailor-made to apply the lessons they'd learned on their own. You can find a trio of successful freelance veterans whom I know well who are now directing communications for a regional agricultural agency, handling editorial duties for a metropolitan city magazine, and presiding over a thriving marketing agency whose foyer is steadily being wallpapered with awards for excellence.

Such case histories illustrate the one rule that governs freelance writing: There really are no rules.

Freelance writing is a chance to invent your own career. It can offer excitement or stability, depending on whether your goal is stimulation or security. It can draw on familiar ground that you know well, or impel you to climb new mountains. It can replace the standard 8-to-5 job forever, or offer a chance for you to reconfigure your résumé with solid credits to carry your career in new directions.

As a career, freelancing offers its fair share of peak experiences. I treasure two in particular. One was seeing my first-born book offered for months in those join-and-take-any-four-for-a-penny book club advertisements. Honest. I never flip through a magazine without making my hypothetical selections, and for just a moment those ads made me feel like a star. The other was on the day B. Dalton Bookseller released its bestseller tabulations for 1986, listing the two top regional titles in each multi-state area. In the district encompassing the Dakotas and Nebraska, both were mine.

Yes, you will have setbacks. I guarantee it! Good work will occasionally be rejected or misused. There will be near-misses on projects you deeply desired. You'll enjoy some of the tasks you take on, and run into a few that are true rats, and learn to tell the difference . . . most of the time.

Projects you love will end, as independent projects always do. For them you'll mourn. Other assignments will threaten to become immortal, and you'll find yourself praying for deliverance.

Some payments will be late, some smaller than you expect—and others thoroughly gratifying. Months may come when you worry about paying the rent. In more successful times you'll gripe about paying taxes.

At first the ups and downs may worry you. Worry? Try "terrify." But if your work is sound and your marketing diligent, and with a light salting of luck (the kind you make yourself), you'll enjoy the scenery far more than you mind the bumps in the road.

Writing is addictive—not only in hypnotic hours spent pursuing elusive thoughts, but for its new beginnings. Infinite beginnings. Next year always holds a degree of mystery. As one door closes, another always opens . . . especially when you keep on knocking.

As freelancers, we have a world of choices laid before us: the security of developing skills that are scarce and valued by the more settled salaried world; the dynamic ability to make things happen in our own lives, rather than flowing along with an anonymous corporate current; and the adventure of not knowing exactly what will come next. If this career were a book, you'd be reading long past midnight. But freelancing isn't fiction, and it doesn't have to end.

Nor need there be limits to geography, to income, to what you can accomplish.

About the figure mentioned in the title of this book: You can believe it. It is well within your reach. It's a reasonable goal, surely not the limit to what one could earn writing wherever you happen to live. My gross income has exceeded that annual figure since the first year I began freelancing in Bismarck, North Dakota; when I moved to Fargo, it came along with me. Had I accepted every assignment I've been offered, it could easily be higher.

You may be sure that including $25,000 in the title of this book has been thoroughly debated. It represents a fair compromise—neither the most that you or I could reasonably hope to earn, nor the least one could expect of a year spent chasing assignments with the longest odds and the highest risk of failure.

It's a reasonable goal. For me, it means I can live the life I've chosen, and still maintain a balanced writing diet—a good proportion of writing for income seasoned with writing more nearly for love. It keeps my options open. It underwrites experiments. It prevents freelancing from turning into no more than a different species of everyday rut, the dread routine that knocked me loose from the corporate world in the first place.

Being able to stay afloat as a freelance writer isn't a fluke. No, it's the once-surprising result of an experiment in writing that worried me ten years ago much as it worries you right now. When I began, I really did not know whether I could do as well on behalf of my own business as I'd done for sundry others. Could I last more than six months on uncharted ground where so many prudent writers fear to tread?

I can do it. You can do it. They could probably do it, too, if they overcame their brainwashed fear of the unknown and set out to try untested and challenging waters.

Learn what your part of the country is waiting to offer you. Make the best of what you've got. Don't ignore the half-hidden opportunities that aren't quite what you'd always envisioned. Stretch you vision—stretch it as wide as your new horizon.

Geography gives you back every opportunity you thought it denied you: Markets for your writing. Research sources and story ideas. Lucrative assignments that bring out your best, and the chance to try new techniques and new approaches.

You don't have to hit the trail to Gotham to gain those options. All you need to do is open the door to the many ways you can use your address and your writing skills to your advantage. Lean hard on your strong points. Shore up the weak ones; New York City and a hot-shot literary agent don't guarantee nirvana, either.

Freelancing is not a low-energy occupation. You have to go after it . . . want it badly enough to make some adjustments in what you expect and where you expect to find it.

But I think the life you'll get to lead is worth every adjustment. I want to dispel your fears and suspicions about freelancing in the country.

You *can* make a living as a freelance writer wherever you live right now, whatever you may have thought a week ago, whichever course you're equipped or inclined to follow. If you want the freelance writing life strongly enough, you'll manage to make it happen right on the spot that you call home. It is real work. It is a real challenge. And it's everything you'd want it to be . . . the best way I can imagine to make a living.

Index

Other Books of Interest

Annual Market Books
    Artist's Market, edited by Lauri Miller $21.95
    Children's Writer's & Illustrator's Market, edited by Lisa Carpenter (paper) $17.95
    Guide to Literary Agents & Art/Photo Reps, edited by Robin Gee $15.95
    Humor & Cartoon Markets, edited by Bob Staake (paper) $16.95
    Novel & Short Story Writer's Market, edited by Robin Gee (paper) $19.95
    Photographer's Market, edited by Sam Marshall $21.95
    Poet's Market, by Judson Jerome $19.95
    Songwriter's Market, edited by Brian Rushing $19.95
    Writer's Market, edited by Mark Kissling $25.95

General Writing Books
    Annable's Treasury of Literary Teasers, by H.D. Annable (paper) $1.99
    Beginning Writer's Answer Book, edited by Kirk Polking (paper) $13.95
    Discovering the Writer Within, by Bruce Ballenger & Barry Lane $17.95
    Freeing Your Creativity, by Marshall Cook $17.95
    Getting the Words Right: How to Rewrite, Edit and Revise, by Theodore A. Rees Cheney (paper) $12.95
    How to Write a Book Proposal, by Michael Larsen (paper) $10.95
    Just Open a Vein, edited by William Brohaugh $6.99
    Knowing Where to Look: The Ultimate Guide to Research, by Lois Horowitz (paper) $16.95
    Make Your Words Work, by Gary Provost $17.95
    Pinckert's Practical Grammar, by Robert C. Pinckert (paper) $11.95
    12 Keys to Writing Books That Sell, by Kathleen Krull (paper) $12.95
    The 28 Biggest Writing Blunders, by William Noble $12.95
    The 29 Most Common Writing Mistakes & How to Avoid Them, by Judy Delton (paper) $9.95
    The Wordwatcher's Guide to Good Writing & Grammar, by Morton S. Freeman (paper) $15.95
    Word Processing Secrets for Writers, by Michael A. Banks & Ansen Dibell (paper) $14.95
    The Writer's Book of Checklists, by Scott Edelstein $16.95
    The Writer's Digest Guide to Manuscript Formats, by Buchman & Groves $18.95
    The Writer's Essential Desk Reference, edited by Glenda Neff $19.95

Nonfiction Writing
    The Complete Guide to Writing Biographies, by Ted Schwarz $6.99
    Creative Conversations: The Writer's Guide to Conducting Interviews, by Michael Schumacher $16.95
    How to Do Leaflets, Newsletters, & Newspapers, by Nancy Brigham (paper) $14.95
    How to Sell Every Magazine Article You Write, by Lisa Collier Cool (paper) $11.95
    How to Write Irresistible Query Letters, by Lisa Collier Cool (paper) $10.95
    The Writer's Digest Handbook of Magazine Article Writing, edited by Jean M. Fredette (paper) $11.95

Fiction Writing
    The Art & Craft of Novel Writing, by Oakley Hall $17.95
    Best Stories from New Writers, edited by Linda Sanders $5.99
    Characters & Viewpoint, by Orson Scott Card $13.95
    The Complete Guide to Writing Fiction, by Barnaby Conrad $17.95
    Cosmic Critiques: How & Why 10 Science Fiction Stories Work, edited by Asimov & Greenberg (paper) $12.95
    Creating Characters: How to Build Story People, by Dwight V. Swain $16.95

Creating Short Fiction, by Damon Knight (paper) $10.95
Dialogue, by Lewis Turco $13.95
The Fiction Writer's Silent Partner, by Martin Roth $19.95
Handbook of Short Story Writing: Vol. I, by Dickson and Smythe (paper) $10.95
Handbook of Short Story Writing: Vol. II, edited by Jean Fredette (paper) $12.95
How to Write & Sell Your First Novel, by Collier & Leighton (paper) $12.95
Manuscript Submission, by Scott Edelstein $13.95
Mastering Fiction Writing, by Kit Reed $18.95
Plot, by Ansen Dibell $13.95
Spider Spin Me a Web: Lawrence Block on Writing Fiction, by Lawrence Block $16.95
Theme & Strategy, by Ronald B. Tobias $13.95
The 38 Most Common Writing Mistakes, by Jack M. Bickham $12.95
Writer's Digest Handbook of Novel Writing, $18.95
Writing the Novel: From Plot to Print, by Lawrence Block (paper) $11.95

Special Interest Writing Books

Armed & Dangerous: A Writer's Guide to Weapons, by Michael Newton (paper) $14.95
The Children's Picture Book: How to Write It, How to Sell It, by Ellen E.M. Roberts (paper) $19.95
Comedy Writing Secrets, by Mel Helitzer (paper) $15.95
The Complete Book of Feature Writing, by Leonard Witt $18.95
Creating Poetry, by John Drury $18.95
Deadly Doses: A Writer's Guide to Poisons, by Serita Deborah Stevens with Anne Klarner (paper) $16.95
Editing Your Newsletter, by Mark Beach (paper) $18.50
Families Writing, by Peter Stillman (paper) $12.95
A Guide to Travel Writing & Photography, by Ann & Carl Purcell (paper) $22.95
Hillary Waugh's Guide to Mysteries & Mystery Writing, by Hillary Waugh $19.95
How to Pitch & Sell Your TV Script, by David Silver $17.95
How to Write Action/Adventure Novels, by Michael Newton $4.99
How to Write & Sell Greeting Cards, Bumper Stickers, T-Shirts and Other Fun Stuff, by Molly Wigand (paper) 15.95
How to Write & Sell True Crime, by Gary Provost $17.95
How to Write Horror Fiction, by William F. Nolan $15.95
How to Write Mysteries, by Shannon OCork $13.95
How to Write Romances, by Phyllis Taylor Pianka $15.95
How to Write Science Fiction & Fantasy, by Orson Scott Card $13.95
How to Write Tales of Horror, Fantasy & Science Fiction, edited by J.N. Williamson (paper) $12.95
How to Write the Story of Your Life, by Frank P. Thomas (paper) $11.95
How to Write Western Novels, by Matt Braun $1.00
The Magazine Article: How To Think It, Plan It, Write It, by Peter Jacobi $17.95
Mystery Writer's Handbook, by The Mystery Writers of America (paper) $11.95
The Poet's Handbook, by Judson Jerome (paper) $11.95
Powerful Business Writing, by Tom McKeown $12.95
Successful Scriptwriting, by Jurgen Wolff & Kerry Cox (paper) $14.95
The Writer's Complete Crime Reference Book, by Martin Roth $19.95
The Writer's Guide to Conquering the Magazine Market, by Connie Emerson $17.95
Writing for Children & Teenagers, 3rd Edition, by Lee Wyndham & Arnold Madison (paper) $12.95
Writing Mysteries: A Handbook by the Mystery Writers of America, Edited by Sue Grafton, $18.95
Writing the Modern Mystery, by Barbara Norville (paper) $12.95

The Writing Business

A Beginner's Guide to Getting Published, edited by Kirk Polking (paper) $11.95

Business & Legal Forms for Authors & Self-Publishers, by Tad Crawford (paper) $4.99

The Complete Guide to Self-Publishing, by Tom & Marilyn Ross (paper) $16.95

How to Write with a Collaborator, by Hal Bennett with Michael Larsen $1.00

How You Can Make $25,000 a Year Writing, by Nancy Edmonds Hanson (paper) $14.95

This Business of Writing, by Gregg Levoy $19.95

Writer's Guide to Self-Promotion & Publicity, by Elane Feldman $16.95

A Writer's Guide to Contract Negotiations, by Richard Balkin (paper) $4.25

Writing A to Z, edited by Kirk Polking $22.95

To order directly from the publisher, include $3.00 postage and handling for 1 book and $1.00 for each additional book. Allow 30 days for delivery.

Writer's Digest Books
1507 Dana Avenue, Cincinnati, Ohio 45207
Credit card orders call TOLL-FREE
1-800-289-0963
Prices subject to change without notice.

Write to this same address for information on *Writer's Digest* magazine, *Story* magazine, Writer's Digest Book Club, Writer's Digest School, and Writer's Digest Criticism Service.